5

BAKER & TAYLOR

REFUSE to CHOOSE!

A REVOLUTIONARY PROGRAM FOR DOING *EVERYTHING* THAT YOU LOVE

BARBARA SHER

RODALE

Book design by Christina Gaugler

Library of Congress Cataloging-in-Publication Data

Sher, Barbara.
    Refuse to choose! : a revolutionary program for doing everything that you love / Barbara Sher.
      p. cm.
    ISBN-13 978-1-59486-303-5 hardcover
    ISBN-10 1-59486-303-2 hardcover
    1. Self-actualization (Psychology)   2. Choice (Psychology)   3. Goal (Psychology)   I. Title.
  BF637.S4S5184   2006
  158.1—dc22   2006000045

Distributed to the book trade by Holtzbrinck Publishers

2   4   6   8   10 9   7   5   3   1   hardcover

We inspire and enable people to improve their lives and the world around them
For more of our products visit **rodalestore.com** or call 800-848-4735

To my grandson Leo

Explorer, Lover, Learner, Teacher, Jokester

I wish someone would just shake me and tell me exactly what to do with my life. I hate getting excited over something and being reminded by a well-meaning friend of all the other things I've tried and failed. Will I ever actually get to use what's inside me? Will anyone know I was here?

Charlotte, a Scanner

Through all the world there goes one long cry from the heart of the artist: Only give me the chance to do my very best!

Isak Dinesen

CONTENTS

ACKNOWLEDGMENTS

Many thanks to my home team: Matthew Pearl, my main editor, who is patient, painstaking, and intelligent and who always helps me say what I want to say (and allows himself to be interviewed because he's a major Scanner himself), and Andrea Reese (another amazing Scanner) who not only takes over all my other jobs, but also reads the drafts and catches those sneaky errors everyone else overlooked. Andrea is also my resident authority on this subject for at least two reasons: first, because she's a top-notch Success Teams leader who has personally worked with dozens of Scanners, and second, because her dad is an acclaimed Diver and her grandmother (his mother) was the greatest Scanner I have ever heard of. I always imagine that household with a big smile on my face. (You can read more about all these people on my bulletin board at www. barbarasher.com.)

Many thanks to the helpful, hard-working editors at Rodale who showed remarkable grace under pressure. And always, a special thank you to my wonderful agent at ICM, Kris Dahl.

I'd also like to send my deepest, most heartfelt thanks to all the Scanners who answered my interview questions, told me their stories, and read early drafts of these chapters (and a few who stepped forward to read final drafts in a last-minute crisis!). I can't begin to list all your names, but you'll probably find yourselves somewhere in the following pages (with names changed to protect the innocent!). It's been a joy to work with such fascinating people.

ARE YOU A SCANNER?

"I can never stick to anything."

"I know I should focus on one thing, but which one?"

"I lose interest in things I thought would interest me forever."

"I keep going off on another tangent."

"I get bored as soon as I know how to do something."

"I can't stand to do anything twice."

"I keep changing my mind about what I want to do and end up doing nothing."

"I work at low-paying jobs because there's nothing I'm willing to commit to."

"I won't choose a career path because it might be the wrong one."

"I think everyone's put on this earth to do something; everyone but me, that is."

"I can't pay attention unless I'm doing many things at once."

"I pull away from what I'm doing because I'm afraid I'll miss something better."

"I'm too busy, but when I do find time I can't remember what I wanted to do."

"I'll never be an expert in anything. I feel like I'm always in a survey class."

If you've ever said these things to yourself, chances are good that you're a Scanner, a very special kind of thinker. Unlike those people who seem to find and be satisfied with one area of interest, you're genetically wired to be interested in many things, and *that's exactly what you've been trying to do.* Because your behavior is unfamiliar—even unsettling—to the people around you, you've been taught that you're doing something wrong and you must try to change. But what you've been told is a mistake—you have been misdiagnosed. You're a different creature altogether.

What you've assumed is a disability to be overcome by sheer will is actually an exceptional gift. You are the owner of a remarkable, multitalented brain trying to do its work in a world that doesn't understand who you are and doesn't know why you behave as you do.

And unless you know who you are, you're going to agree with them! Not only would that be unfair and inaccurate, it could prevent you from developing your gifts and making your contribution to the world. The stakes are very high.

Identifying yourself as a Scanner means changing the way you see yourself in the world. It starts with understanding that you should stop trying to fit into the accepted norm at once and begin learning about who you really are. To help you build the productive future you were designed for, you need a set of instructions. That's what I've tried to create in this book.

Welcome to a new way of looking at yourself...and congratulations! The jury is in. You're not a dilettante and you're not shallow, and you have been found innocent by virtue of mistaken identity. You are now free to stop being judged and live the life you've wanted all along.

Now take a deep breath and let's start over.

PROLOGUE

I should have realized I wasn't a normal student my first week of college, when I looked at the catalog of classes and started to cry.

I was sitting at a table with some high school friends from my hometown, also freshmen, in a dark bar on Telegraph Avenue just outside of the famous Sather Gate, the entrance to the campus of the University of California at Berkeley. There were five of us girls, all 18 years old and trying to act very cool about the pitcher of beer we had legally bought that now sat on our table. Older students sat at other tables, looking sure of themselves, which we almost certainly did not, but everyone was intensely involved in the same activity: leafing through the pages of the *Schedule of Classes*, quickly trying to find the best ones so we could register before they filled up.

What were the best classes? The ones that started later in the day, or had the most lenient teachers, or were the same classes your friends were signing up for. Those were big considerations.

My four friends huddled next to me and pored over the *Schedule of Classes*, trying to coordinate our courses so we could help each other through the first semester on this new planet. Like everyone who was accepted to the University of California, we were all reasonably smart, but as I later discovered, my friends understood how to study—something I had somehow never learned. For this reason, they had a more realistic idea of how many hours of work would be required for each class one signed up for. Unlike me, they personally knew people who had been to college—sometimes older brothers or even parents— and had it on very good authority that college was a lot harder than high school.

While my friends searched the *Schedule of Classes*—a small newsprint magazine that listed in the tiniest print when and where the hundreds of classes would be held—I was reading another book that, in larger print and a more leisurely pace, described the content of all the classes. In easy-to-read English, the book laid out the topics that would be discussed and the books that would be read. It was like nothing I had ever seen or even imagined before. I could feel my mouth drop open in surprise as I read one page after another.

My friends were too busy talking to each other to notice at first.

"You can't take history on Tuesday at 10, MaryLee!" one of them said. "You have sociology at 10!"

"Do they really have classes at 8 in the morning?"

"Why didn't you take trig in high school? I told you it would be easier!"

"Why do we all have to take Bonehead English anyway? Are we the only stupid ones here?" Everyone laughed and turned to include me. But I was in another world. Without looking up from the book, I started asking questions.

"What is a 'close reading'?" I asked. "What is that?! This is about a close reading of Russian literature! What does that mean?"

"Don't worry, you don't have to take that stuff," one said. "You're taking Bonehead English with Sarah, right? You want it on Tuesdays or Thursdays?"

"Oh my God," I whispered, turning the pages wildly. "They have the History of Western Music! Do they play the music or do they talk about it? How do you teach the history of music?! Do you have to read music to take this? Oh look, Ancient Trade Routes of Central Asia! Look! The Golden Peaches of Samarqand! Where is Samarqand?! I want one of those peaches! Or are they talking about a painting? The Geology of History? *The Geology of History?!* Listen: 'The Himalayas rose from the ancient sea of Tethys so now, nearly 6 miles above sea level, there are fossilized seashells 20 million years old'! I'm going to faint. Oh God."

I had walked into the universe of learning. Nothing like this had ever happened to me before; nothing prepared me for this catalog of class descriptions. I had never read about it in novels, and no one had ever spoken of it. I couldn't catch my breath.

"That's the School of Liberal Arts for you," chuckled someone older at a nearby table and returned to his book, shaking his head in amusement.

The School of Liberal Arts. I loved every word in that phrase, even though I wasn't sure what the whole thing meant. Many years later, in a used-book store, I saw it mentioned again in some books I stumbled on about the rise of learning in the Middle Ages. I discovered that as Europe emerged from the Dark Ages, the children of the same Barbarians who had conquered Rome and nearly destroyed literacy (many of them monks and soldiers, senators, and even emperors) were in love with learning—madly in love with learning. They ached to read the few books that existed, and they spent lifetimes trying to piece together the lost masterpieces of Greece and Rome from fragments quoted in later works.

I understood them. I was sure of it. If I had known how, I would have tried to become a monk so I too could reverently copy manuscripts like they did, almost as a form of prayer. I decided then and there that I'd hand copy every book I loved from that day on.

Fortunately, I forgot that goal. I made so many amazing discoveries after I started college that each resolution I made replaced the one I'd made the day before, and I never did hand copy a book, though I loved many of them.

But on that first day reading the catalog of classes, I was as moved by those words as any Barbarian who ever ached to enter the medieval libraries.

My friends were speaking to me, but it was hard to pay attention.

I raised my head and looked up at them, and tears were flowing down my cheeks. They were shocked and contrite. "Oh, don't cry! What's the matter?"

But I couldn't stop crying. "I don't know," I sobbed. "I'm so glad to be here."

They looked bewildered. One friend put her arm around my shoulder. "You are a very strange person, Barbara," she said kindly. "You can't take any of those classes; you have to take the same beginning stuff we're taking. Now let's get down to business so you don't flunk out before you sign up."

After much deliberation, each friend wrote in 5 or 6 classes. I signed up for 10. I flunked 5 of them and barely passed the others. College really was a lot harder than high school, and to be honest, I couldn't understand why they kept having exams at all. It was quite enough to simply discover that there were so many astonishing things to learn about.

I calmed down after a few years and learned the routine, but every once in a while when a professor would say something truly unexpected and illuminating, something I never in a million years could have figured out on my own, I would still sometimes get tears in my eyes because I was actually here in this unexpected universe where people loved learning just for itself.

In a bookstore, months after the event in the Berkeley bar, I found and purchased a small poster, a medieval woodcut of a man at the top of a small ladder that leaned against a tree under a very low, curved, ceilinglike covering. He had stuck his head through a ragged hole in the ceiling and was looking with amazement at a night sky full of stars. I still have that poster. And I still audit classes in any college I'm near whenever I can. In which subjects? It doesn't matter, as long as the teacher is good. They're all interesting.

So what did I do with my fine college education? To what practical use did I put my learning in the years that followed? I did nothing. I just loved learning and wanted to keep on doing it.

I didn't get a job with my education, and I never did anything practical with the other things I loved, either. I didn't write about or teach what I had learned. I never earned a nickel from any of it. My family thought I was crazy, but I think they were proud of me anyway.

I think I once felt a little guilty about that. I mean, I showed promise with some of my poetry, but I never "did anything with it," as the phrase goes. Since then I've come to believe you don't always have to use things you love, and it's not always so practical to be so practical. Now that I've grown up, I realize that all that delicious dilettantism pays its way as much as any degree in medicine or engineering, by making me remember every day—whenever I pick up a book or watch the Science Channel or try to read a map of Asia for no particular reason—that life is amazing and there is no end to the wonder of it.

I like to think that the registration office felt my admiration of learning was commendable, but after a few semesters they did request that I choose a major and stop my attempts to attend every class in the catalog.

"You'll never graduate if you keep this up," they warned. But why on earth would anyone want to graduate? Just to go back to the world where nobody said anything I couldn't figure out by myself? I was perfectly happy to continue on forever, and my study skills were even improving a little. My parents didn't complain much since I paid my own way. In those days tuition was next to nothing. Rent was cheap. My 2-hour lunchtime job at a local hamburger shop paid my expenses easily, and I stayed pleasantly plump on what the boss allowed us waitresses to eat and carry home in addition to our $1 an hour. It was a good arrangement all around.

Finally, I picked a major. Well, I picked two. First I picked math because it looked like the most amazingly gorgeous thing a person could possibly learn on this earth. But I found it incredibly hard to learn, and I simply couldn't locate a trace of the heavenly but unnameable stuff I had thought was in it somewhere.

So I gave up and took an easy major, anthropology (where I'd already gotten some As), and with some disappointment, I went for the grades-and-graduation thing like everyone else.

Through the years, when friends or fellow students inquired why I was taking classes, I could never explain. I felt caught and a little ashamed. The prevailing attitude was that "perennial students" like me were lazy or immature, wouldn't buckle down, wouldn't do the "hard stuff" required of more serious people. I understood by then that I was supposed to study something I could ultimately put to use, but the thought of narrowing my focus and burying myself in one field of study was unspeakably depressing. I never seriously considered it.

And then the sixties came, and everybody relaxed a little. I got older and stopped explaining myself to anyone—and I audited classes to my heart's content. I also noticed that other older students were showing up, too. I guess the enjoyment of listening to those professors never stopped for them, either.

Fast-forward many years, and I had moved into a very different time in my life. I still had my books and I still snuck into classes whenever I could, but now I was a single mom with kids to support and I needed a career. Graduate school was out of the question for many reasons—time and money among them—so I got the kind of work you could get with a BA in the late sixties: working in programs sponsored by the city to help deal with poor people, drug addicts, and ex-convicts, and I enjoyed it enormously. Eventually, I fashioned a career out of some natural ability I had with people, the experience I'd gotten from working in my parents' bars, and a lot of good fortune—I became a writer and what was later called a life coach.

As a coach, I began to notice clients here and there who reminded me of myself as I was that first day in college. They loved too many different things to ever choose one. They never wanted to stop exploring, trying things out, or learning, but they didn't direct their learning toward any goal. They were often bright, many were talented in a number of areas, and they loved to talk about whatever they were involved in at the moment. They were interesting, high-energy, basically happy people. The only thing that bothered them was that in life they had the same problem I'd had in school: They found it impossible to choose a major.

And that's when it began to dawn on me that not only did we behave differently from most people, maybe we were actually *designed* differently. I started reading about famous people in history, like Aristotle and Goethe, da Vinci and Ben Franklin—people whose interests were also all over the map—to see if I could find a clue to help me.

As I looked through the books of their journals and letters, I noticed something odd: None of these people seemed to have the slightest problem about not sticking with one field! They flitted from one subject to another with complete freedom, and they never appeared to feel guilty if they left a project unfinished (even if, like Leonardo, they'd been paid for it!). None of them ever settled on one career, for that matter, and they never seemed defensive or apologetic about it. How did they do that? Who gave them permission to go sticking their noses into whatever interested them?

The only answer I ever found was this: In their time, nobody seemed to think that there was anything wrong with doing everything under the sun. I found no evidence that anybody told Aristotle that it was bad to be interested in so many things. Franklin wasn't defensive, because nobody told him he had anything to defend. Goethe wasn't guilty about writing novels and studying optics and doing everything else that took his fancy, because nobody criticized him for it.

It was a revelation!

There was no way to reproduce the times and places they lived in, but I thought it might be possible to create a loose community that could offer support and a sense of belonging, so I set about giving us a name: Scanners, because instead of diving down into the depths of an interest, we scanned the horizon for many interests. Then, in 1994, I wrote at length about Scanners in my book *I Could Do Anything If I Only Knew What It Was*, and I waited for the book to come out. I hoped it would make a difference.

But I didn't expect what happened.

As soon as the book was published, letters started pouring in. At first, there were hundreds of letters. Ten years later, that number has grown to thousands, and they're still coming. Almost every letter said basically the same thing: "I'm a Scanner! What a relief! I thought I had a disability/was trying to sabotage myself/was lazy/was shallow/lacked character, etc."

The people who wrote me were unbelievably grateful to hear themselves described in positive terms—usually for the first time. For years they had struggled to understand why they were so different from everyone they knew. They had spent years of their lives bewildered and frustrated. Many had gone to therapists for help but couldn't follow the program they were given to choose one path and stick to it. They couldn't understand why they were unable to find the right careers, and they described the same patterns over and over again: Every interesting career they started soon became intolerably boring. Or they had never even tried one because they couldn't make up their minds in the first place.

Scanners who weren't looking for careers had just as many problems because they had too many choices. Should they write, or travel, or make art, or start home businesses? They didn't want to choose one area; they wanted them all.

And why couldn't they stick with anything long enough to finish it? All they knew was that they just couldn't get it right, and as time passed they became convinced they were flawed in some way.

But as soon as they saw themselves described in my book, the lights went on! Everything looked different. As one person wrote, "I couldn't figure out who I was, so I always thought I was doing something wrong. As soon as I read about Scanners, I knew that wasn't true!"

Obviously I had struck a chord. I was getting the word out, and Scanners were starting to wake up to the truth that there was nothing wrong with them. The realization that their behavior was different—because they were actually genetically different—explained so much that it was accepted right away. It was a great start.

But what then? Where do you train to live like a Scanner? What classes do you need for a degree in being a Scanner? What's the logical career path for a Scanner? Where are the guidelines that will show you how to have a good life without having to change yourself?

School for Scanners

Where are the guidelines for Scanners? Plain and simple (unless they're hiding somewhere I haven't discovered yet), there aren't any. If you have a specialty (say geology or fashion), there are schools with majors called geology and fashion to teach you, there are guidance counselors to help you make decisions, and there are recruiters to hire you. There are professional organizations and books and Web sites to help you develop into a successful geologist or fashion designer or whatever kind of specialist you want to be.

There's nothing like that out there for Scanners. If you're a Scanner, you may have gone in for some kind of abilities testing only to find that you scored high in almost every category. Career counselors aren't trained to handle that outcome. So far, the best advice you've been given has probably been, "You can do anything. Just choose one of your talents and get started."

That was also the worst advice.

They might as well have said, "We can't help you at all," because Scanners can't choose. And now you're learning something most of your career guidance people do not know: Scanners aren't supposed to choose.

Until now, this has always left you completely on your own: You aren't guided or assisted in the business of handling your many talents. There is no academic path to train you in the best use of your irrepressible curiosity or to direct your fast mind into a multidirectional specialty. In business, no career tracks or job titles exist for the multitalented, can-do-anything Scanner (the "go-to" people who, even when they're valued by those around them, have no label that indicates who they really are). Our culture's pressure to train specialists simply isn't balanced out by any plan to train generalists (i.e., Scanners).

But you have to start somewhere. I gathered up all the techniques I'd fashioned through the years to help my Scanner clients and went looking for more. I started special discussions on the Internet where Scanners could share their experiences and give each other support. I started giving regular telephone conference-call classes where we could talk to each other on the phone and designed and ran workshops dedicated to Scanners. I even did an hour-long public television special on the subject. More than anything, I wanted to share what I had learned with the people who needed it. I turned into someone with a mission, which wasn't really my style. But with letters like this one, how could I think of stopping?

I have to tell you how excited I was to read your description of a Scanner. That's exactly what I am and now I am working toward balancing my life in such a way that I can fully express myself.

The "permission" to NOT seek after that one and ONLY profession and wander to all of the things that I love is something I never gave myself…I've been trying to conform to the worldview that there is only one true path and I was supposed to find it at 18!

But you communicated that permission very well, and it has taken a weight off of my heart and allowed me to look at the things I love with a totally different perspective, a renewed energy, and, most of all, a joy that had been stifled by guilt for years.

Thank you! Now I have a title for what I previously viewed as a drawback.

I'm looking at my life in a totally different way and not only forgiving myself for being a Scanner but loving it!

I, too, struggled for years about not being able to be "stable." Now I know I am just a true Scanner, and I am the happiest when I can be myself without all the criticism.

My whole outlook of life has changed—thank you, Barbara, for your advice.

And so I dedicated myself to putting together a handbook to help Scanners overcome their obstacles, find ways to let their ideas flourish, and use their many talents. In the process of writing this book, I made it my business to find and meet as many Scanners as I could, and now I've met hundreds of them. They're magnificent. They love life, they're excited about new experiences, and they're the most interesting people you'll ever meet. They're also incredibly generous and have shared with me many tips and strategies they developed to solve the logistical problems of having dozens of interests. You might have developed some of your own. I know I have. Scanners are inventive and enjoy solving problems. But the main reason these people had to design solutions on their own was that they didn't know other Scanners existed; they had nowhere to turn for help.

I think that's why the Scanners I hear from are overflowing with stories and personal experiences: They've kept everything inside for a long time. They wrote about the wounds of being belittled and the frustration of being unable to satisfy the expectations of their families as well as the loneliness of not being understood (and not understanding themselves). But they've also told of their curiosity, their love of discovery, and their almost childlike delight of being engaged in a great project. I've included as many excerpts from their letters as I had room for, but I wish I could include them all because they'd inspire you, but even more, because they'd put a face on other Scanners and provide you with some fascinating company: Wouldn't you like to read letters from Scanners who are teaching school and writing music in Nepal, writing books on making beer, working in the theater, meeting world-famous leaders in Czechoslovakia, or knitting miniature villages for their mom in between playing in their own rock band—after work, of course.

Their words might be the first you've heard from other Scanners. You might catch yourself exclaiming, "That's just like me!" I hope so, because familiar words are what Scanners need to find their way home. In familiar territory, you can begin to celebrate your own identity and start living the full, rich life you're capable of.

This book is a personal homecoming for me, too. It's a signpost that I've come full circle in my life, from the freshman who wept with joy at finding those amazing subjects in the college catalog so many years ago, to the senior who reads and writes and travels and has a very fine time with her dozens upon dozens of interests. And maybe I did put one thing I learned in college to practical use, after all: I found out what it's like to want to learn everything and have no one to show me what to do. In this book, I'm using that experience to understand and try to help you.

Here's my best effort at an owner's manual for Scanners. In it, you'll learn who you are and why you've always been so different from those around you. You'll find out exactly what type of Scanner you are—because all Scanners are not the same—and which of the tools, tips, techniques, and life design models in these pages are right for you. And when you've finished, you'll understand what has always made you different from the people who easily found a path to follow in their lives, and you'll learn how to step over obstacles that have stopped you in the past. And finally, with your arms full of new tools, you'll be free to do what you were born to do: swing into action and use all the creative energy inside you to do the extraordinary work you're capable of.

For a Scanner, that's the best kind of fun in the world.

Scanners like you have always been among us, but until now, few have recognized that they're not just a faulty version of everyone else but a different kind of human. As far as I can tell, you've been "undiscovered" until now. It will be an honor if I turn out to be the first to name you.

What you'll find here is a completely new program, the first of its kind. It's one part rehabilitation to undo the effects of years of misunderstandings and restore your battered self-esteem. It's another part training so that, like a pilot learning to fly a fast plane, you'll learn how to use the unusual abilities you were born with. And since Scanners have to pay their rent like everyone else, it's one more part career counseling—how to find the job that won't bore you but instead will support the life you want to live.

So open your mind, roll up your sleeves, and let's get started. I can't wait to see what you will do with that lovely brain of yours once the gates are thrown open and you're finally free to stretch out to your full speed and explore this big world that you love so much.

PART ONE

WHAT IS A SCANNER, AND ARE YOU ONE?

Chapter 1

ALL ABOUT SCANNERS

Elaine has found a few hours for herself, a rare occurrence, and she's determined to do something she loves to do. Exactly what that will be is still undecided, but it won't be hard to find, because she loves to do so many things.

She stands in front of a large table in her garage, looking at two projects she has started but never finished. To her left are two straw baskets of brightly colored yarn, a tube of glue, and a package of construction paper. Looking at them almost makes her mouth water. She's always happy doing crafts and promised a scrapbook to a friend many months ago. She tries not to look at the shelves behind the table, where her clay rests inside a plastic bag next to some small wooden tools. When she has more time, she'll make that ceramic piece she thought up, a great idea she got while looking through some antique picture books a while back. But she wishes she could do it right now.

She forces her eyes back to the table. In front of her, still in the paper bag from the store, are four books she bought months ago about the history of Poland. Also, in the bag is a package of unopened audiocassettes and a device she bought that will allow her to record conversations on the telephone. She wants to interview the older members of her family, all of whom are immigrants from Poland. There hasn't been a moment to look in the books since she found them at the bookstore. They sit there like a tantalizing dessert, saved for some time when she can relax, after the chores are done. But some of her relatives are growing old; she really should call them soon. She wonders if she should make a phone call right now and at least set up some phone appointments with her family and learn how to hook up the telephone recording system. She misses her Aunt Jessie.

But on the right, sitting on the floor in a tall, narrow box leaning against the table, still in the box it came in, is the electric piano she got for her birthday 3 months ago. She could set it up in 20 minutes if there were just a clear space for it in the house. Elaine knows the piano has to stay set up somewhere, because if she has to bring it out and put it away all the time, she'll never get around to it. But who has time to clear out a space when the whole house needs clearing out?

If only she were five people instead of just one, she'd do everything, all of it, right now, today. She looks with longing at the black-and-white drawing of the electric piano on the box and can almost hear the music. Her voice feels like it's starting to fill up with music and her fingers remember the touch of the keys. Could she just open it right here in the garage and do a little before dinner?

No. Elaine remembers that she promised her 8-year-old daughter a costume for a party coming up in a few weeks, and she really should get started on that and leave all this for another day. In fact, she's had it set up on the dining room table for 3 days, and the family has had to eat on trays in front of the TV set. Embarrassing. She'll do that right now.

But she suddenly remembers that she had another wonderful idea today in the car on the way home from her meeting with a client, an idea about a way to bring in some income that would absolutely work and would cost very little to start, and Elaine feels a familiar sense of apprehension that if she doesn't do something about it right away she'll forget it like all the other good ideas she keeps having.

Every single thing she sees or thinks of sparkles with potential and pulls her attention. She wants to do them all. But she's totally stuck and ends up doing none of them. She might as well pick up the cleaning and head for the market. She sighs and walks outside into the fresh air and remembers she wanted to go for a run today. Her dog, who has been lying on the floor nearby, gets up to follow and wonders what's bothering her. So does she.

Elaine doesn't have attention deficit disorder. She checked it out with doctors long ago. And she knows that when she's involved in any project, she doesn't get distracted by irrelevant things.

So what's stopping her? Why is she so indecisive? For that matter, why is she interested in so many things? Why is she such a great starter but then runs out of steam and leaves a trail of unfinished projects behind her? She doesn't blame her friends and family for smiling knowingly whenever she gets enthused about something new—she lets that roll off her back easily—but it bothers her that she almost never gets to see an end product.

But how can anyone choose between so many interests? Which is the right one? Which is the most important? Another thought comes to her. She remembers that she meant to polish up her Spanish, because she might be able to teach part-time next year, and she can use the income.

Elaine shakes her head, almost resenting the new idea and feeling a hint of despair that there will always be something new and interesting moving into her line of vision; even if she ignores them all and firmly chooses one project or another, these new thoughts have the power to make her unsure of any choice she's made.

Most of her acquaintances know exactly what they're doing with their lives. Why doesn't she just pick something and do it? After all, she's very smart and has been told she could do anything! Why can't she get going?

Does this sound familiar?

Does Elaine remind you of yourself? Do you also wonder why you're caught in this kind of dilemma? Are you unable to figure out what drives you and why you're so different from people who made their choices early and followed one path? Why can't *you* start working on your dreams—and stick to them? How will you ever focus your curious mind on one path when you can't bear to turn your back on anything? What makes you tick?

Believe it or not, there are very good answers to those questions. If, like so many Scanners I've met, you think the situation is hopeless, you're in for some nice surprises. Here's the first and most important surprise: *If Scanners didn't think they should limit themselves to one field, 90 percent of their problems would cease to exist!*

What is a Scanner?

Scanners love to read and write, to fix and invent things, to design projects and businesses, to cook and sing, and to create the perfect dinner party. (You'll notice I didn't use the word "or," because Scanners don't love to do one thing *or* the other; they love them all.) A Scanner might be fascinated with learning how to play bridge or bocce, but once she gets good at it, she might never play it again. One Scanner I know proudly showed me a button she was wearing that said, "I Did That Already."

To Scanners the world is like a big candy store full of fascinating opportunities, and all they want is to reach out and stuff their pockets.

It sounds wonderful, doesn't it? The problem is, Scanners are *starving* in the candy store. They believe they're allowed to pursue only one path. But they want them all. If they force themselves to make a choice, they are forever discontented. But usually Scanners don't choose anything at all. And they don't feel good about it.

As kids, most Scanners had been having a great time! At school no one objected to their many interests, because every hour of every student's school day is devoted to a different subject. But at some point in high school or soon after, everyone was expected to make a choice, and that's when Scanners ran into trouble. While some people happily narrowed down to one subject, Scanners simply couldn't.

The conventional wisdom was overwhelming and seemed indisputable: If you're a jack-of-all-trades, you'll always be a master of none. You'll become a dilettante, a dabbler, a superficial person—and you'll never have a decent career. Suddenly, a Scanner who all through school might have been seen as an enthusiastic learner had now become a failure.

But one thought wouldn't leave my mind: If the world had just continued to accept them as they were, *Scanners wouldn't have had any problems.* With the exception of learning project management techniques, the only thing Scanners needed was to reject conventional wisdom that said they were doing something wrong and claim their true identity. Almost every case of low self-esteem, shame, frustration, feelings of inadequacy, indecisiveness, and inability to get into action simply disappeared the moment they understood that they were Scanners and stopped trying to be somebody else.

It appears that Scanners are an unusual breed of human being. One reason they don't recognize themselves is that they don't often meet people like themselves.

How do you know if you're a Scanner?

Maybe it would be useful to first discuss who isn't one.

Who isn't a Scanner?

Well, specialists aren't Scanners, obviously. If you're someone who is happy being completely absorbed by one field, I've labeled you a Diver. Some clear examples of Divers are professional musicians, scientists, mathematicians, professional chess players, athletes, business owners, and financiers. These people may "relax" with a hobby, but they're rarely passionate about anything but their field. In fact, Divers often wonder how people can be interested in anything but what they're interested in. Sometimes they even make fun of themselves for it, like the racing bicyclist Tim Krabbé described in *The Rider*, who glances up from his gear to look at people walking and says, "Nonracers. The emptiness of those lives shocks me."

By contrast, Scanners rarely think what other people are doing is empty. They're always curious to know "what's out there" and love to poke their noses into just about anything. A Diver rarely spends a moment wondering what he might be missing when he's totally absorbed in his field. On the other hand, 99 percent of Scanners spend a lot of time scanning the horizon, thinking about their next move.

Many people look like Scanners, but aren't

People who continually move from one idea to another often have very different reasons for doing so. Some are simply trying to make up their minds, and when they find the "right" choice, they can easily give up all the other ideas they considered.

Others move between ideas for reasons that surprised me when I first heard them. Here are some examples.

> *I spent years frustrating myself and everyone around me with my constant jumping from one thing to another. What I learned about myself eventually is that I knew deep down what I should be doing all along, but was simply too scared to commit myself to it. The constant stream of alternative ideas was simply an advanced avoidance technique.*

> *I think I've always avoided what I really want to do because I was afraid I'd be mediocre, or fail completely, so I'd keep changing my mind before I produced anything that could be judged.*

Depressed people often make the mistake of believing they're Scanners. Depression can create a fractured consciousness that doesn't allow one to pay attention to anything for long, and some depressed people believe that the cause of their depression is their inability to find something they can care about intensely. But the reverse is usually true: They can't care about anything because they're depressed. One of the main symptoms of depression is the inability to feel desire. A woman who had experience with depressed people told me:

> *The types of attention span problems that have to do with depression are quite different than job-interest attention spans. When you get so you can't read a book (and even newspaper articles are too complicated to remember from start to finish), you can't pay attention during a conversation, and you have no idea where your keys and wallet are when usually you know exactly where you put them, then you need to talk to somebody about therapy and medication, both of which work wonders.*

And then we have ADD. Before knowing who they were, many Scanners assumed that their "problem" might be attention deficit disorder (ADD), simply because everyone assumed that being interested in lots of things was a form of distraction. In my experience, I've found that many Scanners actually do have ADD, but they are true Scanners all the same. I've also met people with diagnosed ADD who appear to be Scanners but are not. Once you understand that a bona fide Scanner has no problem with the normal ability to focus (as opposed to ADD–style hyper-focus), the confusion with ADD usually clears up.

I'm a Scanner and have been diagnosed with ADD. And I can tell you that nothing is clearer than the difference between feeling stuck because I'm having an ADD attack—that is, my mind is in a fog and I have trouble remembering what I'm doing—and being stuck for the typical Scanner reasons of being attracted to so many things that I can't figure out which project to reach for next.

Of course, there are many people who are quite content in their fields and have a few normal interests in addition, such as a lawyer who enjoys cooking and travel, or an advertising art director who collects antiques. But there's a noticeable difference between someone with a normal range of interests and a Scanner.

Who *is* a Scanner?

Intense curiosity about numerous unrelated subjects is one of the most basic characteristics of a Scanner. Scanners are endlessly inquisitive. In fact, Scanners often describe themselves as being hopelessly interested in everything (although, as you'll find out, this isn't so). A Scanner doesn't want to specialize in any of the things she loves, because that means giving up all the rest. Some even think that being an expert would be limiting and boring.

Our society frowns on this apparent self-indulgence. Of course, it's not self-indulgence at all; it's the way Scanners are designed, and there's nothing they can or should do about it. A Scanner is curious because he is genetically programmed to explore everything that interests him. If you're a Scanner, that's your nature. Ignore it and you'll always be fretful and dissatisfied.

It's a whole new way of thinking, I know. And much of the world doesn't see Scanners' behavior as admirable or even acceptable. But it wasn't always this way.

A recent change in fashion

Scanners are the victims of a fashion change in history, and a recent one at that. Until the technology race with the Soviet Union after World War II changed our views, the kind of people I now call Scanners were admired. But by the mid-1950s, a dramatic change had occurred.

When Russia launched Sputnik, the first-ever satellite to be launched into space, the United States went into shock. Immediately our resources were devoted to catching up to and passing Russian technology, and everything else became secondary. University faculties turned into specialized training centers; science and technology—the realm of specialists—reigned supreme. Departments of literature, the humanities, even history were seen as irrelevant luxuries. And with that decline in respect came a radical change in the stature of Scanners. No longer described as "well-rounded," "Renaissance people," or "erudite," almost overnight they were seen as irrelevant, silly, irresponsible. Now, regarding Scanners, this change in thinking is complete. Almost everyone in our society takes it as a self-evident truth—obvious, simple common sense—that Scanners are doing something wrong. Unfortunately, that has come to include Scanners themselves.

It's troubling to speculate on how much unnecessary unhappiness and wasted talent this ignorance of history has caused. That's why it is essential that you never forget that for most of human history, a person with a wide range of knowledge and abilities was highly valued. As you'll see, the pendulum is swinging back.

Now what?

Having the freedom to go after all your interests is wonderful, but how on earth can you actually do it? The revelation that you're a Scanner doesn't automatically propel you full speed ahead on all those things you love: You have to know *how* to manage a life that's full of different talents.

One result of this 50-year-old disfavor with nonspecialists is that role models are rare. Unlike earlier times in history when multiple interests were more common, there's no one who can teach Scanners how to follow so many interests. To be a Scanner these days is like inheriting a fabulous, shiny machine full of gears and buttons and gauges—without an instruction booklet!

How do you travel and become a photographer when you also want to learn Mandarin Chinese, study history, have a great garden, learn to write fiction, and try auto racing, too? It's not at all impossible, but if you've never done it before, it certainly looks that way.

And what about careers for Scanners? Almost no one, least of all a Scanner himself, believes you can find a career without choosing one path and abandoning all others. That's a pure case of tunnel vision, because Scanner jobs are everywhere. Innovative ways to earn a living that favor the Scanner personality—and interesting jobs for people who always called themselves Jacks-of-All-Trades, Masters of None—are showing up everywhere. The world of work is changing, and there's never been a better time to bring the multitalented Scanner into the workforce.

Until now, the manual has been missing

But now there is a manual for Scanners, and you're holding it in your hands. You're going to learn how to do everything you want to do and keep a roof over your head at the same time. For that, you need to undo the problems that were created because you didn't understand you were a Scanner, and you'll get a new understanding of why you're drawn to so many different things and why you leave them when you do. (Clue: It's not because you can't focus, but because you *can!*) You'll learn the particulars of your type of Scanner, and we'll dismantle the myth that has kept you afraid of commitments so you can actually enjoy making them. And if you're way too busy or even frozen in your tracks, if you never seem to start your projects, or if you never seem to finish them, help is on the way.

I think you're going to like what you find: new methods and procedures and tools and strategies for starting up your Scanner engine, and all of them are easy (honest!) and interesting, to boot. When you combine insight with every trick of the trade, you've got what you need to become a truly successful Scanner with a life that matches your unusual and wonderful brain.

Before you get started, I want you to learn to use the most important piece of equipment in your kit, something you'll be using in all the upcoming chapters.

I call it the SCANNER DAYBOOK.

Scanners often avoid getting involved with a new, fascinating subject when it catches their eye. They say things like, "How can I justify wandering off in yet another direction?" But that's a real shame, because they're not breaking any laws or hurting anyone by being curious or enthusiastic by some new thought. And each time they push away an interesting new activity, they're reinforcing the myth that they *are* doing something wrong. Even a short detour to a "frivolous" activity would feel wrong, and so everything waits. As one unhappy Scanner wrote me, "I feel that if I haven't finished what I'm working on, I have no right to have fun." Of course, when you're a Scanner, there is a risk of getting sidetracked and using up the time you need on your original project, but the Daybook can solve that problem, as you'll see.

The Scanner Daybook

This is simply a blank book devoted to what you do each day—as a Scanner, of course. No laundry lists or general journaling, just anything related to being a Scanner—the place to capture your best ideas and also the tangents that pull you off those ideas. In addition, I'll sometimes ask you to work on an exercise that requires writing, and you might want to take notes on anything you find particularly useful inside this book (or anywhere else).

This is your personal version of the Leonardo da Vinci notebooks. If you've never seen them, find a book of reproductions in your library or try to get a glimpse on the Internet. They're an inspiration.

The da Vinci notebooks are a great model for a Scanner Daybook. Leonardo's entries are delightfully out of order, impulsive, and unrestrained. (He even wrote his comments backward! This was possibly to hide his ideas from prying eyes or perhaps because he had mirror vision or maybe because he loved to exercise his brain. I wouldn't put it past a Scanner.) But never be intimidated by his fame, or by anyone else's either. For you, he's just someone who liked to think with a pen in his hand, just like you're going to do.

The blank pages in your Daybook are where you'll capture ideas that could otherwise get lost or keep a record of private little trips and "what ifs" that are always floating in and out of a creative mind. You'll find yourself welcoming these thoughts more and more as you realize you are not required to do anything but write about them. No follow-up is required unless it takes your fancy to do so.

If you find this a trifle scandalous, you're not alone. One Scanner wrote:

> *I call the Daybook my "Guilty Pleasures." Last week I wrote about a special kind of resort I'd love to build, a cookbook I'd love to write (maybe even videotaping myself and creating my own cooking show), and I took some notes on a few careers that looked interesting. I can't imagine why I didn't always do this! It's fun and it helps me think!*

What will your Scanner Daybook look like?

It's important to make sure you own the right kind of blank book to serve as your Scanner Daybook, because this is no ordinary journal. You can carry a spiral notebook to write in when you leave the house, but you need a more impressive book to enter those notes into when you come back home. Get something you like, but more formal than you're accustomed to using—one of those books you're almost afraid to write in. (Don't worry, we'll get you writing in it!)

Make sure there are no lines on the pages and give yourself a lot of space to write on. The larger each page and the thicker the book, the better it will be. You can usually find something suitable in an art supplies store, sometimes with an old-fashioned leather-look binding of the kind you might find in Scrooge's office. Run your hand over the paper to be sure you'll enjoy writing on it and get the kinds of pens that make writing enjoyable to you. If you want to have a really good time, you can put your Daybook on its own stand like one of those huge dictionaries. (If you make notes at the computer or when you're away from this tome, you can always tape them in later. It's creative fun to tape a variety of notes and pictures to its pages and write around them, and it makes an interesting Daybook.)

Writing in your Scanner Daybook is more important than you may yet realize. As the days go by and the entries add up, you'll notice that you're actually taking care of the sides of you that you may have neglected as well as undervalued until now. *But the very act of considering your explorations worth keeping track of begins to change everything you ever thought about yourself.* In place of those thoughts most Scanners carry around with them about their "flitting" or "dabbling," without any extra effort you'll find a growing respect for the way your mind works.

It's good for you, too. Giving that creative mind of yours a chance to have some fun is like giving a plant sunshine and water.

If you've felt under the gun in the past whenever you started something, you'll enjoy discovering that the act of taking some notes or making a sketch on any old idea is too minor to create any performance pressure you might ordinarily feel. But all the same, writing down these fun ideas in a bound book will subtly teach you to value them. Every time you record your ideas and add drawings and projections and fantasies, the early teaching that made you doubt yourself will get fainter, until it becomes second nature to assume it's okay— better than okay—to be fascinated with anything new.

Your Daybook is also a self-study book: Turned loose without any restrictions, allowed to learn or design or imagine whatever you like, what kind of Scanner emerges? Where does your mind really want to go? Your Daybook gives you a free ticket to create anything you like, so the farther you follow your fancy in your Daybook pages, the clearer the answer will be.

In the past, you may have seen yourself simply as someone with an inability to stick to things or follow through on projects, but none of that is relevant here. Getting your ideas down on paper isn't like starting something you should finish; it's like seeing a good movie—only better because you're not only watching it but designing it. That freedom will allow you to be as creative as you like. If, for instance, you're taken by the idea of interviewing your neighbors for their life stories, you'd open the Daybook and write down your idea, and you'd have no hesitation to let it grow. (Maybe you could turn it into a film, or maybe it could be a photo exhibit with audios running of everyone's voice; you could even start schoolkids on a project to save the stories of their families; why not some kind of virtual museum that anyone could add to . . . ?)

Your Daybook lets you go into planning that idea without having to actually produce it. If you decide you want to make a film, you'll find that you've captured the idea at its best moment, when you were the most enthused and the most creative. And if you never take another step, you've had a good time and risked nothing.

Little by little, the process of writing your ideas in your Daybook will change the way you feel about not following up on every one of your good ideas, because it becomes so clear that planning, designing, and making a record of your ideas in something called a Scanner Daybook isn't making a promise; it's the way inventive people enjoy themselves.

First entry

Today, I'd like you to do a trial run. So pick a recent idea, a small one you haven't given much thought to, and do your first Scanner Daybook Write-Up.

Open the book wide. You're going to start on the left-hand page so you have a really big area to write on. Now, put today's date and your starting time in the upper left-hand corner of the first page. At the top of the page, write a title of any idea you'd enjoy playing with, like "Life Stories of My Neighbors" or "The Autobiography of My Cat, George, for Possible Use in a Feature Film." Choose a project that's interesting and has possibilities, but one that you might never develop much past this first description. Leave very wide margins on both sides of each page for writing any additions that later occur to you.

And then, just let yourself go.

Bury yourself in your idea and start writing. Draw boxes with stick drawings or diagrams of anything that seems relevant. When a tangent comes along, follow it, but not in the same area you were writing in. Instead, draw a line to the farthest right-hand area on the right-hand page, ending at the top of the page (to leave room below it for other tangents that might come along), and continue that arrow a few inches into the next blank page. Then look at your watch or set a clock timer and give yourself up to 20 minutes to make notes on this tangential idea.

And then return to your original idea.

Your tangent idea is safe and ready whenever you want it. Now, return to your original idea. You can get information from the Internet and print out whatever you want to keep. You can cut out the most interesting part and tape it right on the appropriate page (with a note that tells where you got it, in case you ever want to find it again). You might want to draw a box around the excerpt with a good dark pen and fill the margin with exclamation points if you feel excited about any quotation. If you find something in a book, write a running report on your thoughts, or copy the essential passage by hand. Make diagrams, paste in photos or clips from magazines, or do anything else that allows you to enjoy the subject you're writing about.

Always try to make your descriptions as complete as possible so that if you disappeared and a stranger found this description, she'd be able to complete the project! Why? Because otherwise, once the passion wears off, you'll forget why you were so excited! Let your thoughts spill out on the page as they come to you, instead of making a list or an outline you won't understand or appreciate later. You don't ever want to look back on an idea and think it was boring or worthless. You've probably done that many times in the past, but the Scanner Daybook is supposed to help you respect your ideas. All of them.

Here's a brief example.

A Great Way to Study Botany!

How about a series of detective novels about a retired botany teacher who travels all through South America, from the US border all the way to Tierra del Fuego at the very bottom of the continent! She could be looking for new plant species and describe them and draw them—like this: [here you might tape in a botanical illustration clipped from a magazine], but she keeps coming across some evil criminal. Maybe he should be a botanist, too! Developing mind-altering plants so he can take over the world!

So each novel could take place in a different country and could include the detective's descriptions and drawings of plants and getting stories from the local people about how they're used. Maybe a cookbook? For some plants. (Look up "poisonous plants for detective mysteries." There's gotta be a book about that somewhere.)

Why not make it into a Web site! Oh! A Weblog diary where I write a new little episode every week, with photos too! Maybe I could get some botanists to help me, and we could each write a different episode and link to some really good botanical sites. That would be so much fun! Maybe it could be a teaching tool and classrooms could use it, just clicking on different parts of the page and maybe hearing a voice, the voice of the teacher, like an audiobook at the same time! Have to ask some techie friends if this is too hard.

If that's what you were writing, you could draw a map on the facing page to show where each episode would take place, and you can come up with some fun titles, like "Miss Bennett and the Case of the Hidden Basil."

Remember: It doesn't matter if you never do what you're describing on these pages, because finishing a project is not the issue here. This is about your vision and the free play of ideas for pure enjoyment.

If you have uninterrupted time to continue working on this idea for as long as you like, that would be very helpful for the purpose of researching how your mind deals with a new interest. If you're not stopped by an outside interruption, the only thing that will stop you will be something internal, and it's very important that you start getting familiar with what that might be.

When you decide to stop, catch the thought you had that caused that decision, such as: "I'm losing interest in this" or "I wish I could continue, but I have to pick up the kids" or anything in between. Write that thought at the end of your description and write the exact time next to it.

And that's all for today.

Your first entry is complete

That's your first entry in your Scanner Daybook. Congratulations! You've learned how to catch an idea *while it interests you*. Now you know how to save a dream, no matter how fleeting it is, no matter how many you may have.

And why should you save your dreams?

There are many reasons. They're pleasant to read, they'll keep you from forgetting a good project you might want to revisit, they'll teach you a lot about what attracts you and for how long, but most of all, they'll allow you to *take every idea and every vision at least one step* instead of discarding it as if it were still-born because it's impractical or impossible.

Scanners shouldn't throw ideas out like trash, no matter how many they may have, no matter how "half-baked" the ideas may be. Respect for ideas is the same as respect for the idea maker: you. (It will also help you respect the ideas of others and might make a huge difference in their lives, too.)

Let's end the notion that ideas have no value unless they turn into a business or have some other practical use. Save them all in a beautiful book like Leonardo did. You might want to give them away someday, perhaps to someone who needs an idea. Or your great-great-grandchildren might love knowing what a fascinating mind you had. Or your biographer might be very happy after you're gone.

Your LIVING QUARTERS MAP

That's all you have to do in your Scanner Daybook today, but if you're feeling energized and ready for more, I suggest this extremely eye-opening exercise for you to do soon, either now or sometime in the next week. This exercise will help replace self-criticism with genuine interest in your identity. Because there's something fascinating I've found in long years of working with people: *Interest is the sincerest form of respect.* It's the most unself-conscious, authentic way anyone can say "you deserve my attention."

In addition, although you don't know it yet, you're in training and your Daybook Write-Ups are part of the program. I'll explain more about that later.

Open up a fresh pair of pages in your Scanner Daybook (remember, in your Daybook, you always start on the left-hand page so you have plenty of open space to write on). Leave a bit of space at the top of the left-hand page for the title of this entry. When I designed this program, I wrote at the top of my page "A Scanner's Home Is Her Workshop," because I found that every single room in my house (even the hallway) has at least one writing surface with paper and pencils nearby! Wait until you've completed this exercise to see what kind of title you come up with.

Now, sit down and sketch out a rough plan of your home in pencil and then, with your Daybook and pencil in hand, walk carefully around each room looking for projects. It doesn't matter if you never finished them or even if you never started them. You know which items were intended to become projects in your own home. When you find one, draw a circle in that part of the floor plan and write the name of the project, such as:

- ❖ Little video player for watching old VHS home movies
- ❖ Basket of interesting clips from magazines
- ❖ Telephone recording hookup and instructions for my telephone classes

"I'm going to get embarrassed if I do that," one Scanner wrote me. "I kind of hate to document how many projects I've started and not finished. They make my place a mess, too."

But that's not the true Scanner inside you talking; that's you worrying about your critics. Scanners, with their love of learning new things and their instinct for potential, almost always live in a "cluttered" space, and it's not always easy for other people to understand what the clutter is about. But I asked you to do this exercise here at the beginning specifically so you could start being proud of that eager mind of yours and all the things it's been drawn to do. Your home is not just a storage facility for your unfinished projects; it's the workspace of a creative mind.

See if you can find photos of the studios of famous artists, like Picasso, and you'll see what I mean. A tidy housekeeper would be horrified at the disorder. Another artist—even a neat one—would have no problem understanding *that he wasn't looking at disorder, he was looking at a functioning workspace.*

Sherlock Holmes, of course, would find an artist's rooms very interesting indeed. So should you.

Let me close with an example from a Scanner just to get you started.

I walked through my living room and saw one antique ladies' shoe sitting on the floor behind a table and remembered why I took it home from a lawn sale. I once saw a lamp made of a shoe just like it, in a magazine. The lamp was beautiful. It also cost almost $400! I had an idea that I could start a whole line of items from found objects. So I circled the spot on my map and wrote

"Victorian Shoe for Lamp." Then I saw my harmonica and remembered I wanted to learn how to play it so I could accompany a friend who plays guitar on the street sometimes . . .

Got the idea? Okay, you do it.

After your Map is complete, you can keep it in your Daybook and add to it whenever you start something new. Or you can do what one Scanner did:

This map of my projects is beautiful! I colored it and even attached photos from magazines and a miniature piano from a charm bracelet. It's a work of art, and I'm going to frame it and put it on my wall! It's like a collage of my soul!

When you're finished, you might see a pattern in your projects, like I did in my Map. Whatever you find, with respect and admiration, write a heading in the space you left at the top of the left-hand page. Nothing deprecating is allowed. Praise is due, and I want your heading to reflect that, even if you have to scratch your head and search for it the rest of the day.

Write in your Daybook every day for a few weeks

I'd like you to write up something in your Scanner Daybook every day for the next week or two, if possible. Once you understand the benefits, you'll start looking forward to these writing sessions, and then it will be okay to be more flexible and skip a day or two.

What will you write about tomorrow? Don't get stressed. This isn't a homework assignment; it's like a coloring book with crayons given to the kid inside you.

Tomorrow you can decide to learn more about fashion, maybe taking ideas from what you wrote yesterday. You might go on the Internet to find, say, "Peruvian Clothing" and even see some books with photos that inspire you to sketch a line of women's clothing based on them. Or you might go in a completely different direction because a television show got you interested in volcanoes. Jump right in!

There's nobody around to tell you to make up your mind or quit fooling around!

Pretty soon you'll stop saying that to yourself, too, because it's so clear that your Scanner Daybook is a protected haven for dreams and ideas and interests of today. With your inquisitive mind no longer under siege, it can start filling out into its real shape.

Now let's find out why you keep picking up and dropping interests in that odd Scanner way you have. It's always made you (and everyone around you) believe there was something wrong with you, and it's time to change that.

Chapter 2

WHAT'S WRONG WITH ME?

Few things are more demoralizing than believing you're running your life the wrong way and feeling helpless to change it. If you keep failing at your attempts to be like all the "normal" people around you, you might feel like a misfit, even a failure.

That's how too many Scanners see themselves, and it's a heartbreaking misjudgment. It's painful to watch these remarkable people be hard on themselves for not sticking to one path in life or to hear them use as proof of their failure the very best things about them: their curiosity and fascination for what is new, their willingness to explore unfamiliar worlds, their exceptional ability to learn new concepts, their enthusiasm for experience—in other words, their love of being fully alive.

In an attempt to conform, some Scanners even try to keep their talents hidden away and quiet, with all the luck they'd have hiding a box of puppies in a library. And with all the unnecessary discomfort, too: Our talents (and those puppies) are so much happier when they're running free. So what's going on here? Who said Scanners had to change?

Well, it's a big misunderstanding, actually, and not the first one of its type in history. We used to think children should be seen and not heard; that left-handed people should be trained to use their right hands; that dyslexics were stupid or lazy. Fortunately, those notions have been set right for the most part, and countless people are now free to live their lives fully, without repressing themselves or being unfairly judged.

Now it's time to right the wrongs against Scanners so they can develop their exceptional potential. If you think you might be a Scanner—that is, if you're someone who loves so many things you've never succeeded in choosing only one and forsaking the others—changing this misunderstanding begins with you. The world will catch up in its own good time, but your life is too valuable to wait for that important event. In fact, you can have a hand in starting to open everyone's eyes about Scanners. It all starts with you. Right here, right now, you must begin to see who you really are.

Pamela's story

I recently read this post on my bulletin board with astonishment.

> *Hi. My name is Pamela. I'm 42, found your books when I was about 27 or 28. Since then I've: traveled to Greenland; driven to Alaska and spent a year there; been whale watching; tracked UFOs for the US Air Force; started several different businesses; bought and sold a couple of houses; been on a ghost hunt in an English castle; read tarot cards at psychic fairs; pulled a loop-the-loop in a fast little airplane; designed and helped build my current house; landscaped my garden with about 10,000 different flowers; worked in a tattoo parlor; become a drummer in a rock band (two CDs out and the third coming up shortly!); raised miniature pinschers; become a certified feng shui practitioner; read nine million books; knitted a whole miniature village as a Christmas present for my mom; taught myself database programming; become a tour guide at the Atlanta zoo; given away zillions of copies of your books to anyone who dared say "I can't . . . "; helped my mom come to terms with cancer . . . three times! . . . and, um, a few other things that slip my mind just now. Just another average bored housewife (ha!). Anyway, now I'm living on 160 acres in the wilds of Alabama (stop giggling), a dozen miles away from the nearest "settlement," and wondering what to do next. So, that's me . . . or part of me anyway.*

I wrote Pamela at once to congratulate her on living such an exciting life and to ask if I could use her letter in my book. I didn't ask if she was serious about the nine million books she'd read, because I was a little afraid of what her answer might be.

"I thought you expected all your Scanner readers to do that," she answered sheepishly.

"Well, I get good responses, but I've never seen one like yours. What did you do before you read my books?"

"I worked in an office I couldn't stand, but then I left and opened a meal-delivery service for shut-ins and started taking medical dictation, did event planning and ran two expos for craftspeople and artisans, was a traveling saleslady for crafts stores for a while, oh, and wrote two cookbooks, which I put up on the Internet."

I was laughing. "Stop, stop," I said. "Tell me what I wrote that had that effect on you so I can tell everyone else!"

And then she said something I've heard over and over again, the comment that caused me to write this book: "Actually, the most empowering thing I learned from all your books was the fact that I was a Scanner...and that it was all right for me to dig into one thing after another as fast as I could. I was beginning to think I'd never amount to anything because I just couldn't stick to one thing, no matter how hard I tried. But now I just know that's the way my neurons are wired...and I love it!"

The power of knowing your identity

Scanners go through an amazing transformation once they begin to understand who they are and realize there's nothing wrong with them. The following is a tiny sample of the hundreds of letters I've received.

> When you talked about Scanners, I almost jumped out of my chair! It was a perfect description of me. I never knew why I couldn't find my "one thing" to love doing until I read your definition of a Scanner. That seems to be just what I am. Now I feel like I have permission to move ahead on as many fronts as I want.

> Thank you! I'm a Scanner! I thought there was something wrong with me! A huge weight has fallen off my shoulders!

> One of the most wonderful things I have learned from you and your books is that there is such a thing as a "Scanner" and it is okay to be a Scanner. In an age of specialization, it is rare to find someone who will champion us.

When I read about Scanners, I felt enormous relief, like someone finally understood me.

Just reading Barbara's description of a Scanner was such a relief to my battered self-esteem.

To be honest, the elated reaction of people who realized they were Scanners came to me as a surprise at first. I had no idea that simply knowing there was a name for them would cause such a complete turnaround in their outlook and feeling of self-worth. Now I've seen over and over what amazing things a Scanner can do with nothing more than the simple permission to be herself. Pamela's list at the beginning of this chapter is pretty impressive, I confess, and not all Scanners have done as much as she has (though I've met many since who have!). Some of you might even get a bit intimidated by how many things she manages to do in her life. Don't be. I bet you don't realize how many remarkable things you've done and wouldn't have thought to list them like Pamela did. Why? Because if you're like most Scanners, you thought they didn't count, or even worse, you believed that since you didn't develop every single thing you started, it meant you were a failure. I hope you're now beginning to understand that you have the absolute right to be who you are: Those puppies are ready to come out of the box now. Let's take a new look at them.

The "WHAT HAVE I DONE SO FAR?" LIST

Take out a sheet of paper or your Scanner Daybook and write a list like Pamela's, with as many experiences or accomplishments, big and small, as you can think of, from teaching your dog a trick when you were a kid, to painting a portrait, to raising your own children or helping someone pass an exam. Include all the projects you started that didn't get finished, businesses that didn't get off the ground, courses you didn't complete, and novels you planned but didn't write. Don't think too long, just write down anything that comes to mind. New items will pop into your head when you think you're done, so don't try to put the list in any kind of order. What you remember is exactly what should be there.

Do it now. Pick up your pencil and start writing. Give yourself about 5 minutes to write, then come back when you're finished.

Did you surprise yourself? Most people do. Chareen, a Scanner who has always been very hard on herself, wrote:

I never really thought I'd done anything, but I sat down to do just a few of these and have so far come up with three whole pages of stuff I've done. Wow! I had no idea I'd done so much.

It's a little strange at first to think of everything you've done or attempted to do as an achievement, especially when you've adopted the scrutiny of our results-driven society. But when you read about Scanners like Pamela and then see how much you've done yourself, a light begins to dawn.

"You mean it's okay? It's allowed?"

"You mean maybe I'm not a failure?"

I'm sure you know how happy such comments make me. But they break my heart, too. Think about it. If realizing that one fact—that you are a Scanner, a bright, curious, probably multitalented person—has this much power, it means that there was never anything wrong with you.

How did you forget who you are?

Ella didn't know she was a Scanner. Sitting abjectly on my couch, she said, "My friends think I'm flaky, my ex-boyfriend called me a dilettante, my parents want to know what I'm majoring in this week, even I ask myself, 'what's my passion du jour?' What's wrong with me? I just can't buckle down."

"Give me some specifics," I said.

Ella told me a story new in its details but familiar in its form. She had enjoyed school from kindergarten through the eleventh grade. "I was a little faster than some kids, but I was never bored, because there was always something interesting to do, lots to choose from. But then, a year before graduation, things changed. That's when everybody started asking questions like 'What are you going to do now? What school has a good department for what you're studying—oh, what was it you were going to study?' Now, years later, everybody I went to school with has found their way. I'm the only one who hasn't. I wish I was like those people who know exactly what they want from the start."

Almost every Scanner says the same thing when we first meet. They see the respect heaped on the specialists in our culture, the ease with which they answer The Big American Question: "What do you do?" And they ache to be the same. You can't blame them. But they don't realize that they're not being completely honest with themselves about this.

At the beginning of my Scanner workshops, I ask the audience a question.

"How many of you wish you were one of those people who have always known what they wanted, who followed one path with certainty and clarity?" Invariably, all the people in the audience raise their hands, nodding their heads almost wearily.

"Are you sure of that?" I ask. They murmur and nod yes, thinking of how easy their lives would be without the confusion they now have to deal with.

"Okay," I say. "Then raise your hand if it's okay for you to do one thing, and one thing only, for the rest of your life."

There's a moment of frozen silence as everyone contemplates such a prospect with horror, and not one hand is ever raised. When they look at my face, of course, they realize I've played a trick on them and forced them to admit they don't really want to be specialists at all. Everyone sits back with relief and starts laughing. I can hear remarks like "That would be awful!"

Ella reacted the same way.

"You're right. I couldn't bear to do only one thing forever. Oh, dear. Does that mean I'm stuck?"

"No," I said. "That means you're free. You've been trying to be like other people, trying to give up your curiosity and your interest in lots of areas. Now you can relax and do what comes naturally." Ella started to look interested.

Now, what's really happening here? Why can't Scanners stick to anything? Why won't they make up their minds? Do they really fear commitment? Do they have some kind of learning disability? Are they hopelessly immature, shallow, afraid of hard work? If not, why don't they make their lives easier and do something about their problem? Having so many interests is difficult by itself, but being criticized for your inability to settle down and being worried that you'll never accomplish anything creates a load that's just too heavy to carry.

But if they're so unhappy, why don't Scanners do something about this state of affairs? Most Scanners really try. They buy books that tell them how to find their passion, and they go to career testing services to find out what they're supposed to be doing, but for the most part, the solutions they're given are designed for a different kind of person. The major effort of each book and testing service goes toward finding out what the person is most talented at—a method I heartily endorse for non-Scanners. People ought to use their greatest talent to find a career. But that doesn't work with a Scanner.

On every aptitude test, I come out above average on everything; there is no one outstanding peak—they are all pretty high. This can be really difficult, as I never know what to choose.

How about you?

Ponder a few questions for a moment. Have you ever taken a career aptitude test and found that you were good at many things—or that they all looked so boring you came up with nothing? Were you disappointed because you'd hoped that something would leap off the page and you'd finally know what direction you should take? Here's what one Scanner wrote me.

I always hoped something would reach out and grab me and say, 'Here I am!' But it never did. I wish someone would tell me exactly what it is that I'm supposed to be doing with my life!

But you'll never settle for only one path. Counselors urge their clients to choose a direction because they can't see how else they can take another step. But Scanners can't choose one direction. It's like telling a parent to choose one child to feed. It's just not possible. A parent knows she has to feed all her children. And a Scanner must find a way to follow every path that interests her. There's nothing else a Scanner can do, for three compelling reasons.

First, Scanners can't have fewer interests

They're designed to do more. Holding them back is like tying an athlete to a chair or putting a 2-year-old child in a small, confined space. It creates havoc, even despair. Elizabeth said it clearly:

If I have to slow down or use only one part of me at a time, I become bored, worse than bored—I feel like a part of me is dying on the vine.

Second, Scanners don't want fewer interests

They light up when they see new things, and they're dying to do something with them. "Well," you might protest, "we all want five desserts after dinner too, but we don't get them. We grow up, and we have to control ourselves, right?"

Oh, so wrong. Scanners want it all not because they're spoiled but for the same reason all your muscles want exercise. Scanners love variety because they have brains that process things quickly and are ready for new subjects sooner than other people. They have special abilities in many areas, and they're built to use them. That's why somewhere inside, although they hate to be stuck and don't know how to justify their behavior, Scanners secretly refuse to choose. They sense they're being stubborn. What they don't know is that this stubbornness comes from a deep sense of integrity.

Finally, Scanners can, so they must, explore many things

Scanners are smart and multitalented; they're divergent thinkers who don't feel Einstein's need to boil the meaning of the universe down to one formula but, like Leonardo da Vinci, would rather expand it endlessly. Most Scanners aren't as attached to stability as other people. They seem to have retained the inborn security of a young child, the same love of what's new, the drive to learn and understand everything they see. While most of us find the prospect of change disruptive, even threatening, Scanners thrive on it. They don't mind being beginners as much as most adults, and while some are driven to master a subject (and then move to another), others are perfectly content with a quick study (after which they, too, move on to another interest).

When you see someone with no tolerance for boredom, who is curious about almost anything new and has the ability to constantly process fresh material, you're looking at a Scanner.

But what exactly is it that attracts Scanners? And why do they so often move on to another attraction before they finish the first?

The answers to those two questions are essential if you ever want to understand what makes you tick. But it's not mysterious at all. To understand a Scanner, you just have to think about bees and honey.

DURATIONS, REWARDS, and honeybees

Whenever people complain that they lack focus, lose interest too easily, can't find their passion, or can't make up their minds about what they want to do, I ask them to consider the honeybee. I'm pretty sure no one in his right mind would ever accuse a bee of lacking focus or losing interest too easily. No one says bees can't make up their minds which flower they want to be involved with or accuses them of being unable to settle on their true passion. We assume that when a bee leaves a flower, it's got a compelling reason to do so. Plain and simple, whether it stays at a flower for 2 seconds or 20 seconds, we understand it needs that amount of time to get what it came for—its Reward—and the time required is its Duration. Any bee that stayed at a flower after it had emptied it of nectar would be seen as derelict in its duties.

When it comes to passion, I think we'd all agree that a bee seems very dedicated to its task—but it's not passionate about any one flower; it's passionate about gathering nectar. If you missed that point, you'd really misunderstand a honeybee.

However, as a culture, we're not in the habit of thinking about Scanners the same way. We simply assume that a Scanner has a problem if he doesn't stay at one interest as long as we believe he should stay—usually for his whole adult lifetime or at least until the job is "finished." But if we don't know *why* the Scanner is involved with a subject (that is, what kind of nectar he's after), we really have no way of knowing what his Duration is, so *we don't know when he's finished*. When I said that to Ella, she brightened at once.

"So no one has the right to tell me when I'm finished! This is fantastic!" Ella said. "I wonder what my 'nectar' is?"

"I don't know," I said. "Give me some examples in your life where you didn't follow through." Some interesting stories came out.

"When my parents needed to understand something obscure about their retirement fund to decide whether to invest it, roll it over, whatever, I sat down at the computer for almost 3 weeks to get the answers for them," Ella remembered. "It was fascinating. By the time I was through, I could have taught basic finance to anyone with my parents' problem and done a reasonably good job. They suggested it, and I thought it was a great idea, too.

"But once I had gathered the information they needed, I was finished. I haven't had the slightest desire to do anything connected with finance since then.

"Even before that, back when I was in college, I got the lead in a play where I had the role of an insurance executive, and I totally immersed myself in the subject. Insurance! You know how dreary and complicated that looks. But suddenly it was fascinating. Until today I'm the only person I know who isn't afraid to read the small print in their insurance policies!"

"So...you decided to go into the insurance business?" I teased.

"Never," she laughed, "it's not for me. But I'll still help other people understand the fine print if they need that."

"Maybe there's a Reward there, too?" I suggested.

"Yes! I'll learn how to do almost anything if someone really needs it. That's a big motivator for me. I never really thought about that before."

Ella was beginning to assemble the information she needed to put her life together.

A bee's Reward is nectar. Ella's Reward is learning about subjects that are completely new to her and helping people with her new knowledge. What's yours? It's not a question you can answer without thinking about it for a moment, but you do know the answer. Here's a bit of peculiar logic to help you. Read it slowly. It works.

ko·an *n: a Zen Buddhist riddle used to focus the mind during meditation and to develop intuitive thinking*

> Q: *How long should you stay at something?*
> A: *However long it takes to get what you came for.*
> Q: *How do you decide what you came for?*
> A: *You don't, you discover it.*
> Q: *How do you discover it?*
> A: *You notice what isn't there anymore when you feel like leaving.*

Another client once told me, unhappily, "When the discovery phase was over, I just couldn't continue. It was like eating yesterday's breakfast. There was no way I could bring myself to finish."

We looked at the moment he lost interest and was unable to continue, and there was the answer. Discovery itself. He loved it, like a new world revealed. It was the riveting experience of confronting something he'd never imagined before. That was the only part he really cared about. What followed felt pointless.

I said, "You did finish. Discovery was your Reward, and when it was over, when you had passed through the discovery phase and gotten your answer, it was time to leave. A house painter leaves when he's through painting the house; he doesn't move in and live there."

As with the bee, you can tell what a Scanner's Reward is by why he's drawn to something and when he stops. When you lose interest in something, you must always consider the possibility that you've gotten what you came for; you have completed your mission.

See if you can think back to some of your past interests and remember at what point you started to lose interest. Can you put your finger on what was no longer there? If so, you can start identifying the Rewards that drive you to anything that appeals to you.

What are your Rewards?

Look at your "What Have I Done So Far?" List with all the things you've done. Now pick up a pencil and see if you can remember anything that interested you, even for a very short period of time, and add it to your List. Then ask yourself these two questions about everything on the List.

1. What was the most exciting or interesting part of the experience?
2. Why did you stop when you did?

Go back and rethink the moment you stopped being absorbed in the project, when you began to lose interest or started having doubts.

What had gone away?

When the magnet that originally attracted you starts diminishing in power, you've done what you set out to do. Your purpose for being there is gone. That's why you lose interest: not because you're flawed or lazy or unable to focus, but because you're finished. It seems obvious, but it never occurs to most of us.

Now, start another column beside your List and title it Rewards. Next to each activity or interest you entered, write down the Rewards you got from that activity.

Here's how some other people answered.

> **Kate:** *I've loved art since I was little, but when I showed some talent, I was funneled into an arts program so I could have a successful career, and at that point, I lost interest. Then I fell in love with acting, but after a while it became more like a business—the business of filling seats. It's been that way with everything I enjoyed doing. As soon as it became practical, it lost importance. I never knew why, but I just figured out what went away. It was self-expression! Taking what was inside me and letting it flow out. I loved that! Since I was a little kid, that was the only part of any activity that mattered to me.*

> **Jill:** *I took up karate and was obsessed until I got my brown belt. And then I just stopped trying to get better. It was kind of embarrassing. Everyone said I had "so much promise." And then I got passionate about Russian. For 2 years, I ate, drank, and slept Russian. But when I felt I could speak and read it comfortably, I stopped. While I still enjoy Russian and karate, too, I don't feel any drive to focus on them. I was told it was fear of success, but that never felt right.*
>
> *But something did go away. It was the challenge to go from ignorance to competence, that steep climb to master something that demands every bit of focus I have. I love that kind of challenge. When it's over, I want to leave.*

When you're getting your Reward from any activity, you always feel happy, absorbed, energetic. And when you are satisfied, or the Reward diminishes, you get bored. It's as natural as sitting down to eat when you're hungry and leaving when you're full.

Isn't everyone involved in Rewards and Durations?

What makes a Scanner any different from anyone else? All people have their own Rewards and Durations, don't they?

Yes, they do. But with the exception of some specialists who have a passion for their field, very few people are as intensely interested in what they do as Scanners. Also, almost no one has such a low tolerance for boredom as Scanners—for them, boredom is excruciating. And, by definition, no one has as many different interests as Scanners. This makes their comings and goings very noticeable to the eyes of others.

But the main reason Scanners are different from others, and the reason they get noticed for not sticking to anything, is because they learn faster than almost anybody.

The typical Scanner runs through her interests in record time because she has a big, hungry brain and her favorite food is learning. Scanners love learning more than anything else. And learning is what they're most talented at.

Of course, there's no major in any college called learning. You can't get a degree in it. And there's no point in trying to specialize in the field of learning theory, because once you understand the issues, you'll leave that field as fast as any other.

Don't worry. I promise you'll find many satisfying, delightful careers and lifestyles for Scanners later in this book. But to take full advantage of those opportunities, you need to know about your own Rewards. Understanding your Rewards is like finding a long-lost birth certificate. It will help you understand your true identity.

What Reward draws you to any activity?

It's not always easy to answer this very important question, but I've compiled a list that will help you. It's made up of the most common Rewards Scanners have mentioned to me. (Open your Scanner Daybook and keep a pencil at hand so you can take notes while you read.)

⬧ Knowing how to do lots of things so I can always jump in and help; makes me feel capable
⬧ Insights, revelations, discoveries, glimpses that make me say, "I never knew that!"
⬧ Anything new: people, places, experiences
⬧ Having impact, being seen (like teachers, performers, ministers, gurus, politicians)
⬧ Exercising intelligence because it feels good
⬧ Sensation: hearing, moving, smelling, seeing, touching
⬧ Using all parts of myself, my logic, my intuition, my empathy, my abilities

- Challenging myself, testing my limits, seeing how good I can be
- Studying anything, like how to make sushi, how to sing medieval songs
- Creating something that didn't exist before, creating solutions to problems
- Vision: imagining possibilities, building prototypes, getting things planned
- Beauty: making things beautiful, having beauty around me, recognizing beauty where it's not obvious
- Building expertise: a reputation, a body of work
- Belonging: finding a community where I can be myself, be part of something I admire
- Discovering what's going on, how things run, what's behind the surface
- Pulling together the big picture, leaving nothing out, seeing relationships between things
- Saving the day: being competent and stepping in to fix things other people don't know how to fix
- Helping others with my skills or knowledge
- Learning by doing, for example, how a carpenter builds a table, how to make maple syrup, how to speak a few words of a language that's nothing like my own

Did this list remind you of some of the attractions you had forgotten or stimulate you to come up with more? Be sure to write them down and keep track of the Rewards you connect with. They are at the heart of your Scanner identity, the fuel that drives you toward everything that interests you. Some of them (like learning) apply to all Scanners. Others are type-specific and will help you figure out what type of Scanner you are later on. For now, you simply need to become alert to Rewards and Durations. They'll help you design the right kind of life for yourself.

And they certainly shine a light on why you act the way you do, don't they? To rephrase something I remember about the I Ching: No blame to the Scanner who loves and leaves many things.

So why have you been told there's something wrong with you?

I hope it's becoming clear by now that not only are you an intelligent, productive person, but you're very good at getting any Reward that's important to you. If you do a good job at what you were designed for, like a bee does, you are a total success. So why have you been made to feel that you were anything less than that? Why have you been given such a hard time by those around you?

I think the answer is ignorance. You've been misdiagnosed as someone who's supposed to do something different. It's as if a wolf were described as an inferior whale! The truth is, when you act like a Scanner, you're not doing anything wrong. You never did.

Plain and simple, the worst thing that can be said about a Scanner is that he doesn't stick to things as long as other people think he should. It looks like *they* got it wrong, not you. If they knew Rewards and Durations, they might change their minds.

Then again, they might not. No matter—the point is that you understand.

Ella's mouth fell open. "When you say it that way, it changes everything! I feel like I just got a pardon after being in jail all my life!" At first she was beaming, but then she became thoughtful. She looked out the window at nothing, shaking her head regretfully.

"What is it, Ella?" I asked.

"Something I never forgot from my childhood," she said. "When I was about 7, my teacher read us a story called *Rusty in Orchestraville*, about a little boy who couldn't make up his mind which instrument he wanted to learn, and so he ended up not playing anything and couldn't be part of the orchestra. That story made me feel terrible all my life. I knew that was me, and I thought I'd never be part of any orchestra."

"That story needs a new ending," I said. "Because I've seen it play out completely differently. In my experience, Rusty becomes a famous conductor. He needed to study all the instruments, because his instrument is the whole orchestra."

Ella smiled at me.

Dear Barbara,

I didn't know why I couldn't find my "one thing" to love doing until I read your definition of a Scanner. That seems to be just what I am. Now I feel like I have permission to move ahead on as many fronts as I want. I have several hobbies (reading fiction and nonfiction, investing, fund-raising for the local Alzheimer's association, crocheting, drawing, gardening . . .). My career is in nonprofit management (accounting and human resources management), where there are always too many things to accomplish and not enough hands and minds to do everything. I love diversification—taking each task or project as it comes and doing my best at it—learning new ideas and better ways of doing things as I go along. There are so many things that I want to try my hand at and accomplish.

Recently, I have been looking into starting a small business. My family thinks that I am going off on yet another wild fantasy. My boyfriend is very supportive. He thinks that, at age 39, I have been successful at enough other things that I should be able to do this if I decide that is what I want.

At some point, I would like to run for an elected office. I have plans in mind for several books. I'd like to have a gallery showing of my art. If this fits with your definition of a Scanner, then I say "Yippee!"

Now you're free to look into anything that interests you

It's nice to know you're a Scanner, isn't it? The freedom that comes with that knowledge is pure heaven. Now, when a new idea comes along, you can allow yourself to get as absorbed as you like. Greet it like a fascinating visitor. Pay full attention for as long as you like, and when you find yourself losing interest, trust that feeling. There's usually a good reason for it. Your Scanner Daybook will give you the opportunity to delve into anything that catches your interest. It will allow you to spend time with this fascinating visitor for as long or short a time as you wish.

Will the world accommodate your style? Will others happily allow you to stop working on something whenever you feel like it? I doubt it, but when it comes to your own projects, who cares? The important thing is that you no longer have to feel terrible because you start so many new things and you don't follow through on them. That's a powerful change of viewpoint and a fantastic way to launch the wonderful life you're about to reclaim. I'm happy to tell you that you've got some very good times ahead.

Or are you having a little trouble enjoying this good news because you can't help wondering if all this fun and games leads anywhere?

Chapter 3

SCANNER PANIC

Scanners always hear a clock ticking. Every time they see their birthday or the New Year coming, they start to panic. If you ask them what's wrong, they usually say, "I can't find the 'one thing' I can stick to. I'm terrified that I'll never find it!"

But that's over, right? Once you know you're not *supposed* to find one thing only, there's no need to panic anymore: You're a Scanner and you'll always be interested in many fields, so your panic should subside, right?

But it doesn't. In fact, once you understand there's no need to find that one right path and that your critics simply don't understand you, once you've accepted the freedom to follow any and every interest you have, something very interesting happens.

Your *real* fears come to the front. And they're more like this:

Will I ever actually get to use what's inside me?

Will anyone know I was here?

I remember bursting into tears when someone told me that she thought everyone had a destiny. "I don't!" I sobbed. I sat in the middle of all the things I'd started and dropped, and they seemed like a worthless waste of time.

Compared with the dread of not using her potential, a Scanner's other fears fade in significance. A Scanner senses her own talents but is pulled in so many directions she often accomplishes very little. As she watches the years pass, the picture of her still sitting on the sidelines when the game is over creates a growing sense of panic.

Scanners are not being dramatic or inventing this danger. When you have unused potential, you're driven to use it. Since, by your very nature, you can't devote yourself to one goal and you don't know how to manage many goals, you are in real danger of living an unused life.

But you don't have to flounder and find your own way anymore. This is your manual. You're on your way to fulfilling all that potential.

You've already completed the first two lessons: You know you're a Scanner, and you know about the Rewards and Durations that drive your behavior. Now you're ready for the next lesson: the Scanner's problems with time.

Scanner's time

In my earlier books, I discussed what I call Time Sickness, a state of mind frequently found in Scanners in which your whole sense of time is compacted into the present moment and you actually forget that tomorrow exists. That translates into the belief that if you put off doing anything you love, it will be lost forever. And when you love more things than you can possibly do now, Time Sickness creates panic.

Panic makes it impossible to see a solution. Panic's secret purpose—or at least its best trick—is to throw a shower of obstacles into the air to show you how utterly impossible all your dreams are.

There's no point in telling you to use your willpower or your reason to "just calm down," because fear is a primitive and powerful defense mechanism not easily controlled.

In fact, the only useful and lasting way I've found to reduce fear is to reduce the danger that's causing it. Let's begin this process now.

Will anyone know I was here?

"I'm nothing but an amateur and that's all I'll ever be," said a woman at one of my workshops. "You only read about experts in the history books. They'll never write about me."

She was wrong about that. Many famous people all through history have been Scanners. The funny thing is that the most famous were both amateurs *and* experts.

Aristotle's story

If you were interested in philosophy, logic, science, physics, astronomy, psychology, prophecy, zoology, theater, and poetry and you lived in Greece a few hundred years BC, no one would have called you a dilettante. They would have called you Aristotle.

Not only could Aristotle never pick a major, he studied things no one had studied before. He taught without credentials in those fields because there wasn't anyone to hand them out.

Aristotle would have liked a Scanner like you. He is said to have given two kinds of lectures: the more detailed discussions in the morning for an inner circle of advanced students and the popular discourses in the evening for the general body of lovers of knowledge. (Which one would you have attended? If you're like me—both!)

If you lived in the 1700s in America and moved between a dozen interests like science, business, music, philosophy, and politics, you wouldn't have been called indecisive or scattered. You'd have been called Benjamin Franklin. He's the author of an aphorism that stirs up panic in every Scanner's heart:

> If you would not be forgotten as soon as you're rotten
>
> Either write things worth reading or do things worth the writing.

Both he and Aristotle did both, and they were not forgotten. But what few people remember is that both these men were complete amateurs. They lacked any kind of credentials that would get them respect or even a job today. That's because most of us have forgotten what the word amateur really means.

am·a·teur *n: from Latin: one who loves*

1. *Somebody who does something for pleasure rather than for pay*
2. *Somebody who has only limited skill in, or knowledge of, an activity*
3. *Somebody who loves or is greatly interested in something*
4. *Somebody who appreciates and wants to understand so many things that she can't possibly specialize in only one field; i.e., a Scanner*

Okay, I slipped in that fourth one because I hope it will actually be there one day, after we manage to restore that beautiful word *amateur* to the high status it deserves.

But what about your family? You don't live in classical Greece or 18th century America. You might feel like the Scanner who wrote this:

I've been laughed at and teased for such a long time. All I want is to stick to something until I can finally get some respect for it.

It's all very nice to be free to do what you want without feeling guilty, and it feels good that Aristotle would have liked you, but he's not here right now and he can't help you with the feeling of failure that's plagued you for so long. What will make your life count in the mind of your family?

It depends on their definition of success.

In Rosemarie's family, what mattered most was being "the best." Getting acclaim. Looking good for the neighbors.

"Was there any special desire that drove you to become a photojournalist?" I asked.

"I did it for acclaim," she said.

I was surprised. "You did?"

"Sure, that's all my family talked about at dinner: who was successful. Not money, but accomplishment, accolades, awards. They tried to be a little different from everyone else, so they weren't impressed with investment bankers—they sneered at that—but with top artists or top scientists. Even my dad's border collies are all about winning awards—activity awards, not appearance awards—but still it's the same thing. Everything is about how you look to the neighbors. That's the whole thing. Forget happiness; just be the best."

A family's definition of success can cause a powerful conflict in anyone. But talented people have a special conflict, and with Scanners it's multiplied with each talent.

How will I ever do all the things I want to do? There are too many!

I can't get moving on anything and I'm afraid I'll die without ever doing what's inside me. When I think of that, I get the worst feeling you can ever imagine. But I don't see any way to change. I've tried over and over and gotten nowhere!

Chances are it will take you a slow reading of this chapter to get your mind to trust what I hope you're starting to realize, but I'd like you to read the next words carefully. *You have no life-or-death decisions to make.*

You don't have to give up anything you want to do. When your panic subsides, you're going to realize there's plenty of time to do everything you want.

You're going to see that you will not be a loser, you won't be left behind, you will use your talents and say your piece while you're on this earth. Your voice will be heard.

You might even get rich and famous, if that's what you care about. And if people treat you like you're different, it's probably because they can see better than you that you're exceptional, and they probably wonder (even if they seem disapproving sometimes) why you're not already rich and famous.

Doing everything you love is easier than you ever imagined. It doesn't appear that way, because panic has thrown formidable-looking obstacles in the way to fulfilling any of your dreams. But a closer look will show that the most common obstacles *don't really exist at all.*

The top obstacles for panicked Scanners

When you hear the clock ticking but you just can't get into action, what's the reason?

1. **You fear critics.** You feel watched, so you're trying to be perfect. Whatever you do never seems good enough, so you drop it and try something else, but you feel like you're wasting precious time.
2. **You've created a "See, it's impossible!" list.** Your list of what you want to do has everything on it but "eat breakfast" and "scratch my head." It covers many pages and proves that you'll never get to do what you really want.
3. **You've inadvertently made the project too big.** You've assumed you'll need a business plan and two PhDs, to say nothing of a huge loan from the bank and 36 hours a day to do all the marketing, selling, bookkeeping, production, publishing, and wall painting that will be necessary—all of which you'll have to do on your own.
4. **You don't feel entitled to just do whatever you want.** You think you don't have the right to do what makes you happy. You should be thinking of other people, not just yourself.
5. **You think you're the problem.** You don't have what it takes or you're not really trying. Or something.

6. **You're pulled in too many directions.** It's impossible to decide which one to take. You're desperately searching for a sign that will at least tell you which one to start with.

If you're nodding your head as you read that list, you've been feeding your sense of panic like dry timber feeds a fire. Let's see if we can get rid of those obstacles one by one and get you into action.

1. **Perfectionists need to admit the source of their conflict.** Too many Scanners say, "I'm my own worst enemy." Be honest. You're not working for your own high standards; you're working for someone's approval. It could be your parents, your high school English teacher, your boss—even your nosy neighbor. It could very well be a voice from your past. Wherever you find a perfectionist, a critic is not far away. But you can waste a perfectly good life trying to meet the standards of someone who thinks you're not good enough *because they can't understand who you are.* I have some tips in later chapters that will help you handle this kind of problem, but for now, just know what's really behind the paralysis caused by perfectionism.

2. **You need to cross some things off your "See, it's impossible!" list.** You might not know it, but you're trying to prove you can't do everything you want. If your list is really long, check to see if you've added on extra things to prove how hopeless it is and justify your despair—and continue to stay immobile. One man at a workshop said, "I'll never be able to do all the things I want to do. I want to swim and run, too. And play my guitar. But I also want to learn a language, and I'm fascinated by botany, and I have to earn a living, too."

    But many people do all those things and more, and they would never think to put them on a list. Your impossible list is saying something else—something like "I'll never get a chance to do what I love; it's hopeless."

3. **You can shrink the size of your project to fit reality by keeping only the parts you love the most.** When we think about what we want to do, we often make the project so big it really *is* next to impossible. If you've done that, cut it down until you have only the elements you love best and try to find a way to do this new, smaller version. If it still includes the heart of the dream, you can do it with complete satisfaction.

    Cyndy wants (among many other things) to relearn her rusty biblical

Greek so she can translate a book into English. But she doesn't have time, and the project is huge. Some people could spend a decade on such a project.

How can she make the dream less of a major production? The heart of her dream was the pleasure of turning out a good piece of work for her church. We found that she can sit down with one important passage and her dictionary and in 1 or 2 weeks turn out an inspiring piece for her church newsletter—and she can start right now.

4. **Doing what you love isn't a privilege; it's an obligation.** Isn't it selfish to do what you love? You might think that it's okay to have a hobby, but if you're a Scanner you want more than that: You want to play an instrument, go to mediation classes, take a holiday in Denmark and another one in Ireland, learn tap dancing, and more! Is that allowed?

Well, if you do these things in place of having a job—if you've burdened someone else with taking care of you and you don't pull your own weight or fulfill your legitimate obligations—the answer is no, it isn't allowed. But if you were that irresponsible, I doubt you'd be looking for permission in the first place. More to the point, by denying yourself the right to do what makes you happy, you may be depriving others of a shot at *their* happiness; and that's *not* allowed.

If you're pulling your own weight, you're actually being selfish by *not* doing what makes you happy. The things that fascinate you exist because of some talent you were born with. You have the eyes to see what many people miss. That's how talent affects all of us. And you owe it to all of us to use your talents.

5. **You'd do everything "right" if you could.** "If I could stick with something, all this mess would go away. If I weren't afraid of failing, I'd be okay by now. If I'd just quit hesitating and spring into action, my problems would be solved." *But don't you understand that if you could do those things, you would have?*

Even if you don't agree, that kind of reasoning goes nowhere and fixes nothing, and it's pointless to think about it. Believing those myths can hurt you. Write these words on a piece of paper and put it up on your bathroom mirror so you see it every time you brush your teeth:

Each time you judge yourself, you break your heart.

Those are the words of Kirpal Venanji, a Hindu monk. And you know he's right.

But how can you let go of all the criticism and move on? It's a good question. Here's a trick that will actually work:

Go ahead and fail.

Yes, that's what I said. And I'm not kidding.

When I was in high school, someone wrote in chalk on the sidewalk "Flunk Now! Avoid the Rush!" We tried hard to avoid flunking back then, but flunking might not be a bad idea for now, believe it or not. After all, you're stuck in your tracks and you're not moving anyway. What do you have to lose?

Don't take big risks or burn any bridges, but do whatever you want, and if it fails, so what? Sometimes the best cure for stress is failure! Write that book or try to create a new Pet Rock, and let it bomb. *If you don't get into action, you've failed anyway.* And we're all much too afraid of failure.

Here's how to fail: Pick any project (you might as well pick the toughest one and leave the easy ones for another time, when you're in the mood to succeed). Then all you have to do is simply refuse to give the project your best effort. If you like, you can work hard at first, but when the time comes for a final burst of speed, just don't do it.

And when you've failed and your critics are watching—oh, how I wish you'd really do this—*flaunt it*. March up to the dinner table and say with a face full of joy, "I totally fell on my face. What a loser I am!"

Go into details until you can see they wish you'd be quiet—and be sure to look happier than you've ever looked in your life. Your critics will mumble that you're crazy, *but you'll take all their ammunition away*. If they fire a few more rounds of criticism at you, agree enthusiastically and start flaunting your failure all over again. Done right, it's a real eye-opener. And it's fun. It might even make you unafraid to fail ever again!

6. **It doesn't make the slightest difference where you begin.** Once you quit worrying about being judged, you can choose the closest goal, or the easiest or the prettiest or any other goal, to start with. You can do a few of them at once, if that's your best way of working. It doesn't matter. *You're going to do them all, anyway.*

How? By using the panicked Scanner's best friend; something so obvious you might blush when I remind you of it. It's called a Calendar.

The WALL CALENDAR POSTER

Nothing drives away the Time Sickness that causes panic better than a Calendar. The best kind is big enough to show everything you hope to do for the next few years all at once. And if it's hung on the wall as a constant reminder, you might find your panic going away.

You can make it yourself right now. Just find a large sheet of paper (or tape some ordinary-size blank sheets together) and with a colored marking pen, divide it into six large squares, one for each of the next 6 years. Why six? Because it's good to know you have 6 whole years to play with. Anything less could worry you by making you feel hurried. Anything greater would be hard to understand. Six years seems to be just right for Scanners.

Mark the year over each square, starting with this year. Nearby, keep a cup full of wide, brightly colored ink markers. When you get a good idea, you'll need to have these markers at hand.

Now, stand in front of that Calendar and think of every project you really long to do (not every one you can think of!). Figure out which ones you might be able to do soon and which ones can wait. Assign a different color to each activity and draw a band of that color on the Calendar in the time you hope to do it. A bright red line for next fall might represent your trip to Rome. A blue one could represent the art class you want to take.

This is a first run only and not written in stone; you're sure to change it frequently. But you've got to start with something real, and a Calendar is the simplest—and strongest—reminder that you will not be cheated out of doing everything you love.

Post that Calendar on your wall where you'll see it many times a day. That's all you have to do. And notice the surprising calm you feel when everything you love is scheduled and will wait for you.

Did you suddenly feel as if your surroundings changed? Instead of floating in space, you just planted your feet on a road with a direction, and all because of a hand-drawn Calendar.

When it comes to demolishing Scanner panic, no piece of equipment is more powerful than a Calendar on the wall that allows you to see, at a glance, the next few years. Here's an excerpt from a letter I got recently.

I physically feel lighter, unburdened, and clearer in my thinking since I put all my projects on the Calendar and decided on the first group of projects to work on. I can now say to that frantic voice in my head—it's okay to wait on that. I'm doing these things right now.

To get anything done, you need structure. That means schedules, timetables, and accountability. Without structure, we all become disoriented; we don't know where we are. If you learn to set priorities and line up your projects in some kind of order, if you develop a sense of beginnings and endings, and if you keep a big, beautiful Calendar on your wall, your confusion will disappear and taking the first step will become easy.

You can do one thing now and another later, or you can line them all up and do a small part of each of them today. It's simply a matter of taking your ideas out of the stratosphere and placing them in your daily life right next to your other activities, like breakfast, picking up the mail, walking the dog.

It might seem obvious, but when you're panicked, nothing's obvious, as this letter from a Scanner will show you.

> *Dear Barbara,*
>
> *Here's an update on your advice on selecting two or three projects and focusing on those. This will sound corny; perhaps obtuse. I never before understood that choosing two or three things was an option.*
>
> *For some reason, there has always been an understanding that I needed to do it all and do it now! Your simple approach has been a freedom boon! It has been especially helpful in directing my "free" time. I know what needs attention now and am able to put the energy and excitement into it like never before.*

Are some of those dead ends starting to open up? Is the panic starting to melt away? I hope so. Because when it goes, you're going to release a lot of wonderful energy into that creative mind of yours, and with structure, you'll be able to use it to do one after another of the projects that fascinate you.

An exciting way to live

In the chapters that follow this one, I'll be showing you in detail how to create your own structure, set up your timetables, and get the accountability you need. I'll even give you tips, tricks, and tools for Scanners—like the Calendar you're going to post on the wall and one other tool I'd like to suggest.

The STICKY NOTE Solution

If something in the pages of this chapter helped reduce your panic, write it on many Sticky Notes and put them everywhere—on your walls, mirrors, refrigerators, and doors; in your appointment book; or on the desktop of your computer—so that every time panic starts to rise again in your Scanner heart, your eye will fall on them and you'll calm down again.

A Calendar, a Daybook, and some Sticky Notes may not seem like a very formidable set of tools, but they will give you a good start. Realizing that there's plenty of time to do everything you love is a very big thing for a Scanner. Remembering that the way to get somewhere is to take one step at a time changes immobility to progress. Don't underestimate the power of these insights or anything that reminds you of them.

Once your panic subsides and you begin working on each of your interests, one after another, you'll let go of the dread that life will pass you by. You'll understand that today, tomorrow, and next year you're going to use every bit of talent, curiosity, and intelligence that's inside you.

And where will you go? When you're involved in doing what you love, the path will always show itself.

Chapter 4

COMMITMENT PHOBIA

What if I sign up for the rest of my entire life to some miserable job where I'm bored to tears and it eats up my life and wastes my best abilities?

Getting stuck in the wrong career is like a horror movie where I've been buried and no one can hear my screams!

When it comes to commitment, many Scanners draw the line. The horror of wasting their lives looms in front of them, and avoiding commitment itself is often the only thing a Scanner will commit to.

But the stand they've taken against commitment is based on some odd misconceptions and outdated rules that rarely apply to anyone anymore. That means Scanners who avoid commitment are taking an unnecessary detour from the very thing they want: a life full of learning, exploring new fields, and starting something new whenever they feel like it.

Now, just a minute, you might be saying. How can anyone have a life like that? And even if it were possible, how on earth can he do it once he's made a commitment?

It's easier than you think. You simply need a fresh understanding of what commitment really means—and what it doesn't.

Joanne's story

Joanne is avoiding what she believes is commitment. Any choice she'd make feels like it has great and irreversible consequences.

"I can't choose any career. What if I pick one that's second best? And what if I change my mind, which I absolutely know I'll do? See, my problem is that I want to be a psychologist, a composer, a writer, a teacher, a world traveler, and a painter. But every time I begin to walk down one of these paths, sooner or later I get this horrible thought: 'Am I *sure* that this is what I want to do with the *rest of my life*?' And that's the end of it."

"And the worst part about making a mistake?" I asked.

"Oh my God," she said with horror. "Where do I start? First, it takes years and money and training to go into something new, and if you find out it's wrong, you're stuck! I've already done that more than once. I can't stand to do it again. I remember so well the feeling of boredom and the realization that if I stayed, I'd be bored for the rest of my life!"

"Well, if all that were true, I could hardly blame you," I said. "Forget the rest of my life. I wouldn't want to do something for a week if it bored me. But you've made a lot of assumptions here that I don't think are true."

"Like what?" she asked.

The commitmentphobe's list of mistaken assumptions

1. You must choose one and only one path in life.
2. Everything you love has to be a career. Doing something for pleasure doesn't count.
3. If you're not in love with your job, it will be a living hell.
4. You have to get it right, because every career choice requires a huge investment of time and money.
5. Once you make your choice, you serve a life sentence with no chance of parole.
6. If you're not passionate to the point of obsession, you'll never be content to give up all your other interests.

These mistaken assumptions add up to a contract signed in blood and carved in stone, inspired not only by misinformation but by a dread of wasting one's life and by the desire for a single passion so great it can make a life sentence tolerable. No wonder Scanners refuse to make commitments.

But there's one problem with their conclusion: *Not one thing on that list is true.* Let's look at each of them, one by one.

Mistaken assumption #1:
You must choose one path for your entire life

Well, for one thing, Scanners can't choose one path and that's all there is to it. But more to the point, *almost nobody else chooses only one path for an entire lifetime, either!*

Look around you and what do you see? Almost no one stays at one career "forever" anymore. All these notions belong to a time that disappeared long ago. More and more lawyers and teachers—the mainstays of career commitment—become dissatisfied every year, and many of them are out looking for new careers as we speak.*

"My daughter has to decide on her major, and she's having a terrible time choosing what she wants to do for the rest of her life," a concerned mother wrote me recently. All I could think was, "Oh my, what have you been teaching your daughter?"

What a massive burden for anyone to carry—and an imaginary one at that. Even the most successful people can be certain of changing career directions several times in their lives.

Mistaken assumption #2:
Everything you love has to be a career;
doing something for pleasure doesn't count

Someone on my bulletin board wrote, "I love bodybuilding, but I love doing research, too, on almost anything! Is there a way to combine them? Can I become Conan the Librarian?" making me burst out laughing. Many clients, though not as funny, have the same concerns.

"I'll never find a career that allows me to renovate houses, work on motorcycle engines, be a poet, design computer games, and write screenplays," one of them said to me.

"No, I don't imagine you will," I said. "But why does everything you love have to be a career?"

"You mean just *do* them? For the fun of it?"

"Is that as illegal as you make it sound?" I asked.

---

* I have found a number of different services for helping lawyers and teachers find new careers. I recently read that 40,000 people become lawyers every year, and 40,000 leave the profession because they are dissatisfied.

"But how do you pay the rent?"

"Pick the one that makes a living and doesn't take up too much time, and do the rest on your own time," I suggested.

He thought for a minute. "That's a good idea...but then everything else would just be a hobby. I'm very serious about everything I love."

"Leonardo da Vinci seems to have been serious about everything he loved, too," I said. "Pretty much the only thing he was paid for was painting until he was in his sixties. I'm sure he was never paid for designing his airplane or his submarine. Does that make them 'just hobbies'?"

He was thoughtful. "No, but what *does* it make them?" he asked.

"It's a question I'm sure Leonardo never gave a moment's thought," I said. "Maybe we should all follow his lead on that one."

Mistaken assumption #3:
Every career has to be what you love
or it's a living hell

If you're a Scanner, you might not stay interested in any profession unless it's loaded with variety. If you go to medical school to become a doctor and your motivation is money, you're likely to be disappointed. In fact, you might get disappointed even if you love practicing medicine, judging from the many doctors who stop practicing in today's managed-care environment, which doesn't seem to allow them to practice medicine the way they had hoped.

But if you're in love with the idea of being a doctor or a lawyer, you should do it anyway! Why? Because if you're creative, you'll find a way to use that profession one way or another. Doctors become politicians; lawyers become writers or work in the theater with actors and directors and are often sought after as business partners.

I know accountants with lives any Scanner would envy. My friend Eddie works 3 or 4 months a year and goes on international bike trips, on scuba-diving expeditions, or to photography school the rest of his time. A Canadian accountant fulfilled his secret dream of becoming a cowboy after finding out that ranchers needed accountants just like any other business owners. He now spends much of his time on the prairies of Canada, rounding up cattle with other cowboys. (He works on the rancher's books in the evenings.) Teachers become public speakers and go on the lucrative lecture circuit—often as motivational speakers! And I know a psychologist who has fulfilled her dream: She works with the National Football League, counseling the players.

Mistaken assumption #4:
Any career you choose requires a huge investment of time and money

If you assume that's so, think back on all the people you knew in high school and college. How many people do you think graduate from college and go on to do what they studied? Or look at the flip side: Think of all the interesting careers you've seen people in and ask yourself how many of them actually trained for that career. I think you'll find that many people fall into a job and turn it into a career through a series of unexpected events.

It's not wise to invest in training for a career before you know these things:

1. What kind of work will you actually do?
2. Is training really required?

People usually sign up for school before they know these answers. Why? Although it's difficult to study when you have other obligations and it's costly to go to school, many people choose this path because it's so clear and simple. For a certain number of years, all they have to do is what's required. And the feeling of being in rehearsal seems to lower stress, too. But you can wake up with an awful hangover. Try doing informational interviews and, even better if it's possible, do some volunteering or intern work in the actual workplace you're contemplating. You might save yourself a lot of time and money that way.

Mistaken assumption #5:
Any career you choose is a life sentence with no chance of parole

This assumption, too, could use a reality check. You probably learned it from someone who grew up in the 1950s or 1960s or worked for a company like IBM that tried, longer than other corporations, to take care of their employees from "cradle to grave." They don't do this anymore. You might want to look around at people 50 years old or younger and check out how long they've been at their latest career.

The truth is, you can't find a job that's a life sentence anymore, even if you're looking for one. What about lawyers, doctors, financiers, that sort of thing? Well, I've already mentioned how often they leave their chosen professions, but even those who stay make up a very small percentage of all employed people. Many people, Scanners or not, find it best to carry their skills with them like a plumber carries his tools. Others simply step forward to help, no matter what their position, and are recognized and given completely different jobs than they ever trained for. Often these are jobs that don't offer any training but hands-on experience—sort of like planned (or accidental) apprenticeships.

Mistaken assumption #6:
If you can't find something you're wildly passionate about, you can never be content with one job

This myth is created by Scanners, I'm sure of it, who often bemoan the fact that they've never found one passion so great it would make them forget everything else they love.

I keep waiting for this deep voice to call down from heaven and tell me what I should do!

But that voice isn't coming, because there is no *one* passion so great that a Scanner can happily limit herself to it. I don't have a deep voice and I'm not calling down from heaven, but I can tell you exactly what to do if you're a Scanner: Do everything that interests you.

But some people get completely wrapped up in something, focused and intense, happily involved. Can't Scanners have that?

Of course they can! In fact, Scanners become more deeply involved with their interests than most other people. If you're a Scanner, you've felt that way a dozen times. What you might not understand is that every one of those "passions" was legitimate and right.

But what you've been looking for is an all-encompassing passion that lasts forever. And that's where I want you to do some fresh thinking: Just take "passion" and turn it over a few times to see what this concept of yours is actually made of. Because, coming from a Scanner, the word "passion" always concerns me.

"I've never found anything I'd sacrifice for; I've never heard the voice of God telling me what to do, seen fireworks, or had the feeling that I've come home and can stop searching," a Scanner told me recently.

"Don't you enjoy the things you're trying?" I asked.

"Well, yes, I do, a lot actually, but none of them turns out to be right."

If you've ever thought the same, think again. Maybe what you're trying out isn't supposed to be right. Maybe learning about new environments is what makes you happy, what's right for you.

Most Scanners miss that point and don't realize that they've already found the right kind of life for themselves. The fly in the ointment for the Scanner above was that he thought each activity he enjoyed was supposed to be the big passion, the final choice, and that was ruining his enjoyment.

"How would it feel to forget about finding your big passion and enjoy the delightful fact that you can learn anything you like and your life will be filled with variety and excitement?"

He looked at me like a little boy who's been told he can ditch school and go to a movie. "Can you do that?" he said with a slightly guilty smile.

Yes, he can and you can, and you *should*, because the elusive search for one great passion can blind Scanners to a dozen *real* passions they experience every day. Passion (a word so misunderstood I prefer to call it interest or enthusiasm) is a gift all Scanners have. It's part of their makeup. The notion that it's meant to last forever should be discarded with relief. Remember that well-known adage "Be careful what you wish for," and be happy you didn't get it this time.

You might find the perfect combination of all your interests and have a very enjoyable career. Or you might discover that what you really love is learning itself. The only true "passion" Scanners have is the passion to use every part of themselves, to exercise their curious brains, to follow anything fascinating until they've found out what they wanted to know.

And then to leave it.

So if you're a Scanner who's been commitment phobic, please listen carefully: You're not going to find one passion so great that all the others will disappear, and you wouldn't like it if you did. You will find many passions. You're not expected to make a commitment to follow one career or lifestyle track to the very end of your life—your genetic mandate is to make many commitments and enjoy each one to your full capacity. One path will never be enough for you.

A more typical course of events

If you can shrug off your misconceptions, you'll see all around you the course that so many careers actually take.

Annick: *I've been a Scanner since childhood . . . and I was so impressed with every college and university course available to me way back when that I opted for a humanities degree at San Francisco State University more than 20 years ago. The SFSU humanities major was rather forward-looking in those days, as it embraced an academic philosophy of multiculturalism and diversity before it was the trend. It allowed me to pursue a traditional liberal arts education with an emphasis on comparative world history, literature, sociology, the arts, and more.*

I then fell into a career in fund-raising, marketing, special events, and philanthropy, beginning with my first postgraduate spot at San Francisco's public television station. One thing led to another, and I found myself in Chicago as a health and social service fund-raiser. I also had a four-year stint helping a major international bank give away their millions in a program of institutional giving and public affairs.

I'm now living in Portland, Maine, and employed part-time as the assistant to a local arts agency administrator. It's a fascinating spot in which to learn about a new city, a new field, and an entirely new way of life. I'm not sure where this situation will lead as I am presently reassessing every aspect of my life in my mid-forties.

The Scanner in me has always had a strong interest in international affairs and especially in European life and culture. I have recently discovered my Irish roots and spent three frenzied years tracing ancestry records, which culminated in securing my Irish citizenship and passport.

While I am loving my new life in Portland, the island of Ireland continues to have a strong pull on my heartstrings. I'm "sussing out" all the various possibilities and hope to end up on that side of the pond at some point . . . even if it's just for a few years.

I used to be bothered by this business of being a Scanner . . . but now I realize that it's just some sort of natural plan and an unfolding of who and what I'm meant to be.

Does this mean Scanners never have to commit to anything?

It absolutely does not mean that. *Scanners must commit to everything that interests them.* You possess a valuable eagerness to explore what's new and an ability to be fascinated where too many people see nothing at all. Those are gifts. Don't even think of squandering them. Not only do they give you great pleasure, they add to your wealth of knowledge, and knowledge is like money: You might not know yet what you'll use it for, but you can be sure it will come in handy sooner or later. Who knows? You might someday add a piece to someone else's puzzle and make his dream come true. You'll surely bring a fresh perspective to any situation you're in. Anytime you bring fresh thinking to someone's discussion, you could be doing something of inestimable value.

A Scanner is like a passionate artist or a great lover. Good artists and lovers give their whole hearts to the object of their interest; they hold nothing of themselves back. A Scanner must do the same. As a Scanner, you must always focus completely and give yourself wholly to anything you have chosen. And when you feel the desire to do something different, you must commit yourself to the next thing you want to do. Anything less would be a waste of talent.

How does that work if you're considering a career? The same way: Love it or leave it. However, there is one big difference between making a commitment to exploring everything that interests you and making a commitment to a career: You need to know something about a career before you choose it. So, here's another important tool for Scanners.

The CAREER TRYOUT

The big problem, I believe, isn't that people don't make career commitments; it's that they make them too soon. Instead of learning everything they can before they sign up, commitment is seen as some kind of virtue, an act of character or willpower, almost like planting your flag in the ground and pronouncing that you will pledge yourself come hell or high water.

You wouldn't buy a house that way or decide what city or country to live in, and you wouldn't choose a surgeon that way if you needed an operation. (You wouldn't even buy a pair of jeans that way!) Hopefully, you'd try to find out as much as possible before you decided on any permanent commitments.

But few of us remember to try out a career. Here's one way to do it:

Go to your Scanner Daybook and write a first-person, present-tense fantasy of what you imagine your workday will be like. Imagine you are actually in any job you're considering. Place yourself where you imagine you'd be working and put your brain and hands to work, like this:

"I'm standing by a drawing table working on a graphics presentation of a concept that's not easy to understand. I'm finding ways to illustrate it that will make it very clear, and that's fun. I arrived at work at 10:00 a.m., as I do every day. In an hour we'll have a meeting with all the people on my project, and I'll show them my ideas..."

Once you've done that, you'll understand what you want. Then you can start interviewing people in the field to see what really goes on.

But what if you don't have any idea where you'd be sitting or what you'd be doing? *Then you're not ready to say yes to the position.*

You're not ready to say no, either.

And isn't it wonderful that you found that out before you signed on? Now, how can you find out more? Well, I guess you could change your name and sign on as a temp or wear a disguise and work in the mailroom for a few months. Not always possible, I fear, but it would certainly give you an inside look at corporate culture. More realistically, you can talk to some people in the position and do a reality check. How do you find such people? Call anyone and everyone you know to ask if they personally know someone in the position you're considering. The person who grooms your dog or tutors your niece probably has a family member working in the company you're looking at. Call whoever will respond cheerfully to hearing from you and offer them a "degrees of separation challenge" to find someone who knows someone who knows the inside of the place you're thinking of going.

And if that gets you nowhere, start hanging out (in your best corporate disguise) at a nearby lunch restaurant or after-work location and watch, or even get to know, some of the employees.

Because if you don't know where you'll sit or what you'll actually be doing, it's way too early to consider any commitment, and your fears are absolutely appropriate.

Will you stay forever?

Here's the short answer: no. You know as well as I do that unless the job has variety and learning built into it, sooner or later you'll get bored, and if you're a Scanner, you have zero tolerance for boredom. It hurts your brain.

If you've heard that everyone has to put up with boredom and that it's not so bad, it wasn't a Scanner who told you. To a Scanner, boredom feels like being shipwrecked on a tiny desert island with no humans and one palm tree. Curiosity, creativity, and learning are essential to Scanners, and without them they become depressed.

But you can't always avoid boredom, or you'll get stuck doing nothing. If you're a commitmentphobe, that's where you are already. However, a Scanner has so many resources, you can always find a way to make a job interesting, at least temporarily. Here are a few tricks and tips some veteran Scanners have suggested.

1. Set yourself the challenge of finishing your work early, and spend the rest of the time in private explorations that fascinate you.
2. Find a way to do interesting things for the company: Write the newsletter, organize events, set up a Web page, or do Internet-based research—anything that will make the job more interesting.
3. Take on the project of exploring the company culture. That can be interesting in itself but also useful for that screenplay you're writing. Keeping track of the dialogues you overhear—that's great material!
4. Use your job as your social life so you can dedicate yourself to a solitary passion after work.

Or you can try one of my favorite solutions for Scanners contemplating any career. Before you choose a job, see if it's compatible with this four-step system I developed for my clients: the LTTL SYSTEM.

I first used this system in a small Scanner workshop, and it was so successful at overcoming commitment phobia that I now use it with many of my Scanner clients. I think you're going to like this one. The letters stand for Learn, Try, Teach, Leave.

In your Scanner Daybook, write up a one-page plan for every career or interest you're considering, using the LTTL System. For example, let's say you're considering a job overseeing operations for a large company. You'd write something like this:

Step 1: Learn. For 6 months, I'll learn how to run the central office of a national graphics firm, coming up with new systems—but only on paper.

Step 2: Try. After the learning curve levels out, I'll try to get my new systems implemented, perfect them, make sure they run, or build the prototype to iron out all the kinks. This might take 2 more months.

Step 3: Teach. When it's clear that everything I've designed works brilliantly and the company wants me to stay and run it, I'll explain I can stay only long enough to teach someone else to do the job. Maybe this will take a few more months, and what I teach each day will go into the employees' manual I've arranged to write for the company. (I'll naturally be very well paid for these services I'm rendering.)

Step 4: Leave. On this day, I'll have my farewell party, at which I'll receive tearful good-byes and be given a severance package, which allows me to live for 1 year without working. I've arranged for this by showing the bosses how much money I'd be saving them.

During my free year, I'll pursue my own interests and keep an eye out for the most interesting job opportunity in a different field entirely, at which time I'll repeat the entire process.

For the purposes of illustration, I haven't kept this explanation 100 percent realistic, but I know for certain that the LTTL System is completely doable in a form you'll find useful. Just reading it might have given you a new perspective on the whole issue of commitment, as it's done for so many other Scanners.

Because if a "commitment" looked more like the LTTL model, I doubt you'd mind making one. Signing up for a dreary work life is something no one should have to do. And no one should blame you, a Scanner, for loving only the designing and learning aspects of your job. Scanners need to learn, to invent, and to tinker with things. That's how they're wired.

Rarely will a Scanner be happy sticking around to turn the switches on and off or keep the system humming. To require execution and maintenance of Scanners is not a good use of their ability. Talent is hard to find. A smart boss knows and respects it.

The Scanner's best hope: a smart boss

If you don't have a smart boss, maybe you should go out and find one. If you're starting to see the outline of what you might like to do, the next step is simply to package yourself, do some networking wherever it's possible, and offer your services to someone. Every smart boss wants to hire and hang on to talented people. If you're around someone who doesn't care, you're in the wrong place.

Daniel Pink, author of *Free Agent Nation*, has noticed a new phenomenon he calls the Peter-Out Principle, which "decrees that when the fun peters out, the talented walk out."

So don't get stuck in your parents' view of employment. The times are definitely changing. I hope the words "What will I do for the rest of my life?" will soon fade from your memory.

Here's a suggestion: Whenever you're thinking about making any big career decisions, remember the LTTL System and change the word "commit" to the words "try out" or "audition" a career.

However, there is one commitment you should make right up front: Commit yourself to give everything you've got to whatever you do, no matter how little time you have to do it. Holding back isn't good for anyone, but for someone with energy and imagination, it's especially unwise. To feel right, you must commit to the fullest life you're capable of. With the gifts and resources you've been given, any lesser commitment would be a terrible waste of brainpower and talent.

When it comes to your search for a career or a specialty, you won't have any trouble making commitments as long as you never forget these facts:

Fact #1: A Scanner can choose many specialties. She can combine them or do them in sequence, do one as a job and another as a passionate hobby, or a dozen other combinations.

Fact #2: A Scanner can use any decent job to support what she loves to do—and do it on her own time. That's what most musicians and puppeteers, writers and inventors, historians and small business owners do. I call it the GOOD ENOUGH JOB (see page 136). You'll find it mentioned often in the pages to come.

Fact #3: A Scanner can invent her own career. Don't look on a career list; what you want isn't there. Don't worry about personality or preference indices, either. You already know what you like; you just don't know how to find it. You can create your own career and read stories in this book about people who have done just that.

There's no need to hold back anymore. You never have to allow anyone to lock a door behind you, and no one really wants you to these days. But even if they did, you've got three keys right in your pocket, those three facts you just read. They'll keep you as free as you want to be and unafraid of commitment from now on.

In the next chapter, we deal with a very different kind of problem: What can you do if you're too busy to do *anything* you love?

Chapter 5

TOO BUSY TO DO
WHAT I LOVE

Dear Barbara,

I'd love to follow your advice and go after all my dreams, but I don't have time to go after any of them. By the time my wife and I are finished with getting the kids off to school, fulfilling the demands of our jobs, maintaining our home, paying bills, and helping the kids with schoolwork, we can't decompress enough to remember what we want even if we had the time to do it. How do you do the things you love when you don't have time in your life or space in your brain?

Signed, Loving Dad, Husband, Employee, Home Owner, Citizen

Many of us are simply too busy to find a moment for our dreams. When you have too much to do, finding time to get involved in things you love isn't an option. Even when you do have time, you can't remember how to use it for yourself. Add kids to the equation and you've got a life with no free time at all. That's reality.

Or is it?

In this chapter, you're going to learn some things that may surprise you. First, feeling hurried and harried isn't entirely the result of having so much to do. Many people do just as much in a state of calmness. Second, when you're too rushed to think clearly, you lose any sense of what doesn't have to be done and pile on more work than necessary. You even need more downtime when you're constantly in a state of controlled alarm, because you're not nourished by what you're doing; you're drained by it.

But talk is cheap. How can a busy person do anything about it?

The truth is, overworked people are scared. They're scared of forgetting to do something, or not meeting a deadline, or letting someone down. They're scared of being overwhelmed, of things careening out of control. That's why they never think to make their lives easier or more fun; they just add on more responsibility.

Jeff's story

When Jeff stepped out of his car—arms full of groceries, two kids fighting in the backseat—I could see his nerves were frayed. And who could blame him? "This goes on every day," he said as I stepped up to take a bag from him. "All day!" He skillfully got the family into the house without interrupting their fight (I was filled with admiration) and herded me into the kitchen—I choose that word carefully and you'll see why. "There's no schedule on earth that's going to make me less busy. Consider this a challenge."

But I've had a lot of practice with people like Jeff, and I spotted one clue right away—as I said, he *herded* me. He had a symptom common among people with too much to do: Instead of reducing the number of tasks on his plate, he added to them. That is, instead of rushing into the kitchen and letting me follow him or pointing in the direction he wanted me to go, he herded me as if I'd try to escape out the window.

When I pointed it out to him, he blushed and apologized. "I'm sorry, I just get in control mode and I'm on automatic pilot."

"You mean you forget that anything can get done unless you push it. What a heavy load you carry! No wonder you're so busy! Have you ever considered letting things run on their own and using some of that energy toward things you really want to do?"

"Sure...and then I wake up. Come on, Barbara, do you think I could paint or write a novel with all this going on? Or start my own business? Who would take care of the other stuff? You see what I have to do just to keep this house together. And boom, there goes my weekend!"

That's reality when you have little kids—or is it? Why does it feel like you are driving an ambulance and someone's life is at stake when the problem is only lunch or diapers or getting the babysitter home? Why are some people in the same situation calmer than Jeff is? Although Jeff's feelings are so common that everyone who has ever been in his situation remembers them well, this need for control is a little odder than it appears to be.

What's wrong with Jeff?

Jeff's tension can't be taken at face value. Overwhelming feelings of busyness are never what they seem—the situation seems to be causing the nervousness, but the opposite is usually true.

Yes, Jeff is busy; but all the same, he does a lot of things he doesn't need to do. He confessed to me that he wastes hours every night searching the Internet for "get rich quick" schemes, for example. Also, he thinks he has to give his kids all his attention when he's with them and doesn't realize that if he did what he loved while he was with them, they might get a lot of value out of it.

Jeff said, "Sometimes I stay awake at night thinking of all the terrible things that could happen if I didn't keep everything under control."

"Were you always like that?" I asked.

"Me? No way. I was always the 'kid without a care.'"

"So what happened to him?" I asked. "When did all that change?"

When did you become this busy person?

It's a question I ask every exhausted Scanner, and the answer is always revealing.

"I was the baby in a big family of hard workers, but nobody noticed what I did; so except for school, I was a really free kid. I'd often wander over to the church theater and offer to do anything they needed, from moving furniture to painting sets to helping the actors learn their lines. I loved that." Jeff also loved animals and spent hours at a neighbor's house, playing with their dogs. He learned guitar on his own and wrote songs, and even wrote a musical when he was a teenager. And then one day, when he was 14, his last sibling left, and he was the only one at home.

"My folks were old by that time and sick, but my dad still worked really hard, and my mom wouldn't stop taking care of the house. I woke up to the hardship in the family, and that's when I stepped out of Eden," he admitted. "I gave up all the fun stuff and tried to figure out how to make enough money for my dad to retire.

"Since then, I've been very driven. I always feel a sense of urgency, like I have to stay on top of everything or there will be some kind of calamity."

We don't all experience Jeff's kind of responsibility before we become adults, but many of us have feelings that are strikingly similar. I think we're all shocked to find out how much we're responsible for when we grow up, and even more when we have children. We feel like kids trying to be as capable as grown-ups.

For all of us, there was a time before we were given responsibilities. Some of us lost it when a younger sibling was born; others, when we entered school. Some not until much later. But there was a point when you stepped out of that Eden of having nothing expected of you and into a sudden need to stay ahead of your mistakes. The shock of that change is rarely given the respect it deserves, and I think it's the source of many missteps that busy people take.

Let's start out by trying to locate when it happened for you. Without giving it too much thought, try to remember the last time you were free of that busy feeling—doing things you enjoyed without having to schedule them. How old were you? Describe the feeling of freedom you had.

Now memorize that feeling. Because I want you to visit it at least once a day.

Remember when you sat on the steps as the evening grew dark or played with your dog and had nothing else to do—and visit that memory, because when you forget what easiness feels like, you're always in emergency mode and can't even think of what you really want or how to find the time to get it. It's like trying to read a book of poetry in a burning building; it just doesn't occur to you.

But the building isn't really burning. It only seems that way.

When you find you simply can't relax, something special is going on

Stress and anxiety are the cousins of fear. Fear comes when you have a sense of danger. Overly busy people describe that danger in roughly the same way: I have to shop, pick up the kids, get dinner and homework, and then get that report ready because tomorrow I have to present it and I'm not ready—and the dog has to go to the vet, and my sister broke her foot so I'll pick her up on the way to work...

And what they mean is *something is about to go out of control and the result will be disaster.* That fear puts us into survival mode and prevents us from calmly finding solutions. But if you could find what's blocking you and visit the feeling I want you to memorize, you'd be able to lighten your load.

Let's look at why you make yourself busier than you are.

◈ You pile it on to prove you're not a bad person.

◈ You pile it on to see how much you can handle.

◈ You want to push yourself until you collapse (then "they" will know how hard you work).

◈ You're speeding and it feels utterly necessary, but you can't remember why.

Where is that feeling coming from? You might be holding down feelings of fear or helplessness, even a sense of loss of that easy childhood you can barely remember. The control you're afraid of losing is often the control over that feeling. That little kid inside you is reacting just as he or she did when you were first shocked by responsibility and afraid you wouldn't be able to handle it. Man or woman, when you're too busy and stressed for too long, sometimes you want to put your head down and cry, and somewhere inside you know it.

What you don't know is that a few tears would melt your stress like hot water melts an icicle. Even a sincere, sorrowful sigh will help. What do you have to cry about? Maybe nothing more than you're tired of being worried all the time. Any kid knows that.

The MICRO NERVOUS BREAKDOWN

It doesn't matter how strong and competent you are, when you're operating on automatic pilot and you're fueled by stress, you're going to hurt somebody or trip on something. If you want to think clearly, be calm and be smart; schedule a Micro Nervous Breakdown at least once a day. It's easy and no one will ever know about it. Try it and you'll see what I mean. Here's what to do.

1. Find a restroom where you can shut the door and have some privacy.
2. Close your eyes, take a few deep breaths, and silently say, "I hurt." And "Ouch."
3. If you feel the slightest sensation in your eyes or your chest, pretend to

yourself that you're crying and sigh a few times. If you can shed some tears, that's even better but not necessary.

4. If you can't feel anything, pretend you're an 8-year-old kid with all the same responsibilities and silently say, "Somebody help me. I'm too little to carry all this. I'm going to screw up." That ought to do it.

5. Give yourself two or three moments to feel any sorrow that comes to the surface, silently release your feelings, and notice how your tension melts away.

You'll know you're finished when you sigh a different kind of sigh, the one that says, "Whew. Well, that's over." Stand up, walk out, wash your face—and you will find something very surprising. Your stress is gone, and you're not having any trouble slowing down and being relaxed.

This is a simple little procedure, but I think you'll be amazed at how different it can make you feel. The fear of being overwhelmed is often caused by trying to push down these kinds of feelings, so once they've been released, there's nothing to fear anymore. It's almost as if the frightened child inside you needed to cry, and once he did, the fear disappeared.

These can be hard feelings to face, but if you face (and release) them just once—instead of avoiding them a thousand times— the payoff is huge. You'll have the secret of being active instead of merely being busy.

You can see the difference at once. You'll feel surprisingly comfortable and not harried or hassled at all. (In fact, it might be a while before all your energy comes back, so don't do this just before a bicycle race.)

Of course, you'll have to do it more than once. Handling this feeling is like weeding your garden; you have to do it whenever the new weeds pop up. But if you stay current, you'll find, over time, the garden becomes cleaner. You'll become easygoing and patient more and more often. That's good for you and everyone around you.

You'll be surprised at the other benefits, too. You'll be easier on yourself, for one thing. You'll be able to think calmly and find ways to lighten your load instead of ramping up the stress as you did before.

The busy Scanner's bag of tricks

Here's a grab bag of tips, tricks, and tools to help you find time to do those wonderful Scanner projects you've been missing.

Make your mental to-do list and then cut it in half. Pick up the kids and go home without shopping. What will you eat? Who cares? Bananas. Breakfast cereal. Forget their homework this one time and make them help you with yours. Explain what that report you brought home is supposed to do and why you're worried about it. Bring them in as rescuers. If they're over 6 years old, they can actually help, and they'll give great advice. In the meantime, you'll be saving time by making that report come alive for you, and tomorrow you'll remember your kids' faces when you present it—and you might be smiling.

Get more help than you need. Find a retired person in your community who drives and pay him to be your dog's uncle so he can step in whenever you want him to—and let him take the dog to the vet. Hire a car service to take your sister for her checkup.

"But that's a waste. Really, the vet is on my way to work and so is my sister," you might say, because *you've forgotten how nice it is to drive to work with nothing else to do.*

And that's the big danger with people who are too busy. You lose your memory of the luxury of doing less than your full capacity. You lose your common sense, too. In fact, you probably do whatever you can to keep the pace of your life always at high speed, like having an ambulance parked at the curb with the motor running—just in case.

Grab your time first. Here's a tip that will help if you work outside your home. When you walk through the door at night, don't visit with everyone first and hope you'll have time for yourself later. That time might not come. Instead, go somewhere private and do your own work first. What if you've been so busy you haven't come up with any projects yet? Then it's a good time to pull out your Scanner Daybook and write in its pages like Leonardo da Vinci. When you're finished, come out and greet your family all over again. It's as easy as that. I'm not making this up. Here's a letter I got from a working mom who is writing a book.

> *When I come home, I say hello, kiss everyone, and go to the writing room first thing, for a full half hour of work. Then I emerge, change clothes, and start my family life. I'm moving steadily along on my book. Try it, it works!*

Ignore everything but your favorite parts. There's one really good way to do lots of your favorite activities in the time you have, no matter how little that may be. Go for the reward that matters to you. *Do only the part you love the best.* You can probably do that in a matter of minutes. If you don't have any minutes, close your eyes, focus, and fantasize the best part for a full 30 seconds. (You'll be surprised how long that will feel!) You must keep dreams alive and healthy until there's more time. It will put a smile on your face.

Learn to sort and dispose of what comes at you, fast. When too many things come toward you at the same time, you can't decide which one to address, so you just give up and do something else. This is a Scanner's hazard. Quick rule: Learn to sort things in your mind as they come at you. "Urgent. Later. Someday. Not possible. Get help on it. Forget it. Yummy." Just stand there and bat them into the right place.

Carry a PORTABLE DREAM DECK with you everywhere. Keep this low-tech tool in your pocket so you can catch your thoughts and ideas on the run. Busy or not, people tend to get their best ideas when they're doing something else. You can carry a package of 3 x 5 index cards held together with a rubber band (stick a pen between the cards). This will let you capture any ideas that fly through your mind, no matter where you are. (You might also consider keeping one brightly colored card to record your successes; that is, the times you beat out your worry and had a little fun.)

And here's a fun way to customize your Portable Dream Deck: Instead of using ordinary 3 x 5 cards, carry Rolodex cards that fit into an alphabetical address stand. When you get home, just put them in a special Rolodex file you use only for this purpose. Your ideas will be easier to find, and you'll have a nice, fat index of ideas to leaf through whenever you have extra time and you're stuck for something to do.

That's a nice thought, isn't it?

The SETUP

This one is my favorite tool, and I saved it for last because it just might save the Scanner in you. Two minutes here or there for the projects you love may be all you ever find, but the trick is to be ready for them. And the Setup will make you as prepared as a fireman with clothes at the ready and a pole to slide down when the fire alarm rings. It's simple, but it can change your life: Just get every single thing you need for any project set up in advance and ready to go. Put it all together in one place. Then forget it until you have a little time.

And I mean "little." Take short, frequent visits to whatever you love. You can make a sketch or write a line of poetry for even *2* minutes, and if you're completely focused (no multitasking allowed), you'll find it's enormously satisfying. Slip in these brief visits as often as possible. The results will astound you!

One first-rate way to do this (but we rarely think of it) is right in the middle of your time with your family. I call this technique How to Paint a Masterpiece during Commercial Breaks. All you need is that same miraculous Setup and a small corner of time.

Jeff found a way to do painting with this Setup, but the technique can be used with any of your interests. In the corner of the family room, set up a ready-to-go painting corner with a canvas, brushes, and palette of colors and *never put it away*. Keep the brushes in water so they need only a wipe-off to be ready to use. Cover the palette with plastic wrap so it's always ready. With your project completely set up and ready to go, you can actually stand up, walk over, and paint for a few minutes during every commercial. Sounds ridiculous? Try it. It's fun!

Then sit down and watch TV with your kids until the next break. Of course, you might want to keep painting after that, but you won't be sequestered away from your family, feeling guilty and lonely, either. (Jeff's kids liked this process so much they started doing their household chores on commercial breaks!)

You can do the same thing with redecorating a room, writing a cookbook, scanning photos for a greeting card project, or creating a storyboard for your next home movie.

Don't forget to check on your feelings

You don't need to be a parent for life to run you ragged, and I hope all busy and stressed Scanners will take my suggestions to heart whenever they find themselves turning into control freaks. The child inside every stressed person needs attention every time you're feeling harried, frazzled, and rushed. And if you've tried to cure burnout by taking time off and doing nothing, you know it doesn't work. Boredom doesn't cure emotional exhaustion, especially for Scanners.

But when you get the hurt out of your system, you'll find the space in your life to do something you love. Creativity and learning cure burnout. Involvement in a fascinating project will heal you.

As my friend Gudrun wrote me, "Editing a new book has excited me in these last weeks, and it is true! I felt so tired before and thought I needed some rest, but no! I need more things in my life that excite me!"

To sum up all of this, here's my answer to Loving Dad, whose letter opened this chapter. I think it will bring my point the rest of the way home.

Dear Loving Dad,

I know what you're talking about from firsthand experience. I was a nearly broke, single working mom with two kids, grimly fighting against being overwhelmed by the demands of my life. But one day I learned something that changed my viewpoint forever. One weekend day, the three of us were at the park on roller skates, holding hands because we were all pretty wobbly, moving along like awkward robots, when to our horror, a hill appeared under our feet and we lost what little control we had and began careening down the hill. We were moving way too fast and were frozen with fear until we managed to veer off the path onto some grass, where we fell down and broke into hysterical, relieved laughter.

As I sat up, still laughing, I caught my boys looking at me with happy smiles and happier eyes, and it hit me like a lightning bolt: They loved to see me laugh. And they didn't see it very often. That's when I realized something I'd never thought about before. Kids need to see their parents happy.

No matter how little time you have, if your kids saw you enjoying yourself, it would be very good for all of you. If they saw you going after a dream, they'd know they wouldn't have to feel guilty going after theirs. Too much self-sacrifice makes you a bad role model.

Start thinking about how you can relax some of the roles all your family members play. Let them make your lunches sometimes. (You can live on peanut butter, honest!) Instead of only helping them with their homework, once in a while read aloud from an old travel book you love about someone who went through the Amazon jungles or sailed across the sea. Something you'll enjoy at least as much as they will.

When you're driving them to school, instead of worrying about their backpacks and their apples, occasionally remember aloud when you wanted to be in musical comedy and see if you can sing all the verses to your favorite song from Guys and Dolls *before you reach their school. If your dream was (or is) to be a standup comic, try out your jokes on everyone—and let them join in or let them groan. If you wish you knew how to build an auto engine or play a violin or have your own television show on the Internet, tell your kids all your obstacles, see if they know some way to help you overcome them, and listen to them with the same respect you'd give any adult. (If they don't come up with anything when you first try it—after all, they'll still be new at this—thank them for listening and helping you talk it through.)*

Just be sure you're not being a camp counselor or a cheerleader; i.e., be real. Really think about those dreams while you talk about them. People will be pulled into your vision if you can imagine what you describe.

Soon they'll be telling you their dreams—but, first, you have to show them how. And you have to mean it.

It's not really a matter of having enough time to enjoy yourself, because nothing has to be a big production. You can have 3 minutes' worth of an immensely good time in those little moments that exist in the busiest of lives. That's all the time it takes to eat a hot fudge sundae, get your back scratched, or get your kids to explain the words to a hip-hop song.

It's good for you, too. You'll stop believing a responsible grown-up must sacrifice doing what he loves. And then, one day when your load gets lighter, you'll find that you haven't forgotten what you wanted to do. In fact, you'll be ready to roll.

Signed, Loving Mom, Writer, Dog Owner, History Lover, Citizen

That letter is for you, too, good reader. I hope you take it to heart.

And now we come to a Scanner with plenty of time who won't do what he loves anyway. Sounds strange? It's more common than you think. In fact, you might find that you're often in the same predicament.

Chapter 6

I WON'T DO ANYTHING IF I CAN'T DO EVERYTHING

"I think I should find a new career," said Ralph, an unhappy engineer who came to see me. He wanted to know if he was in the wrong field and admitted that engineering had never thrilled him.

"What else have you considered?" I asked.

"Well, maybe I could go into architecture. But that takes a lot of training and there are so many other things I might like just as well. How do you choose?"

"Maybe you don't have to choose," I said, ready (as I am with all Scanners) to help him see that he could, and should, do it all.

"That's just it: I *don't* choose," he said. "I don't do anything at all." Ralph never got past daydreaming about things that interested him. He never took one step toward any dream, because to him that meant giving up every other dream. "If I pick architecture, I can't be a graphic artist. If I pick either of them, I can't be a lighting designer or a writer or an inventor."

Is this beginning to sound familiar? Have you ever felt stuck because the world is so full of fascinating options that choosing one—even something you wanted with all your heart—would only make you feel deprived?

As I said earlier, that's like starving in the candy store. But a lot of Scanners do the same thing.

"I wish I could live 200 years," a young woman told me at a workshop. "Maybe that wouldn't be enough."

"Some people want to know a little bit about a lot of things," a man wrote on my bulletin board. "And some want to know a lot about only one thing. But I want to know a lot about everything. And I don't see how I can possibly get that in one lifetime."

The one thing these people all had in common—aside from believing they wanted to do absolutely everything—was that they were doing practically *nothing* that interested them. Instead of trying to find a way to squeeze in at least a few of the things they loved, they had pushed everything out of reach, and many, like Ralph, spent their days in activities they didn't like at all. Now, why on earth would they make a choice like that? I was intrigued.

"You want to help me understand that, Ralph? If you'd been putting a little time into some of the things that interest you..."

He finished my thought, "I know. By now I could have written a novel."

I started to get it. "But then you wouldn't have been able to do all the other things? Is that it?"

"It's crazy, but that's exactly what stopped me," Ralph said, shaking his head.

Ralph wasn't crazy by any definition I knew for the word, so there must have been some thinking behind his behavior that was directing it. What did Ralph assume or take for granted that resulted in this illogical behavior? I would have to go snooping.

I came up with some discoveries that set Ralph free and might help you, too. If you're one of those people who think the very number of things you want to do is so huge there's no point in doing any of them; if the sheer number of options before you has you overwhelmed, even paralyzed; if Ralph's behavior makes sense to you—then you, too, are depriving yourself of a lot of happiness, for no good reason. I think that might change in this chapter. First, let's look at how you got here.

How did you get into this dilemma?

Scanners are smart, multitalented people. How do so many of them get so stuck? Interviewing Ralph carefully, I saw some answers begin to emerge. The first, and probably most influential, reason was that he honestly believed there was absolutely nothing on the face of this earth that he wasn't interested in.

I understand part of his dilemma. I have to stop myself from buying more books than anyone can possibly read. Whenever I see a book that doesn't interest me, I'm relieved. My list of maddeningly desirable new subjects grows smaller every time I actually try them out. I figured if I could persuade Ralph to use my reality testing, he'd start seeing things differently.

"You know," I ventured, "most people really aren't interested in *everything*. But even if you're interested in a huge number of areas, there are ways for you to taste them all, depending on what it is you want from them."

"That's where I'm different. I've almost never seen *anything* that didn't interest me."

"You did say 'almost,'" I answered hopefully.

"It doesn't matter," he said and came up with the second reason this kind of Scanner refuses to take a bite from the smorgasbord of things that he loves: "I don't want to just do a little wine tasting. I want to go *deeply* into *everything*. That's just not possible. Life is like those nature shows where the cheetah comes on a herd of gazelles. If he went after all of them, like you say I should go after all my interests, the cheetah would wind up with nothing."

"What if you loved only, say, two dozen things, and what if you didn't try to make any of them into a career—you know, you did them evenings and weekends and on vacations, for years and years until you really got deeply into them? Would you be willing to try them out? That way, you could keep your job until you found something you loved more."

"Sounds nice, and I'm not trying to be difficult," he said, "but I'm not interested in two dozen things or 200 things. Listen, my wife made me move 1,200 magazines out to the garage last fall because there was no place to walk in the hallways. I try to stop buying magazines, but there's always something on the cover that's just too interesting to pass up. When I get them home, I read them cover to cover, and I just have to know a lot more about every single thing I read. Sometimes I think I'll go back to school and get some new training and go into a new field—and then I think, 'Why am I doing this? This is going nowhere.'"

But by now I had a very good idea what was going on with him. "Do you read a lot of women's magazines?" I asked.

He looked confused. "Huh? No."

"Do you read sports magazines, then? Or hunting and fishing magazines? How about quilting magazines? I see a lot of them in the stores these days."

"Okay, okay," he conceded, "it's true I'm not interested in absolutely everything. I'm a nut for technology magazines." He went on to explain that he'd see an article about a new breakthrough in electric lighting and be dying to know more, but when he turned to the next article about microscopic instruments being developed for surgery, he was equally intrigued. And so on with almost every article in the magazine.

"By the time I'm through, I'm so frustrated. There's just so much out there, it's overwhelming sometimes," he said. "It wouldn't matter which one I chose, or which 10 I chose, I'd still end up disappointed. So what's the point?"

Ralph was deeply disappointed, ironically, because life was so full of riches. Now, how do you fix that? What do you give the man who wants everything?

Well, maybe you give him these two secrets:

1. Scanners don't really want everything.
2. Scanners don't really want the depth they imagine.

I know two things Ralph doesn't. One is that no one really wants to do *everything*. The other is that Scanners are often confused about how much depth they actually want in any one subject. Scanners who sincerely want to spend years burrowing deeply into something go ahead and do it. They're called Serial Specialists, and you can read about them in Part Two of this book.

But Scanners who think they want to spend years doing something and end up doing nothing are suffering from what I call "deprivation overshoot." They've been hungry for so long that they feel they'd have to eat a whole ox to feel full. But the truth is that they can eat only what their stomach will hold, no matter how hungry they are. The sad thing is that the fantasy of getting as much as they want actually creates more deprivation; because of it, they get nothing at all. But the reality is that it doesn't take much real food to fill up an imaginary hunger a mile wide. I sensed that if I could get Ralph to take a little bite, we might pull him free of this unfortunate cycle.

If you understand Ralph and know about that kind of self-imposed hunger—intellectual, creative, love-of-learning hunger—I'd like you to do an exercise. When you're done, we'll come back and work on getting you off your hunger strike. I promise that you not only will be able to go as deeply as you like into as many areas as you choose but also just might run low and have to go shopping for some new interests!

The Scanner's BIG LIST

There's a book called *1,000 Places to See Before You Die*. To a Scanner, doing is a lot more fun than merely seeing, so let's adapt that idea and see how many things you can think of that you'd really love to do: the 1,000 things you *believe* you want to do before you die. I'd like you to write a more active list; not places you want to see but interests you'd like to explore: things you want to do, learn about, make, collect, create—you get the idea. Later, you'll be able to use this list when you actually have an empty period of time and can't decide what to do next. But its first purpose, right now at this moment, is bigger. Do the exercise and you'll see what I mean.

I tried it out on Ralph.

"Write down all the things you can think of that you'd love to know more about," I told Ralph, and he took out a pen and paper.

"It's everything, like I said," he answered.

"Okay, so it will take a while. I've got a lot of paper. Let's get started."

He took about 10 minutes and wrote down 30 items or so on the sheet of paper. Then he tried to remember some of the magazine articles that had intrigued him and came up with around 20 more.

"I'm sure you'd come up with a hundred more if you had your magazines here to look through."

"Two hundred," he said, almost defensively.

"Okay, 200. Now we've got about 250. I was hoping we'd get to a thousand."

He smiled. "Well, I guess I'm not interested in *everything*, but 250 is still too many, right?"

Before I tell you the answer we came up with, try it out yourself.

Make your Big List

Open up your Scanner Daybook and give yourself four to six blank pages or get a large piece of paper, as big as possible, so you can add to it at will. Then, in the upper left-hand corner, writing as small as you can, begin a numbered list of anything and everything that interests you, that has ever interested you, or that might ever interest you if you live to 105 years old. Really do this, because writing them down makes them real, and part of the problem has been that you've kept them somewhere in the fog of assumptions, where they're easy to lose.

Think before you write any entry. I don't want you to write things like, "I want to learn about 1. African history, 2. Asian history, 3. European history . . . 78. Physics, 79. Math, 80. Quantum mechanics . . . 120. Hungarian, 121. Greek, etc." This isn't an exercise to see how many things there are to do on earth. It's an exercise to see how many things you would really enjoy spending time with. You should include:

◈ Everything you've done already
◈ Everything you wish you could do for the first time
◈ Everything you wish you'd be doing all through the years to come
◈ Everything you'd like to do once or twice only

That means that before you make an entry, you must sit for a minute or so, with your eyes closed if you can, and imagine yourself actually involved in that activity *in real time*. (Alternatively, you can write for 2 minutes in the present tense: "I am opening my book on medieval safety pins and reading the first page. It's about a crypt that was found in 1345 . . . the afternoon passes and I'm still turning the pages . . .") Be there, as much as you possibly can.

If the fantasy feels as good as you had hoped, it passes the test and can go on the list. If it's scary but thrilling, it also goes on the list. But if it's just the title of some field that appeals to you, be sure to think about it carefully before you write it down.

If you like, you can give yourself a few days to finish this exercise. Carry a small notebook with you and jot down interesting things that pass the test. Then bring the list home with you and add the new entries to your Big List in your Daybook.

When you're done, sit back and take a long look at how much of that paper you've covered up. If you didn't cheat, I'm betting you'll discover that you're truly interested in only a few dozen, at the most a hundred, activities. Possibly, just possibly, more.

But not everything. Nowhere near 1,000 things.

And that means you've just scored a very big win in the game of What's Possible, because no one can do everything. You knew that. That's why you were doing nothing. *But everyone can do many, many things.*

Think about it. Maybe you don't have to feel stuck anymore. You may be interested in many, many things and you might add to their number every year, but it will never exceed, in real time, the realm of possibility. Now you can get started on the first one or two (or three or four) that are most easily within reach, today if you like, in the knowledge that you'll be able to do the same with other activities on your list. And you've got a great chance of getting through most, maybe all of them. And a fine chance of actually feeling profoundly satisfied in every one of your interests.

Incidentally, it's not a bad idea to open up another page in your Scanner Daybook or keep that notepad with you and start a list of all the things you *don't* want to do! It's amazing how satisfying that list will be, as well! Every item you write down should make you feel better. "Pole-vaulting. Oh good, I don't have to do that one!"

But shallow wasn't what you had in mind, was it?

I love new experiences and trying new things, but I would also love to get into the very depths of a subject.

I tend to learn things quickly and move on again pretty quickly, but it leaves me a little empty if I don't go deep enough.

How about that depth you wanted in each of your interests? I promised we'd return to that after you did the exercise that has disposed of the first of your obstacles: the notion that you wanted to do absolutely everything. But getting rid of that notion is only half the battle. You may have narrowed your interests down to a smaller number—or to whatever happens to pop up in front of your nose that catches your interest—but how will you ever be able to learn everything you wanted to learn about those things? Nobody has that much time. Or do they?

Here's yet another nice secret. Remember your Rewards and Durations? The amount of time you need, your Duration, always depends on the Reward you're seeking. It might take a bee 10 seconds to get the usable nectar it wants from one flower and maybe take 10 flowers to fill its tank and send it back to the hive to empty its cargo. What about you?

As I've said, if you're like most Scanners, you have a peculiar sense of time. You live in the present moment. With the focus being on today, Scanners get tasty bits of experience that other people pass over. But there's a troublesome downside. We operate as though today is all we're going to get. Maybe we can think about the coming week, and we certainly plan our work and home projects and our vacations and paying off our debts, with a clear picture of the coming years.

But if we wish we could travel to China, read *Little Dorrit*, and learn to play the fiddle, we forget everything but the present. It feels like everything has to be done all at once, right this minute. We think we have to eat an entire elephant by nightfall and have forgotten that it's done bite by bite. No wonder we feel overwhelmed.

Of course, a Scanner misjudges time in other ways, too; ways we'll be discussing in future chapters. You might remember a time you scheduled for yourself to clean all your closets, edit all your home videos, and put in a vegetable garden on a long holiday weekend—and be shocked after 3 days at how little you got done. Scanners often think things take less time than they really do.

On the other hand, Scanners also think it takes a lot more time than it really does to go past the surface into a subject they love. They are convinced that it's impossible to explore to their own satisfaction more than one or two areas—ever.

"Okay, tell me how I could do even a few dozen things that interest me," Ralph insisted.

"Well, it depends on what you want to get out of them. Not everyone is after the same Reward," I said. "What are we talking about?"

Regarding the technology magazines he loved reading, I asked how much time would it take for him to learn what he really wanted to know about each of the articles that had fascinated him. I also had him create a fantasy scenario where he was doing just what he longed to do as if it were happening right now.

"Where are you standing?" I asked. "In a classroom at MIT? In a library in Berlin? Make sure it's the place that makes you happiest. We're looking for satisfaction, and the feeling of happiness is the best guide to what will satisfy you." I waited a moment, interested in hearing what his best possible scenario would be for each subject he loved, and what emerged surpassed my expectations. He smiled and his face almost glowed. But the scenario he imagined was not at all what he had expected.

"Not a school or a library. That's not what I really want. But if I could spend an afternoon, just one long afternoon, and maybe one more the next day, in the lab talking to this guy who designed this new kind of electric lightbulb—if I could ask questions and let him tell me what he was doing, the story of what he was looking for and what happened, the story of this discovery of his, and maybe just enough detail so I could really understand the basic principles—that would be amazing. I would enjoy that so much. It would be like hearing about a great adventure, like I was there when each discovery happened, and that would be completely satisfying. More than satisfying." He stopped for a moment and opened his eyes.

"Now that *is* amazing," he said. "A couple of afternoons. That's all I'd really need."

What were you thinking while you read about Ralph's fantasy? Did it make you curious enough to try it yourself? If so, get your Big List of "1,000" things you want to do before you die.

Now, one at a time, take a slow, careful look at some of the items on your list and think about how long it would take for you to get *what you want* from each one. You don't even need to know what to call the Reward you're after—it just has to be what you really want from that experience. To get the most out of this experiment, you have to imagine yourself actually doing that activity, have a sense of where you are and what you're doing. Don't limit your conclusions to the quick answers your mind deals you. If you take the time to actually walk through a fantasy, you'll get more information than you can from any amount of theoretical information. Keep the following questions in mind:

- What do you really want to know about this area of interest?
- What would you most enjoy doing with that information (if you had a magic wand)?
- Who would you love to talk with about this subject if you could talk to absolutely anyone?

Then, after you finish imagining each item, note on your list how much actual time would realistically be needed for you to be satisfied. Would it take an afternoon as it did for Ralph? Or an hour, a weekend, a month, 5 years? Once you understand what you're looking for, the answers will come easily, because the truth is that you know them already.

Even if it's only in your imagination, when you think about the reality of doing what you'd love, something happens. That feeling of deprivation you thought you had to live with goes away and you start understanding what it feels like to be satisfied.

Soon those assumptions you made about wanting everything, needing a lifetime to investigate each thing you wanted, and most of all, the hopelessness of doing anything at all will be gone, driven away by the bright light of reality. And you'll be just a step away from ending your self-inflicted deprivation, choosing one of the once-unattainable items of your list and actually starting it. Today.

Be sure to hang on to that list. You might want to do what Ben did with his list of dreams.

> *I created a system similar to Barbara's "lost and found for your dreams" box; but instead of tossing notes into a box, I keep a journal with lined pages for my dreams. Each dream gets a line, and as I do them I put a check beside them. This allows me to go back and see what were once dreams and now have become a reality. All my dreams go into this journal, from something as simple as "own a teakettle" to something outlandish like "develop a space tourism business." And yes, I now own a teakettle, and it makes me very happy every time I use it. And in the case of my space tourism idea, it turns out to be not so crazy after all, now that billionaire Richard Branson is doing just that!*

Search for common themes

It can also be useful to look for common themes among your many interests. Ralph found that everything he loved involved the same elements: He loved learning by talking to creative people about what they were working on; he enjoyed every aspect of having the principles explained to him one-on-one by someone who was passionate about his work; and he loved the stories, the step-by-step retelling of how they had created their inventions. Discovering that these themes were at the heart of his dreams was a huge step for him.

If you have any trouble finding what your favorite activities have in common, go back and make a list of the things you are *not* interested in (as I did when I asked if Ralph read women's magazines). That can clarify what your interests have in common very quickly.

Now, how can Ralph make that dream real? He knew the answer before I did.

"I can actually write to some of these inventors if they're in my field. I think they'd answer my letters. But I know that I can go on Internet newsgroups every time I see an article like this and find the people who are doing it.

They're often right there. Or other people will be online who know about the technology. I'm not the only one who's turned on by these articles. A lot of people like me are reading them. I could have a great time chatting with them. I don't know why I never thought of it before. And who knows? If I get to know them a bit, I might go over to their school and talk to them in person one of these days."

"How much time do you think you'll need for each thing you come across?" I asked.

"Well, if I replace my frustrated wandering around the Internet with discussions on bulletin boards that I really care about, I might get everything I want and it will hardly take any extra time at all."

"Great!" I said. "Every time you see an article about something new and exciting, you can head for the boards. As soon as you find the place you're looking for and send out your question, you can go back to the magazine. That way, you won't get overwhelmed again."

So what about that engineering job he wanted to change? It turned out not to be at all unpleasant once he started doing what really interested him. But when he thought it was all he was going to get in terms of interesting, challenging ideas, it simply wasn't enough.

"I really don't mind my work as long as I've got something exciting like this going on, too," he said. "If I can find a way to talk with creative people online every day, this job will be just fine."

Your INTEREST INDEX BINDER

Now you need a new tool to help you keep track of all these ideas. Keep the Big List of all your interests in one three-ring binder. This is an index of every new interest that shows itself, all in one handy place. I'd start with a three-ring binder that has a 1-inch spine and a number of blank sheets. You can have dividers to separate pages, but a small sticky note attached to each sheet will save space.

Each sheet will have a different interest on it. If you were reading a magazine, like Ralph does, and came upon an article about a new breakthrough in electric lighting, you'd create one sheet for that topic and keep a log. The top entry would have the date and the title and location of the article, with perhaps a brief note about the most compelling point or the most important question you had, perhaps what you'd like to do the next time you're free. The goal is to keep all new interests in one place, like an index. There are many ways to do this on your computer, too, if that's more comfortable for you.

What's it for? When you have a few open moments, you can look in your Interest Index Binder to see which subject attracts you and then go online to follow an interesting discussion on that subject where you can ask some questions or read what others have said.

The result: You'll stop worrying that you'll never be able to follow up on your interests and will be able to continually revisit the most interesting ones far more often than you thought was possible. That means you'll be going into them as deeply as you want to. (You won't be afraid of "losing" an interest, either.)

And when one binder fills up, you can start another—and put the previous one on a shelf where you can always find it.

And while we're talking about binders...

Here's a first-rate tool that you'll be hearing about in coming chapters. It's perfect for someone who has dozens of interests and likes to investigate each of them more than is allowed by putting one crowded page in the above Index Binder. What I'm talking about is 20 or 30 THREE-RING BINDERS or as many as you have room for.

If you haven't used them in the past, you're in for a delightful revelation when you create a different binder for every interest. Having lots of binders is part of the system. Every time you get inspired by a new interest, you reach for a new binder and give that new interest a home. When you start feeling stressed because yet another interest has arrived, one you can't possibly devote yourself to in the way you want to, create a binder for it and put it on the shelf. The relief you feel after doing something this simple will surprise you. But it's another way of knowing nothing will be lost and everything will wait for you when you do have time.

The best kind of binder for your needs has clear "windows" on the outside where you can slip in notes and change labels easily if you decide to discard any subjects or move them to larger binders. For these beginning binders, you want those with the narrow spine, about half an inch wide. They're less intimidating if they don't fill up, and they allow you to stack dozens on one shelf.

If you do a lot of your delving on the Internet, keep three-hole paper in your printer and hit the "print" button whenever you want to keep something. Put that printout in one of your blank three-ring binders, write the topic on a piece of paper, and slip it into the window on the spine. This little tool will make you a very happy Scanner.

There are a number of uses for this system, and I'm sure you can see the possibilities for your own, but here's a letter that might bring the idea home better than any further explanation.

Dear Barbara,

Before you advised me to think of myself as a researcher, my apartment was frightening! Everything had potential, so nothing could be thrown away.

So, what's happened is like a little miracle! I have two wall shelves of three-ring binders! Every new interest gets a binder! I pull them out of a box the minute I feel myself shifting to a new interest. (And, for the first time, instead of worrying that I'm some kind of wild-eyed neurotic, I'm letting myself enjoy these new things!)

Every time I'm interested in something, I cut out clippings and tape them in there; I add printouts from the Internet, too. In the past, I'd have written a few notes about how I'd write a book or something and lose the notes as I moved on to something else. It was very distressing and felt like I was getting nowhere.

But all that has changed because of these great little three-ring binders. If I look up from my desk right now, I can see the binder about photographers holding about 20 pages printed out from the Web sites of news photographers and magazine photographers.

Instead of spinning around like a whirling dervish, I've slowed down, way down, and ended my frustration. I think it's because I know nothing will escape! Now, instead of feeling hopeless about ever looking more deeply into an interesting subject because there were so many, I've been spending hours on each of these. You don't know what a huge difference this has made!

There you are. Now you can quit depriving yourself of what your hungry mind has been craving. Enjoy yourself.

Chapter 7

I CAN'T GET STARTED

I'm so glad to know I'm a Scanner and not just a mess. But what do I do now? Quit my job and jump into the unknown?

I spend my time planning all kinds of things I'll never do. The next day, I'm planning something different. How do I stop planning and actually do something?

It's great to know you're a Scanner. All the energy you've directed toward trying to change into a different kind of person and all the time you've used up being bewildered or angry at yourself have opened up and are now yours to use. Think of it: time and energy you didn't know you had for creating a wonderful future. You're free to take your first step toward the life you've been longing for.

But how do you take that first step? What *is* the first step? Which goal should you choose? How can you be sure it's right?

It's nice to finally stop blaming yourself for being a Scanner, but the distance between that knowledge and taking your first step might seem as big as it ever was. You can see obstacles everywhere, both real obstacles and imaginary ones.

What can you do about those obstacles?

Obstacles are either real or they're not. The ones that aren't real are based on misinformation or emotions, and they're the ones we have to track down first.

You'll find that real obstacles are a lot easier to get around, and we'll deal with those, too.

So let's get started on a search for the ones that aren't real. They need a little scrutiny, a little sorting out. Then you'll be ready to address your real obstacles. You might be very surprised to find out how easily you can make them disappear.

Laine's story

"I can't get into action," said Laine, an executive secretary for a local shipping company. "I never get past thinking about what I want. I just sit around making endless lists of possibilities about a dozen directions I could take, but I never end up making any moves. Anyway, I can't risk quitting my job and jumping into the unknown, so what's the point in getting started?"

"That was quite a leap!" I answered. "You went straight from fantasizing with a pencil in your hand to jumping off a cliff! If my only two options were making lists or quitting my job for the unknown, I wouldn't move either! But who told you those were your only choices?"

"What else is there?" Laine asked.

"How about hanging on to your job for a while and putting your toe in the water first?" I suggested.

There was a long silence. "I don't even know what you mean," she said.

"I mean forget about jumping. After your workday is over, go out and get some information. Leave the world you know and find a way to hang around in the world you're interested in. Find Web sites and see if there are any conferences coming up that you could go to. Ask your librarian to help you find trade magazines in areas that interest you and take the time to read them. Get involved in an online discussion group with people who are already insiders. That's a no-risk way to learn something about those things you dream about. Just pull some reality into that listing and planning."

So many people (and Scanners in particular) are stuck for the same reasons as Laine. It's one of the biggest tricks our fears play on us: They make us forget how many safe steps you can and should take before you even think of leaving behind what you have.

"But if I don't jump, I'm afraid I'll never move," you might be thinking. Well, think again. Grand gestures make good fantasies, but when it comes to actually doing them, most of us aren't that reckless. We've seen what happens when people get reckless, maybe even experienced it ourselves. So by keeping the risk levels high, we aren't forcing ourselves into motion; we're forcing ourselves to do nothing.

Making lists and plans without actual information is just an extension of the fantasy; for many Scanners, daydreaming with a pencil in your hand is a way of life. In fact, it's a way to avoid action when your dreams look impossible. Real planning, on the other hand, the kind with facts and appointments and deadlines, is totally different. That kind of list is an action in itself.

Now, how do you go from writing down ideas to making something happen? Let's look at Laine's case. One of her ideas is to start an online clearinghouse for small-town recyclers, a central information exchange that would keep them abreast of the latest technical developments and government rulings, maybe even allow them to keep in touch with other small-town recyclers. She got the idea while she was in charge of the recycling co-op of the township where she lived and was certain there was a great need for what she'd envisioned.

"But I have lots of other ideas, too," she said, "about totally different things. Too many things!"

"Just for the sake of discussion, let's look at this one first," I suggested. "I know of a really fun way for you to design the kind of plan that actually *makes* you get into action. Once you learn to use it for one project, you'll be able to use it for all the others. Don't think of this as some huge undertaking; think of it as nothing but a practice run. Okay?"

"Oh. I guess so," she said hesitantly.

Action. The very thought freezes many of us in our tracks.

As a dedicated Scanner, you can be forgiven for refusing to move when you believe it requires abandoning your other dreams, but you've already seen that such choices are unnecessary. Even so, it can be hard to actually leave the gate.

You, too, might be thinking, "Which goal do I try first?" So I'll say it again, because fear can make us hard of hearing: *It doesn't matter which goal you try first, because this is only practice.* Later you can decide which of your goals to actually do first—remember, you'll be able to go after *all* of them—but you can learn how only by picking one and doing a practice run with it.

With that barrier to action removed, you may be running out of excuses—but I know many of you are still feeling plenty of hesitation and are not ready to take your first step. Laine, however, prided herself on being a rational person.

"If I could get my plans in order, of course I'd move. There are just so many things to consider," she said.

I held out a letter I'd received that morning. "Tell me what you think of this," I said. She took it and put on her glasses to read.

Barbara,

My obstacles are things like this: What if I write an e-book and nobody buys it? What if I offer my services as an information researcher, but I have to go out and "market" myself to lots of people and I don't like talking to lots of people, so I don't do it? What if nobody will buy my photography because it's invisible in a sea of competition? What if I learn how to be a good Webmaster and then technology makes my services obsolete? I'm trying to find a career that is a perfect match for me, and in the process I'm drowning in a sea of "what ifs." I'm paralyzed by the very analysis that is my most marketable talent. What do I do now?

Signed, Ed

Laine put the letter down and looked at me. "Well, he's just driving himself crazy. Do you think I'm doing that? That I'd be afraid to move even if I worked out a good plan?"

"I don't know," I answered, "but making the risk as high as you did by assuming you'd have to leave your secure job to take the first step makes action almost impossible, doesn't it?"

"I guess it does," she said, thoughtfully.

"I wouldn't feel too bad about it," I said. "Action in the direction of a wish is frightening. Most of us create a much more elaborate defense than yours. 'I want to work with animals, but I'd need a degree, so I'd have to change jobs to have time for school, but then I won't have enough money so I'll have to find a cheaper place to live, but I can't do that until I pay off my credit cards...' We weigh ourselves down with so many obstacles we can't even buy a goldfish bowl."

She started to smile and I wanted to keep her smiling, so I handed her an amusing clipping I'd saved from a newspaper. "Even the European Union does it," I said. This is what the clipping said:

Innovation Gives Finland a Firm Grasp on Its Future
Economy Offers a New Model for Old Europe
By Robert G. Kaiser
Washington Post *Staff Writer*

> *"Right now," said Himanen, the young Finnish intellectual, "Europe is like a once-fit top athlete who has fallen out of shape. Instead of taking action, the athlete keeps writing new strategic plans on how to get back into shape: 'I could go running, I could go swimming,' and so on. Sometimes it feels that the European logic is: 'When I'm in better shape, I will start exercising.'"*

As she read the article, I was thinking about how difficult it can be to move from thinking to taking action and how many reasons we can come up with to avoid doing it. Of course, Scanners aren't the only people who get stopped by "analysis paralysis," but their problems are multiplied by the sheer number of goals they have.

Muriel: *I made a vow to myself earlier this week: to list the top three things I want to accomplish before the end of this year. But the top three kept changing! And before I knew it, I had a list of eight top things. If the number keeps growing, I'll never accomplish any of them.*

Katchal: *How much hand-wringing and kvetching and procrastinating do we really have to do to get started on a goal? Why do so many of us subject ourselves to the impossible expectations of forcing every passing interest into a six-figure career and put off starting until we figure out how to make it pay? What if we could just do what we want to do without all the worry and emotional angst that's holding us back?!*

Good questions. What's the big deal?

Getting into action is a very big deal

Our defense mechanisms are designed for caution. You don't see them operating in babies, which is why babies need to be watched at all times. But caution grows with experience. Adolescents can be reckless, young people can be bold, but neither of them are as big a danger to themselves as babies. The more you know about tripping, the more carefully you walk.

This answers Katchal's question, above, when it comes to taking real risks, but why would the same caution exist for projects with no risk at all? Why would anyone hesitate to write a novel or design a line of clothing for herself? Because by the time your defense mechanisms are fully developed, they don't want you to do *anything* new or unfamiliar. They don't want you to bungee jump, which makes sense. But they don't want you to sing in front of an audience in your living room, either.. And that doesn't make sense.

Defense mechanisms are primitive and powerful, and they think everything new is a survival issue. Right or wrong, they affect you.

But if you give in to your defense mechanisms' sillier prohibitions, you won't do anything interesting at all. How do you get into action when you really want to and it's not dangerous at all?

Here's a down-to-earth, three-step system that can work magic on inertia.

Three magic steps

If you're a Scanner who can't stop thinking and start doing, I'd like to propose three small steps that, used together, will get you into action every time.

Step 1: Learn to use a new kind of planning (the BACKWARD PLANNING FLOWCHART), which won't replace action but will actually nudge you into taking real steps.

Step 2: Let this flowchart expose any hidden fears you might be feeling that make you avoid action, so you can take steps to reduce the danger.

Step 3: Set up a REAL DEADLINE, a "drop-dead date" when you must be ready. This is also known as making an appointment with a living human being and will provide you with both the companionship that reduces stress and the accountability that makes you move even when you do feel stress.

Used together, these three steps will transform you from a planner and list maker into an action hero. They're quite amazing.

Here's how they worked out with Laine, who was finally willing to try a practice goal.

"In my experience," I said, "I've found that it's not nearly as frightening to be in action as to hover around it."

"I can believe that," she said. "But I don't believe in going off half-cocked and unready."

"Neither do I," I reassured her and introduced her to the first magic step, the Backward Planning Flowchart.

The Backward Planning Flowchart, SUCCESS TEAMS, and Real Deadlines

This is my own version of a flowchart, which I designed while preparing to run my very first workshops in 1975. (It was one of the most popular parts of my first book, *Wishcraft: How to Get What You Really Want*, which is still selling well after 25 years, partly because of this flowchart. If you want a more detailed diagram, complete with little circles and lines, you can find the original Backward Planning Flowchart in that book.)

I had found corporate flowcharts too hard to understand or use and started from scratch by setting up a goal and asking myself, "Could I achieve that goal right now? If not, what would I need first?" I kept drawing circles with goals written inside them and moving back to draw more circled goals—asking those same two questions each time—until I finally reached a step I could actually take immediately.

And when I reached a goal I could do right away, I drew a big arrow pointing at it that said "Now!"

The process got me out of my chair and actually taking steps—no mean trick—and I was very proud of myself for thinking of it. I was also very excited to think I had found a way to help everyone move from inertia/paralysis into action.

I tried the Backward Planning Flowchart out with a little team I'd put together and used an imaginary dinner party for practice. "Okay, we're going to have a dinner party for 12 people. Can we do it tomorrow night? If not, what would we have to do first?" We worked at a blackboard, noting how we'd first have to invite people to come, and we'd need to buy and prepare the food. To take those steps, we'd need telephone numbers and to decide on the menu. It was great fun and so simple anyone could do it. I could see it was potentially quite powerful, and I couldn't wait to use it. But when I actually introduced it in my first Success Teams workshops, way back in 1976, the response was not what I expected.

For some hours, the people in the workshop had been helping each other come up with fun ways to accomplish goals. There was a lot of laughter and the heady air of enticing possibilities everywhere. Everyone was having a good time and looked at me with expectant smiles to see what I had planned for them next.

And, as planned, I said, "Okay, let's make it real. I want you to each set a goal and a tentative date when you'll achieve it. Let's say you want to sing your first torch song on 'open mike night' at a local club in 3 months." Everyone listened with enthusiasm while I drew a circle at the far right corner of a chalkboard.

"To show up at that club and sing, you'd need a couple of things," I continued. "You'd need the permission of the owner of the club, and you'd need to know how to sing, correct?" The audience looked interested and nodded their heads as I drew lines to two circles and wrote "permission" in one and "able to sing" in the other.

"Now," I continued, "to get permission, you'd have to talk to the boss," and I drew another line attached to a circle. "And to talk to the boss, you'd have to find a club. So," I turned to the audience, "can you find a club that has an open mike night?" Most of the people nodded affirmative. "Is there anything you have to do first, or can you do that tomorrow?"

"It's pretty easy," one woman said. "You just look in the Yellow Pages of the phone book."

"Great," I said. "Then this line is done. You've got a step you can take tomorrow. Now let's go back to the beginning and look at the second thing you'd need to actually perform at this club: to be able to sing."

In the same way, moving backward to first steps, I drew out the path to being able to sing a couple of songs, including getting a singing coach and choosing the songs.

When I was finished, they looked at me as though I was a very clever person and I felt pretty good about my invention. I told them to each draw the same kind of Backward Planning Flowchart full of circles and lines for their own goals, and I gave them about 25 minutes to give it a try. As they picked up their pens and started to work, I turned away and began looking through my notes. A few minutes had passed when I sensed an odd change in the room. I turned around to look at the people as they worked on their sheets of paper, and I realized no one was laughing or smiling anymore. They weren't writing, either. I watched for a minute and then I said, "Is something wrong?"

Everyone looked at me with such worry in their eyes that I felt terrible. Finally one woman raised her hand and said, "This isn't fun anymore; it's getting scary." Everyone nodded in agreement.

I realized she was right. What I'd thought was a rather clever transition from wishing to actually achieving a dream—a kind of magic moment of transformation—was actually too powerful. It forced action where everyone had been playing.

I didn't want to lose the great momentum that had been building, so I immediately told some stories to make them laugh and shake the tension. Then I put them into teams of six and set up nightly phone calls and weekly meetings with each other, and when they felt safer, I showed them some ways to make their first action step so tiny and nonthreatening that they stopped being afraid.

You'll notice I didn't suggest any positive thinking, because I don't think it's reliable. As I said in Chapter 3 ("Scanner Panic"), and you can't hear too often: *If you want to lower your fear level, lower the danger level.*

Once they saw how small those first steps were and understood they'd have support at every step from their teammates, they stopped being worried. By the end of the workshop, they were again excited about their ideas and looking forward to meeting with their new buddies. I got heartening letters about the great accomplishments those original Success Teams produced for years after that workshop.

But I never forgot what I learned that day: Scheduling any kind of action is a change of universes from writing lists and making plans. It's never a small matter. And it's always a jolt to one's system. To keep moving, you need many techniques and tools.

For example, always have a target date for each part of your goal. A calendar without deadlines is exactly like playing tennis without a net. (You might ignore a target date that no one but you knows about.) Support combined with accountability creates a Real Deadline. This letter from a Scanner says it nicely.

Something that I had not realized before is that Support gets us past Resistance. I have been too isolated. I am realizing that my ups and downs really seem to depend on whether or not I have a support system. I think structure is the key to why I like work. The paycheck is kind of a built-in motivator to focus me, and the boss is a support system. I have to get to work.

I also loved the period when I was going to school full-time, and I think a major reason is that I had appointments, deadlines, and a great support system at that time. My best friend had also quit work and was going back to school, and we'd walk to school together, cheer each other on, and take classes together. Also, in my biology class I got involved in a study group (what a marvelous thing) that met at my house and was of course a great support group.

Do you have that kind of support in your life? Every time I see someone who cannot move, I find out he's trying to pull the whole plan off all by himself. That's not how we're designed. On our own, we'll often opt to avoid any kind of action, and we play tricks on ourselves so we don't realize what we're doing.

Isolation is the dream killer. It will stop you every time.

Those workshops I described were designed to create Success Teams. They were (and are to this day) extraordinarily successful. When it comes to actually making dreams come true, nothing compares with having a weekly meeting and a team on your side. If you can't find or create a team, get a single buddy or hire a coach and set up regular meetings. Knowing they're waiting to hear from you will lower your anxiety and make you get into action.

(While you're at it, don't underestimate the power of your APPOINT-MENT PLANNER. That's the tool in which you write your dentist appointments, and if you didn't, you'd never go to the dentist. Write in every appointment with your coach or teammate. You'll be motivated to remember what you're supposed to do because other people will be waiting for your report.)

I told you the story of that early workshop for three reasons: First, because the Backward Planning Flowchart is such a hugely useful tool and telling a story is a great way to teach it to you. Second, because you might be avoiding action without realizing it, and the Backward Planning Flowchart will shine the light of day on your hidden fears. (Nothing will flush a bogeyman out of the shadows like a round of Backward Planning.) And third, I want you to realize that the prospect of imminent action—making Real Deadlines with your Success Team—will reveal any of your fears. Talking about them gets you nowhere, but action makes them melt away.

Getting unstuck

So, just as an experiment, draw a plan that moves backward from the goal until you get to the steps you can do tomorrow, no matter how small they may be. And while you do it, pay careful attention to how you feel. Are you enjoying the first stirrings of getting unstuck? Or can you feel yourself starting to freeze in your tracks?

That's what happened to Laine.

In our session, she decided to "practice" action by selecting her recycling goal. "I'm not sure this is really the project I'd choose to do first," she explained, "but I see that I have to choose something or there's no way to get started at all."

The following week, she spent about three or four lunch hours and evenings at home after work on the Internet finding out everything she could about local recycling and took careful notes.

At our next session she said, "I almost made a PowerPoint presentation to make myself feel respectable but realized I'd do just as well with notes on a pad of paper and it would create a better mood when I presented it."

She had also gathered together the phone numbers of some of the people she had worked with as a volunteer in her town's recycling program, looked in her calendar for available times, and scheduled a tentative date for a meeting at her home. She showed me all her notes.

"That's impressive," I said. "You're good to go."

"I don't know," she said. "I'm having serious doubts about this project."

"Why?" I asked.

"Maybe it's not as important to me as I thought," she answered, not looking at me.

"Do you think there's anything you're afraid of?" I asked.

"Of course not," she replied emphatically. "We're not talking about skydiving, just gathering some people at my house to talk."

I nodded agreement. "And you'll be calling the meeting, so I guess you'll open by explaining what it's about?"

Her expression changed slightly, but she said, "Well, yes." There was a moment's silence, and she said, "You know, they might have already come up with an idea for this. I'd feel a little silly if I didn't know about it. I'd better do some checking around first." And then she looked at me and said, "I don't think I even care about recycling!"

"That was sudden," I said. "What uncomfortable moment did you just imagine, Laine?"

"I imagined them looking at me like I was an idiot," she confessed. "I don't really know these people all that well, but they look very capable. How do I know *I'm* capable?"

"Hello?" I said. "Are you kidding? You know perfectly well how capable you are. You've told me so a number of times yourself."

She looked at me, with a small, ironic smile on her face. "I'm scared. I'm the new kid on the block. Maybe they'll snub me in some awful way. Oh boy, I never realized that."

"Is it a difficult bunch of people or a closed club?" I asked.

"Not at all. These are very nice, welcoming people. It's one of the reasons I've been so active in the recycling program. I just got some kind of flashback to my childhood, I guess. Go figure. Me. Afraid."

And she looked much more relaxed. "You know, I think I'll call one of them to help me with the plan. If we're working together, I'll have to do it, like when my friend shows up at my door to go jogging."

Laine had worked through all three of the magic steps. First, she used the Backward Planning Flowchart to identify the first steps. This got her so close to action, her fears were exposed and she saw what they were, which reduced the danger. And now she had come up with the third surefire way to stop being stuck: She decided to hook up with a buddy for support and the accountability of Real Deadlines.

Ending the great debate with REALITY RESEARCH

If you find that you still have a need to do the "But What If..." routine and you can't talk yourself out of it, here's a way to bring in the kind of data to turn your analyzing into something very useful. I call it Reality Research.

Instead of wondering if your idea is a good one or a bad one—and going around in circles with an internal debate that can't be resolved—go after some real answers, like that great Scanner Ben Franklin was so fond of doing. He knew he could only get so much information about electricity by thinking about it or reading about it. Finally he had to go out into a storm and fly his kite.

While I don't suggest that you spend your time in a thunderstorm, I do advise you to follow Franklin's style of finding things out by stepping away from the desk and out into the world with Reality Research. You can wonder forever how many teeth a horse has—or you can find a horse, open its mouth, and count its teeth.

Here's how Reality Research works.

Let's say your inner risk analyst presents you with this question: "What if I write a book and no one likes it?" Instead of using that question for a stop sign, follow it with this one: "What's the best way to get the answer to that question?" And go get some answers.

That's it, plain and simple. If you make it a habit to ask that one question, you'll be in action. And not the reckless, jump-off-a-cliff kind of action you're too wise to follow, but the kind of action that brings in real answers.

To continue our example, let's say the answer is: Try to find out if people like it by showing them a sample.

That's a very big answer. To show a sample of your work to people, you need a chapter of the book you haven't written. To create even one chapter and show it to someone requires writing up a table of contents and a description of what you'll be saying in your book. Combined with your chapter, that will be a very good thing to show people so you can find out if they like it. I do it all the time, in fact. What I just described is also called a book proposal.

To answer the question "What's the best way to get the answer?" requires action. There's no way to think it into being. And action has magic in it.

Try it with your own project. Set yourself a tight deadline (pull in a friend to lower the danger level and keep you honest, and maybe to help). Then create enough of your idea so you can show it to some people.

Will that give you a surefire answer? No, but it will get your project out of the ditch and back on the highway, where you can get started. And that's what you were after, remember?

That's the whole secret. That's all you need to go from planning to getting started toward anything you want to do. Let's try a quick run-through, shall we?

◈ Pick one "practice" goal right this minute.
◈ Create a Backward Planning Flowchart and put a tentative target date for completion of the steps over each circle.

- Check to see if you have any "holes" in the Flowchart (missing steps or lack of information or fears that might stop you).
- If so, do your Reality Research and get some answers.
- Get a buddy or other Support Team to check on your Real Deadlines regularly.
- Take the first step.

You might be surprised at what comes of this little test run: You could actually turn one of your dreams into reality, just like that. Whether or not that happens, I can guarantee that going after a practice goal by taking real steps will change the way you look at action forever. And it will change more than just your viewpoint—it will change you, too. You'll become too self-conscious to let yourself get away with your "But What If..." games without going after real answers, of course. But trying out this process will forever expose the two mysteries that have so often stopped you in the past: (1) why it's so hard to get started, and (2) how to get started anyway.

The night of Laine's meeting, I got a call from her. She had teamed up with one of the women she knew best, and together they had prepared the list of telephone numbers and a "calling script" to get them through the first awkward moments of each call. Between them, they called everyone on the list.

"They're coming over tonight," Laine said, "and I'm nervous. They might think my idea is stupid. But they're good people, maybe they won't. The woman who helped me has become a friend, and she'll be there. So I've lowered that danger level as much as I can."

"Good for you, Laine!" I said. "Going from wishes to action is a big move. It can be very intimidating."

"Yes, it's still a little scary, but you forgot to tell me one thing."

"What's that?" I asked.

"That it's exciting to finally get moving! You know *something* is going to happen."

Start small, start now

So the moral is: Start small ... but start *now*. Move back to first steps, contact a buddy or set up a team, and start taking your first, small steps. That's the hardest part. Once you become unstuck, no matter how slowly you move at first, the hard part is over. With the support and accountability you'll get from a buddy or a team, you'll be able to take bigger actions: Make a call, show up at a meeting, write a letter, even make a speech. Once you get into motion, everything changes.

Now let's take a look at Scanners who might have no trouble getting started on a new project—they start projects all the time. They just don't seem to finish any of them.

Chapter 8

I NEVER FINISH
ANYTHING

For me, starting something is the most exhilarating part. Optimism, the promise, the passion, the absolutely giddy feeling of excitement that always happens for me when I begin a new thing. The trouble is, very soon the gloss disappears, the hard work has to begin, and I start to feel lost.

I look around my house and see all the unfinished projects I've started with such gusto and never got back to. But they're sitting here staring at me, reminding me of my failure to complete another project!

I work enthusiastically and then crash, and the whole thing looks stupid, so I give up.

Why don't Scanners finish what they start?

If you identify with the quotes at the top of this page, you are not alone. Enthusiastic starts that fizzle out are almost every Scanner's major concern. Why don't Scanners complete their projects?

Gillian, an Australian homemaker and mother, was recently discussing this problem on my bulletin board.

"I always think I've found my passion and I get so fired up," she wrote, "but it never lasts. If only I could find something that would stick and never let go!"

But a few hours after she wrote those words, she seemed to find exactly what she was looking for. Someone mentioned a relative who was a midwife, and Gillian responded with excitement.

"That's something I've thought about for years! I know I'd love that. If only I knew where to start."

I happen to have a neighbor who is a midwife and a world-renowned lecturer and teacher of midwifery, so I immediately put her in touch with Gillian. And then Gillian, who had previously been a daily presence on the bulletin board, simply disappeared.

It's not uncommon to get cold feet when the perfect contact shows up virtually on your doorstep, but it usually passes. However, Gillian was gone too long. Concerned, I finally e-mailed to see if she was okay. She answered promptly.

"Thanks for asking. I'm fine. I did act on talking to Georgia and the midwifery council here. I learned that my idea of what I would enjoy in being a midwife is different from the reality. I guess at my heart of hearts I am still waiting for *the* thing to show up rather than *a* thing, though I am not sure how I would recognize it even if it did exist."

I pulled her back to the specifics. "What part of the program didn't you like, Gillian? Was it different than you had expected?"

"Oh, midwifery isn't the problem; I am," she said. "I'm the same with everything. Last year I started a newsletter and shut it down after two issues. I just felt worse and worse the more I got into it. I like to plan, but I don't like to act. I feel like I was born a runner but I now live in a wheelchair. The desire is there, but I'm incapable of follow-through."

I scolded her lightly for her tone. "Gillian, everybody loves planning better than action, and no one wants to continue a newsletter after the first two issues. What exactly happened?"

But I couldn't get a real answer, just a litany of the typical labels too many Scanners pin on themselves. She said she tended to be lazy, to drop the ball, to have a short attention span, even to be stupid.

Out of curiosity, I went looking for her other messages on my bulletin board, and here are some excerpts from what I found.

> *My middle child has severe allergies and I spent many, many hours research-*
> *ing the immune system, chemical sensitivities, making my own lotions and*
> *potions to use on her skin, how to keep our home healthy, etc. That was 5*

years ago, and my little girl is doing great! (I even started a successful little business making and selling natural bath/beauty products, but the work got too repetitive so I stopped.)

I was going to study metaphysics. Got right up to Wittgenstein and when he said philosophy was ended, I had to agree with him.

I once got interested in physics, life, the universe, and everything. My math is beyond lousy, but I read most of the popular books on the topic. Wanted to know what the basis of matter is.

I got really caught up in becoming a wealthy investor and about all the different theories on personal finance. I saw it was all simple and constant, and once I learned that, I lost interest.

There was more, but I had seen enough. Gillian was clearly neither lazy nor stupid.

But she had it all wrong when she said she never finished anything. She finished everything she started, just like those honeybees I mentioned earlier.

The reason you stop when you do: You got what you came for

If you're like Gillian and you start new projects with a rush of enthusiasm but soon lose interest, you have almost certainly finished what you started. It just doesn't look that way to anyone else.

True, sometimes you may get overexcited and become scared and stop before you get what you came for. Your subconscious defense mechanisms hear all that excitement as an alarm and try to protect you by making you crash. You shouldn't give up at those times because after a while, your interest will return in a calmer form, and you can continue.

Most times, you don't lose interest until you get exactly what you came for. Remember the Rewards and Durations discussed in Chapter 2 ("What's Wrong with Me?")? When a honeybee gets the nectar it came for, it loses interest in that flower and heads over to another one. When a Scanner leaves a project, it's for the same reason.

Now why does it appear to the world that you've quit too soon?

You might have taken in the information faster than everyone else. Some Scanners (and non–Scanners as well) are simply too fast for the programs they're in. They finish early and lack the patience to wait for everyone else.

Maybe you're a visionary or a leader. Scanners love beginnings and can set the course and inspire the crew. For them, that's the only interesting part. They don't want to take the voyage. They'd rather start something new.

Perhaps you're a designer. "I'm great at starting, conceiving, and planning things, but once I figure out the design problems, I lose interest. I guess I don't want to do the hard work that comes after that," a woman told me.

"Maybe you're a designer," I answered. "Maybe someone else wouldn't think the follow-through was such hard work."

I think she stared at me for a full minute without a word. "No one ever said that to me before," she answered, finally.

There are many reasons Scanners finish before anyone expects them to, but they all have the same pattern: While the interesting part was there to keep them, Scanners stayed. When it was gone, they left.

But none of these reasons explained why Gillian had stopped pursuing her interest in midwifery so abruptly. After some persistence, I finally got a clear answer from her.

> *I read one of my sister's nursing manuals on birth when I was about 15 or so, and I was surprised a baby ever gets born safely with all the things that can go wrong. I guess I've been fascinated with the process ever since.*
>
> *I wanted to learn midwifery because I thought I'd be training to be a medical advisor through pregnancy and do research into abnormal births. I was eager to learn everything, the medical field, human biology, especially if it could help bring a dependent little baby safely into the world.*
>
> *But the program doesn't focus on medical research—which is certainly fine. But when I realized that, another big enthusiasm fizzled out. I can't seem to stick with anything.*

Her conclusion: Something was wrong with her. But how did she end up there? Nothing could be simpler. Gillian wanted to learn medicine and use her knowledge to rescue babies. She'd already shown that she could do it with her independent studies about allergies and the improved health of her daughter. But what she wanted wasn't in the midwifery program. So why on earth would she want to continue?

It was so obvious. Why didn't she see that?

I explained how odd her conclusion was, given the facts. "You know what you want. You found it wasn't there. Now you can look somewhere else. That's what you're supposed to do."

The problem wasn't Gillian. But she, and so many other Scanners, do have a different problem: If they wanted to buy a pair of shoes and accidentally walked into a pet store, they'd blame themselves for not wanting dog food. And when they walked out empty-handed, they'd call themselves quitters.

And that *is* a problem.

But something Gillian said in one of her letters gave me a clue to what might help to solve that problem:

> *I started a newsletter and shut it down after two issues. I just felt worse and worse the more I got into it.*

Have you ever had that feeling?

If you're a Scanner who can't stick with anything, I already know the answer—you most certainly have had that feeling. But have you ever thought about what it is?

I'll tell you one thing I know: This feeling is the cause of every Scanner's unexpected ending. The dread of being locked away from their main source of energy and joy—learning, discovering, sleuthing, creating—makes Scanners pull back from every job or project, no matter how hard they try to stay.

Nothing could be more important than understanding when and why you have this feeling. It's at the heart of what makes you a Scanner!

But understanding the when and the why is not something Scanners want to do. Because the feeling is so unpleasant, they just want it to stop and never willingly stay long enough to see what it is. The result? Not only don't they understand what that bad feeling is, they automatically assume it's a flaw in their makeup, a lack of character, even a desire to fail. Like Gillian, they conclude there's something wrong with them.

If that rings even the littlest bell, I want you to stop what you're doing and start an important investigation.

Name that feeling

Go somewhere quiet for about 20 minutes. Pull out your Daybook and pick up a pen. Now think back to the times you tried to stick with a project after you had lost interest in it. Pretend you're in that situation again and recreate the experience of having to focus your attention on the task. How does that make you feel? Does the feeling get more intense the longer you continue this fantasy? What is that feeling about?

Describe it the best you can. Be sure to take your time. This will not be fun, but if you do a thorough job you won't ever have to do it again. Continue writing until you've described everything you can about what you were feeling.

When you're done, read what other Scanners have said:

> **Rosa:** *I felt like I was being locked away from everything that would make me happy. I wanted to struggle to get free.*

> **Howard:** *I knew if I stayed at what I was doing, my life would be drab and boring.*

> **Renee:** *It was like going down a tunnel and thinking I'd never see the sun again. That was such a bad feeling.*

If you wrote something similar, you've named that feeling. For the sake of easy identification, let's call it the Bad Feeling. Confronting it is very powerful stuff, because that feeling drives you away from every project once you've lost interest. It's what stops you from following through even when you want to. The Bad Feeling is the first half of the mystery behind what makes you a Scanner, and it's important that the next time you feel it, you'll know what it is.

Identifying the Bad Feeling lets us draw a few conclusions about why you, and all Scanners, don't "finish" what you start.

◈ You leave a project because staying would feel intolerable.
◈ Staying would be intolerable because nothing you want is there.
◈ If you stayed, you'd have to accept being unhappy.
◈ And trying to accept being unhappy is just crazy.

That's what your feeling is telling you. It's not to be taken lightly. The profound discomfort you feel comes from deep inside your very powerful and primitive survival mechanisms. They're telling you that if you stay, you could harm yourself—and, as I'll show you in a moment, they're probably right.

To blame yourself for these Bad Feelings doesn't make any sense at all. To ignore them doesn't make sense, either. It's time to stop criticizing yourself for not following through. When you allowed those feelings to drive you away from a project, you were doing the right thing!

How many times have you said that to yourself before right now? If you're like most Scanners, the answer is none. So take a little time to enjoy it. You were right all along.

But what if a chance at success comes along? Don't you have to take it no matter what you feel?

You could be wasting a great opportunity!

Opportunity. Sometimes that lovely word carries a very dark message. We've all had the painful experience of seeing one of our ideas or inventions show up in the marketplace under someone else's name because we didn't follow through on it. *Obviously, we think, if you don't stick with something—no matter what feelings you have—you can pass up your chance of becoming a success. When you don't seize opportunity, you're a quitter, even a failure.*

Actually, that's quite an assumption, the notion that you must "do" something with every project that interests you or you've wasted your time and your talent. It deserves a closer look.

Why does every bright idea have to be an opportunity to become accomplished, rich, and famous? Even if you were the kind of person who finishes everything you start, you couldn't harness all your ideas anyway.

Artist Vik Muniz says it best: "Ideas make you do a lot of work. It's like I have a whole bunch of people in my head telling me what to do, but there's only one guy to do it all."

Even with a load of helpers, no Scanner can develop every idea or become a specialist in every field that interests her. After all, you're a Scanner, and you would never want to be kept away from all the other great ideas you could be having!

But what's the point of getting wildly enthusiastic and diving into all these new ideas if you're not going to do something with them? Why would you continue to do this?

Are you being frivolous? No.

Is something else going on? Yes.

It's the other powerful feeling at the heart of what makes you a Scanner: the Good Feeling.

Jess: *The most wonderful moment in the world is standing on the edge just before I plunge in and thinking about all the wonderful things that might be waiting for me there.*

Lucia: *My favorite feeling is the one I had when I had gotten rid of almost everything I owned and all I had was a round-the-world open-dated plane ticket, a few thousand dollars, and my backpack. That's the feeling that drives me on in all my interests—that "What's going to happen next?" feeling.*

Mark: *When I see a puzzle, my mouth waters. I'm like a dog with a bone. I can't wait to gnaw on it until I get the answer!*

Dianne: *I love East Coast music from Canada. Actually, I love it so much that it makes me feel like I'm going to burst into tears sometimes. It's the only thing that I've ever experienced that makes me feel that way. Anyway, I stumbled upon a new interest: the Irish whistle. I've decided that I want to learn how to play it, and then I want to compete in the All-Irish competition (and win), and then I want to be invited to play with my favorite East Coast bands. Or become a recording artist.*

I almost can't breathe right now because I'm so excited about the Irish whistle. Will I be fantastic and finally realize my ongoing dream of fame and glory? Could this be it, the thing that I've been looking for? Or will it just be something else that will be fun for a few months and I'll drop it and move on to other things?

If you're like me, all you can think when our whistle player talks about dropping her interest in a few months is, so what? It will be worth it. And where can I buy one of those whistles?

You see, your mind gets fired up for its own reasons, and they aren't always connected with accomplishment. Dianne may want to be a champion at the Irish whistle, but happy dendrites firing off in her brain might not care about that at all.

On the other hand, if the path to championship continues to be stimulating, joyful, and delightful, Dianne will follow that path because she'll be pulled by the power of the Good Feeling.

Name that other feeling

You've already described the Bad Feeling. Now it's time to do what Jess, Lucia, Mark, and Dianne did: describe the good one. Open your Daybook and think about how you feel when you're in full-speed-ahead Scanner mode, when you're completely captivated by something and want to do it more than anything else in the world.

Then pick up your pen and describe the sensation you're having in the Daybook, *and write slowly and thoughtfully so you'll never forget it.* It's time to claim the feeling that draws you like a powerful magnet to what is new and unknown, because it's the most joyous part of you, and it's the other source of your identity as a Scanner. You see, not everyone feels as bad as you do when you're stuck with a project that doesn't interest you. And not everyone becomes as fascinated and delighted by something new and interesting.

That's what makes you different. Your mind loves new ideas for its own reasons.

Maybe coming up with ideas is just the way your brain dances. Instead of thinking "This could be a great opportunity for success!" why not enlarge the meaning of "opportunity" to include the Good Feeling? As in: "This could be a great opportunity for my brain to boogie!"

If your brain cells are having a good time, they must be hearing their own kind of music. Let them dance.

Which leads me to a radical bit of advice

I'm convinced you're not supposed to finish 99 percent of the projects you start under the influence of the Good Feeling. *But you should start them anyway.*

I have something to say to you now that might shock you and will certainly shock anyone who's been trying to "reform" you. In the previous chapter, I told you that action was important and that the two most important rules are: Start small. Start now.

It's time for you to know the whole process:

Start small.
Start now.

Start everything.

And don't bother to finish *any* of it.

What?!

You heard me. If you wake up with a great invention and you have a fantastic way to market it...or if you realized you could help the families in one inner-city block start their own home businesses and you have a plan to set them all up with computers donated from giant corporations and a way to train all their kids to be computer techies...or if you just came up with an amazing idea for a Self-Confidence Video Game so powerful that it can get shy people to step up to microphones and make speeches...and...and...well, you get the idea.

If that happens, start up the engines.

Pull out your Scanner Daybook or open one of your three-ring binders and do a full da Vinci Write-Up. Lay out the idea in all its splendor. Don't let anything or anyone interrupt you. Get every good idea down on paper, with diagrams and drawings and anything else you want. Find information on the Internet and print it out on three-hole paper. Take the idea as far as your enthusiasm and imagination allow and don't stop until you collapse and your brain is empty.

You'll be brilliant. When you're in love, you're a genius. Everyone is.

What should you do with these beginnings?

Save them, show them off. Celebrate them. And be grateful that you're a Scanner. Not everyone can have this much fun with nothing but what's between her ears.

And never again criticize yourself for not finishing your ideas. Drop that burden off your shoulders. It should never have been there in the first place.

Because you were never the problem.

Gillian knows that now. She's taking another look at all the projects she dropped, and instead of wincing because she didn't take them further, she's starting to see things very differently.

> *Scanners feel the pressure to choose "it" when they're not made for such a thing.*
> *At least that is my understanding. Some things they will follow through more*
> *than others, some they may even turn into a career, but maybe they never will.*

That in no way means they are weak willed, cognitively deficient, or any other label you would like to put on it. We just have many and varied loves, our wow button is pushed far more often than others, and thank God for it.

I hope you'll soon feel the same way.

Okay, that's what I had to tell you. It's the same thing I tell people at every one of my Scanner workshops. And, after a few moments of stunned silence, someone invariably says:

But I bought all that equipment!

I know you don't want to get petty about such little things, but what about all those beads you bought for your new jewelry ideas (and you only made half of one bracelet, a year ago)? And what about the pile of photographs you developed yourself? And all the pans and chemicals? That took days! And you never did it again. What about those voice-over audiocassettes you made when you were sure you could do that for a living—a couple of years ago?

Well, you could throw a work party and bring a bunch of friends in to try to revive some of your semidiscarded projects, and that might work for a while. But sometimes you have to admit you're finished and there's nothing you can do about it. If it's a personal project, it won't be a disaster.

But if you can feel the loose strings hanging there, if your incomplete projects call out messages of reproach every time you pass them, there's a special tool that will fix the problem. It's called the SCANNER'S FINISH.

The Scanner's Finish

This is a very different way to wrap things up than we're usually taught. Here's how it works: When you know chances are good that you will not be working on a project again, you simply gather together all the parts, wrap them up in a parcel of brown paper, and tie it with a string. Then attach a large label explaining what the project is, what the goal was, at what stage the project has been put away, and, should it ever be continued, what the next steps should be.

Then you can walk away without regret. You've signed off on it, without pretense of returning. Your Scanner's mission has been accomplished.

Although it may not seem finished to anyone else, it's finished to you. It's your project. You did it by choice. You have the right to decide when you're done.

You've also created the possibility that it won't be wasted by leaving instructions on the outside. In fact, if you have the nerve, you can give the parcel as a present to someone who needs something to do. But there's something even better you can do with your little parcel. You can start a collection and call it your LIFE'S WORK BOOKSHELF.

Your Life's Work Bookshelf

For a place to hold your new parcels, you need a bookshelf or a closet with empty shelves in it and a small sign attached in plain sight that says "My Life's Work Bookshelf" or "My Autobiography" or "Souvenirs of an Adventurous Mind." You can even treat it like a collection of a composer's or writer's works and call it your "Oeuvre." That has a nice ring to it.

Every time you have a parcel you've made with your Scanner's Finish, you'll place it on this shelf as a way of creating a small display, almost a museum, of all the ideas and projects and plans you loved and worked with.

If this system looks a bit simpleminded, look again. The meaning is more profound than you might think. It could be the first time you're admiring that wonderful Scanner mind of yours. It's possible neither you nor anyone else has ever done this before.

Before completing this book, I gathered together a group of Scanners on a Sunday morning for a question-and-answer session, just to make sure I had covered all the important issues that confront Scanners. I had the session recorded so I could listen to it later, and during the session I discussed the Scanner's Bookshelf as a way of learning to respect the output of your thinking. I said something like, "The plans and ideas that fall out of your mouth are like diamonds and rubies, but in a culture that only values immediate success, no one sees them that way. That's why you have to carefully save them when you're ready to move on and keep them on your Life's Work Bookshelf. Those are your works, a record of your creativity's travels."

The whole time I spoke—it was more than 3 hours—I noticed the sound engineer listening with unusual intensity. When the session was over, I walked back to thank him and to ask why he'd listened with such focus.

He said very seriously, "I realized today that my wife is a Scanner. I never knew her ideas were like diamonds and rubies. I'm going home to build her a bookshelf."

If you still wish you didn't have to "waste" any of your good ideas, consider this jolly Scanner idea from my bulletin board.

Marlowe: *Follow-through is not my strong suit. Until there is a market for half-finished projects, I am going to have to find a way to fix this problem.*

Cyrano: *Okay, here's the half-finished-project idea. Set up a listing place for half-finished ideas that have been abandoned reluctantly. Put them up for "sale." The seller would sell all rights and give the buyer all his ideas, papers, and other records. Probably no money would change hands at the time. Instead, the seller would receive some sort of royalty on any income (or maybe revenue) the idea generates when implemented.*

Or maybe the more altruistically inclined would be content just to see someone else make their idea come to life. Not me, though—I want a cut.

That's what it looks like when brain cells dance. An engineer from my latest Scanner workshop suggested that I put up a Scanner's Web site with a free library of half-finished ideas for others to put into action. That's an idea that might get some follow-through!

Just a minute. What about those pesky bosses and teachers?

Right about now you might be saying, "It's all very well to follow your heart, but you get paid/graded not on what *you* think is finished but on what the *boss/teacher* thinks is finished."

And you're right. Even if you feel you have excellent personal reasons for wanting to stop, *you still must be able to finish a project sometimes without feeling like you're in prison.*

In the first place, you'll be called on to finish projects no matter who you are. From finishing repairs on your screen door to finishing a term paper or a project at work, that's real life. Your natural tendency will be to tap into self-discipline and force yourself to tough it out. But that can create too much unhappiness in a Scanner, and unhappiness isn't good for you. It's wiser to find a method that's right for you, and I have some ideas that might help.

Second, knowing how to finish what you start—even if you're a dedicated Scanner and don't intend to do it very often—is a great confidence builder and one of the best tools in your kit. It gives you the freedom to choose what you want to do. If you *choose* to drop something you're doing, that's okay; but if you *can't* finish a project, that can create problems. But what if that Bad Feeling is waiting for you as it always does? Won't it stop you again?

Maybe not.

Now that you've named that feeling, you'll find it's lost much of its power. You won't want to claw your way out the window every time you're stuck with an uninteresting job to do. But it still won't be fun.

What will you do about the tedium?

If beginnings are a source of delight to you, sticking with something when the delight is gone is like waiting for a mechanic because your car broke down in the middle of nowhere—and the other passenger is someone you don't want to talk to. If there's no way out, you'd better pull out your deck of cards and start telling jokes until help comes.

The name of that someone is Boredom. Boredom is the mind's way of rejecting anything that lacks nutrients. It's unpleasant for everyone, but it's hell on earth for Scanners. Boredom needs to be tackled; you need to learn its moves and develop your own.

Here are some strategies to keep you involved in a project even when the best part has gone.

The bored Scanner's bag of tricks

Eat your vegetables first but remember that dessert is coming. When you're stuck with a dreary task, use tempting new projects as your reward for finishing uninteresting ones. That way, digging through the dull project has an exciting purpose.

Bring in a buddy. I go through many rewrites when I'm doing a new book, and when I run into a tough stretch, I toss it back and forth with my proofreader/editor like a hot potato. Nothing eases the pressure like knowing you can send an incomplete version to a friendly reader and get it back loaded with comments and edits.

Keep track of how far you've gotten. It's important to know how far you've gotten and how far you have to go or your task feels like it stretches to the horizon. Decide in advance what marker will indicate that you've only got 75 percent, 50 percent, or 25 percent left to do.

Invent a fantasy to make it more interesting. Sometimes you can bring a new approach to the same task—experimentation is always interesting. Pretend you're going to teach it in a class tomorrow to people who know nothing about it and will adore every word you say. Or pretend it's a precious thing you must finish before the aliens arrive from outer space and snatch it away for their evil purposes.

Take notes on overheard dialogue. The more boring your environment is, the more usable it will be for that novel or screenplay (or poem or anthropology paper or reality show) you've always wanted to write. Observing banalities gives you the distance you need to avoid feeling oppressed. If you're gathering dialogue, banalities can be quite entertaining.

Work in short sprints. Use your kitchen timer and work on your project for 15 minutes at a time. Or give yourself 30 minutes to work on it today, tomorrow, and Saturday. Make a deal with yourself and stick with it until you're finished.

Keep looking for more tricks. And share them with the rest of us.

Remember, you're not required to finish everything you start, *but you are required to know how.* You'll need that knowledge one of these days, when you find something that's really worth finishing. Until then—and even after that time—never forget to appreciate your love of beginnings and the joy they bring you.

And that's it?

But what about everything you've been taught about "buckling down," disciplining yourself, doing something with your life? If you let Good Feelings and Bad Feelings make your decisions, that's nothing but self-indulgence, isn't it? To accomplish anything important, people have to ignore their feelings and stay single-minded and purposeful—don't they?

Let me answer you with a look into the mind of a very successful researcher and author. Here's a quote from Jamie Shreeve's review of *Monkeyluv* by Robert M. Sapolsky in the *New York Times Book Review.*

Robert M. Sapolsky, a neurologist and primatologist at Stanford University, writes essays in his latest book based on what he describes as "hit-and-run obsessions"—topics that infect his mind for a couple of months, causing him to research endlessly and drive his poor wife to distraction with monologues on the subject until he eventually writes the obsession out of his system, leaving room for the next one.

Dr. Sapolsky's "obsessions" are just one example of all the Scanner behavior that you and those around you have deplored for so long. I could give you many other examples (and I do on my bulletin board at www.barbarasher.com). You'll find that your troublesome behavior is shared by some very clever and accomplished people!

If you've reached the conclusion that you should give up your attempts to conform to the norm and you're ready to get the most out of your curious mind and your many talents, it's time to take a new direction. Instead of changing yourself as you once wanted to, you're going to change your surroundings. You need to roll up your sleeves and direct your energies toward creating an environment for yourself that will support you exactly as you are.

Which brings us to Part Two of this book.

What comes next

To arrange your life so it can support your remarkable potential, you need to do some more learning about who you are. You've gotten a good start in these past chapters but in order to gear up so you're ready to do everything you're capable of, you must look more closely at your unique style, your particular problems, and your specific needs.

Scanners are not all alike, as you shall see.

PART TWO

WHAT KIND
OF SCANNER ARE YOU?

Hello, Scanner!

I hope you've stopped believing you must limit yourself to one career, one lifestyle, one passion and that you understand you weren't designed that way. You may have been unhappy that you could never make up your mind, but some part of you has always refused to choose. What's your problem? You might not have one. What you do have is an unusually fast, curious mind that loves to solve problems and explore new ideas and too many aptitudes to fit into one job title.

Now you have the exciting task of designing a lifestyle with all the space you need; one that's arranged to let you make full use of your considerable talents. But just what is the right lifestyle for you? The answer is different for each type of Scanner.

Scanners aren't all alike. Even the Rewards that draw them are different. Most Scanners share their love of learning about almost anything at all. All creative Scanners love making something that didn't exist before. Many Scanners wish they belonged to a community of people like themselves. But in other, more specific areas, you see a surprising variety of Rewards. One type of Scanner (the Serial Master; see Chapter 16) loves the challenge of learning to speak a foreign language like a native or perfecting the techniques of glazing a clay pot or becoming a black belt in karate. Another type of Scanner (the Sampler; see Chapter 19) loves to see how things are done by actually doing them. This Scanner wants to build one small boat, write and illustrate one children's book, create a rock garden—once. Becoming an expert at something would feel limiting to him.

Scanners also have distinct strengths and weaknesses. The Plate Spinner (see Chapter 13) has a dazzling ability to work on a dozen problems at the same time but never finds time to develop his own projects. The Wanderer (see Chapter 18) is remarkably receptive to new people and environments but lacks direction in his own life.

What makes one type of Scanner different from another?

You'll meet one kind of Scanner who explores a new field for a week or two and another who needs years to learn what she wants to know. Some Scanner types move from one interest to the next and never look back. They may say they haven't really lost interest in anything they were once passionate about and they often keep all the tools and materials they used, but after a little probing they admit they want to explore new areas. Other types have many interests, but they always circle back to pick up the same ones over and over.

These differences aren't superficial. They create the foundation on which a successful operating style must be built. In the past, you've always been advised to follow the plan that worked for everyone around you: Pick something and stick to it until it's finished. But you can't do that. You have too many interests, for one thing. And you mean something very different by the word "finish." Scanners differ among themselves about what they want from any project. You might want to solve real-life problems and nothing else. Another Scanner loves mysteries and only wants an insight into what's behind them. Chances are good, however, that neither of you knows how to conform to the world's demands or fulfill your own.

But wait until you see what happens when you're given the right tools and a good set of operating instructions. With a schedule that finally matches your natural pace and a career that gives you room to be who you really are, you can turn your life around.

How to use the upcoming chapters

Identifying your Scanner type is not a neat and tidy matter. You're almost sure to find yourself in two or three, even all, of these chapters. I'm still learning so much about Scanners—I make exciting new discoveries every day—that this typology has to be tentative. The truth is, I've never encountered a Scanner who was only one type!!

But you'll get everything you need if you simply read through all the chapters. You'll find useful tools (and interesting careers) in every chapter, and some appear in all of them. So read straight through the coming pages and toss anything that looks promising into your shopping cart for a Tryout when you're ready. By choosing what works and discarding what doesn't, you'll end up with the perfect program for you.

What if you can't figure out what type you are?

It won't affect the way you use this book or the success you'll have with it, but pay attention. You could be operating in a way that doesn't naturally suit you. Some years ago, teachers were expected to train left-handed students to use their right hands. I had some lefties in my family, and they usually had a hard time of it. More than their handwriting was affected—their ability to learn was thrown off. It's simply a bad idea to try to be someone else. If you've done that up to now, start relaxing a little until you gradually revert to your authentic self. If that hasn't worked before, don't worry. You're about to learn techniques that could change everything right now.

As you discover all your unique Scanner characteristics, try to remember this: You were designed by a master. Nature didn't make any mistakes with you. You must explore the workings of who you are, not who you believe you ought to be. That means you must respect your tastes, your ideas, and your inner clock. Like every other creature in this world, you were designed to do something well. If you're a Scanner, you were designed to do *many* things well. Don't try to change yourself into something else. Just observe what you do without judgment and try to understand yourself. The more you know, the better your chances will be of creating the life that fits you perfectly.

With that in mind, let's see what kind of Scanner you are.

Chapter 9

ABOUT CYCLICAL SCANNERS

I'm a repeat offender. I have four or five major areas I'm interested in, and no matter how often I drop them, I always get interested in them again.

If I ask you to list what your interests are and you have no trouble doing it, you're probably a Cyclical Scanner. You know all the things you love to do most—unlike the Sequential Scanner, who is always discovering a completely new interest.

Your list may have only a few items on it—like the Double Agent in the next chapter, who is torn between two lives—or it may have 20, but the list isn't endless. You know what you love, and you usually return to each activity over and over again.

I've identified three types of Cyclical Scanners. I'll start the discussion with the Double Agent, a Scanner who typically has only two things he wants to do. All Scanners can use the techniques the Double Agent needs, but the Double Agent has his own set of obstacles, his own gifts, and his own conflicts—and needs to find a career that may be unlike other Scanners.

The second type of Cyclical Scanner—Sybil—makes up the largest group of Cyclical Scanners by far. Each Sybil has many interests and is torn between them to the point where she often does none at all. Sybils can be plagued by confusion and clutter but are more concerned about having nothing to show for their lives.

The third and final Cyclical Scanner type is the Plate Spinner. This is the fastest of the Cyclical Scanners. Like the carnival performers whose name I've given them, they can keep many projects in play at the same time. Although they're often the stars of any place they work, they have just as much trouble doing what they love as any other Scanner and are more likely to put their dreams off for some day in the future. (Not a wise choice but, fortunately, not a necessary one either.)

Let's step into the lives of the Cyclical Scanners and see if you recognize yourself.

Chapter 10

ARE YOU
A DOUBLE AGENT?

I had to choose between what's right and my dream. You can't just do what you want. You have to think of others.

Should I keep my practical job or do what I love? If I do the first, I'll be unhappy. If I do the second, I'll be broke!

I want two different careers and can't possibly do them both. I'm stuck like the fabled donkey between two bales of hay, going hungry because he can't make up his mind.

Are you a Double Agent?

- Have you given up a dream because it's unrealistic?
- Would you love to live in more than one country or have more than one career?
- Do you believe life is full of hard choices?
- Do you ever consider just quitting your job and starting over in something you love?
- Would you hate to be seen as selfish? Are you stuck because a change would cause too much sacrifice for the people you love?
- Do you sometimes think your problem would be solved if you were two (or more) people?

If you answered yes to most of the above, you belong to a special group of Scanners I call Double Agents. I use that name because they sometimes have fantasies of being two people: one who does the right thing and another who is free to live her dreams.

A typical Double Agent Scanner feels her main choice in life is between breaking her own heart and breaking someone else's.

Unlike many Scanners, Double Agents don't need to change what they're doing with any frequency. In fact, they'd be willing to live at least one of those lives forever, if only they could. Their obstacles seem insurmountable, but in fact, they're the Scanners with the most easily resolved conflicts of all.

But if you're a typical Double Agent, you're convinced the problem is hopeless.

Helen's story

Helen, a woman who drove me back to my hotel after a workshop in Houston, spoke sadly: "I loved living in Africa. Being in the bush for 2 years made me feel completely alive in a way I'd never experienced before, and I haven't felt that way since I returned home. But I can't live in Africa anymore, and I guess I should be grateful that I had a few fabulous years of that life."

"Oh, too bad," I said. "Why can't you live there anymore?"

"My parents are getting older, and I can't bear to leave them on their own. And I don't want to miss their last years with me. They're the best people in the world, and if I'm far away when they need me, I couldn't bear it. I'd regret it for the rest of my life. Giving up Africa breaks my heart, but this is more important. So that's that."

She turned into the driveway and stopped, ready to say good night, a little embarrassed for having bothered me with her story. But I was curious about something.

"Is there some reason you can't go to Africa for a shorter time now and then, say 3 weeks, maybe a couple of times a year?" I asked.

She paused and sat back a little. "Well, I really never thought of that."

There was a moment's silence in which I could almost hear the wheels whirring in her head while she went through this new idea. Then she broke the silence and said in a resigned voice, "I can't get that kind of time off from my job. I'm sure about that."

"Ah, I see," I said. "Too bad. But wait a minute. Didn't you say you've only been back in the States for a year? Do you already have a great job?"

"Hardly," she laughed. "I'm an administrative assistant at the local hospital. No benefits. But it's a job, and I need one. And I know they won't let me take 3 weeks off."

"Looks like you have the wrong job. Have you tried to find one to suit your needs a little better?"

Again there was that surprised pause. "Like what?"

"I don't know, but unless your hourly rate at the hospital is unusually high, it seems you could do the same work as a temporary worker and pick your own schedule. Or maybe you could even pick up contract work, where you're hired for a project that might take a few months to complete and when it's over, you take a few months off. And of course, you could always teach school and have your summers free, right?"

It was dark outside, but the hotel lights lit her face as she turned and looked at me, and I could see an idea dawning in her eyes.

"You know, my brother and his wife and kids would love to come to Houston and spend time with the folks during holidays," she said with some excitement in her voice.

After that, nothing could stop her. She said good night as politely as possible, but I could tell she was ready to stop talking and swing into action and would probably be making phone calls on her way home.

Either/Or Thinking

If you, too, are someone who has forgotten other ways of working besides the 2-weeks-vacation-per-year model, chances are you're stuck in Either/Or thinking. It's not an unusual way to think by any means—unless we're talking about Scanners. Scanners are typically creative and not ordinarily tied to rigid thinking. They're the quintessential "out of the box" people, if only because they're aware of so many different fields.

But over and over, I found Scanners like Helen who shut down their thinking before they went looking for other solutions, and I never understood why. Remember, the only thing I did for Helen was suggest that she go to Africa for a shorter period of time, since she couldn't live there all year. That's not rocket science. And then I realized we've all done the same thing in our lives, and I began to understand.

Your heart can shut down your brain

When we have what appears to be an unresolvable conflict like Helen's, we've fallen into a trap that I call the Either/Or Fallacy. The moment Either/Or hijacks our thinking, all of our natural resourcefulness disappears. If ever there was a dream killer, Either/Or thinking is it.

What about that fable of the donkey who stood between two piles of hay, unable to decide which to eat, until he finally starved to death—can you see the fallacy? Someone forgot to tell that poor donkey he can have both those piles of hay, one at a time. He can finish one and start on the other, or go back and forth, munching to his heart's content, until they're both gone. He can then head out and eat a lot more bales of hay.

But Either/Or thinking puts you into a trance. It sneaks in when you're not looking and monopolizes your thinking with artificial limits. Once it takes over, you don't even try to imagine better alternatives.

And why does this happen? Because you're so disappointed you can't think straight. So you square your shoulders, bite the bullet, do the right thing, and tell yourself you're not a kid anymore and it's time to stop indulging yourself.

But there's a part of every Scanner that never grows up. When Scanners fall in love with an idea, they fall in love with the intensity of children. Disappointment hits them deeply. So when they run into a conflict about something that matters to them enormously—Helen's love of Africa couldn't compete with her love of her parents—they see only one possible outcome and give up the fight.

But, like Mark Twain's obituary, reports on the death of your dream are premature. We each have our own history of disappointment that began when we were children, and it has an influence on how we operate today. But if you're an Either/Or thinker, it would be good to remember that you're a grown-up now and no longer have to give up so fast.

Either/Or thinking kills too many dreams too quickly. But if we could get you to start holding the decision door open for much longer than you're used to, you'd stand a really good chance of beating it. Here's a little game you can play that I hope will change your way of thinking forever. (Try it with friends and family, too. I bet you can all use the practice.)

The "Busting Open Either/Or Thinking" Game

If your thinking falls into the narrow "Gotta be this or that" pattern, you need to get into the habit of looking for more solutions. Read the instructions for this simple game and you'll see what I mean.

Step 1: Imagine that you've looked in the cupboard and found nothing to eat but a package of spaghetti, a can of tuna, and a can of dog food. You say the following to your family: "Either we can have spaghetti or we can have tuna for dinner."

That's your Either/Or statement.

Step 2: Now see how many ways you can change that Either/Or statement to one like this: "Either we can have spaghetti or we can have tuna salad—or we could come up with other choices…"

Step 3: Come up with as many alternatives as you can. (If you play with friends, give points for every alternative they offer. Try it with kids. They'll win all the points.)

For example, Alternative #1 might be "We could have neither tuna nor spaghetti."

We could pick up the phone and have pizza sent in. Or we could get off our couch and go to the store or to a restaurant. Or we could call a friend or relative and invite ourselves to their house for dinner. Or we can give everything to Fido and start a weeklong juice fast.

Alternative #2: "We could have both tuna and spaghetti."

You could eat one and I could eat the other. Or we could open the tuna and put it over the spaghetti. Or we can eat a very small tuna dinner now and a very small spaghetti dinner later. Or we can order vegetarian food from a Chinese restaurant, add the tuna, and put it over spaghetti. Or we could invite a friend to bring a third choice and make a tuna casserole.

Alternative #3: "We could try eating the dog food with either the tuna or the spaghetti."

Alternative #4: "We could go to the market and exchange what we have for canned chili with beans."

Can you think of any other alternatives? (At this moment, I confess that I can't.)

When you finish reading my example, try it yourself using your own issues. Helen, for example, would say, "I want to live in Africa and I want to live in Houston," and one of her solutions would be "live in both places at different times of the year."

This game may seem a bit silly, but I've found that if you play it a few times a day for just 1 week, your thinking will open up in a remarkable way. Think what that could do: You might stop giving up on your dreams and start making them come true.

Carmen's Either/Or conflict

See if you can help solve this Either/Or conflict. My client Carmen, who worked in North Carolina, had a dream of working with big cats (that's lions and tigers, which gave me pause, but I never question love). She longed to take a yearlong program offered in Oregon, where she could learn to work with the big cats, but, unlike Helen, she was completely locked up in a very successful industrial design career.

"It's 50 weeks a year at work and 2 weeks off for vacation, and that's that," she said. "I'm considering just quitting and taking my chances at getting work somewhere, somehow."

"Not so fast," I cautioned. "Like suicide and divorce, quitting is always an option, so let's make it the last one, okay? Maybe you can be a Double Agent and do both at the same time. Do you do much traveling as part of your job, or even better, do you have (or can you get) any big accounts in Oregon?"

"No, in my company the work is all on the East Coast. And I'm pretty much chained to a computer at the office," she sighed.

What would you advise Carmen to do? Take a moment to see what you come up with. When you're done, read the rest of her story.

If you thought Carmen should keep her job and telecommute from the West Coast, you guessed right. Telecommuting is a way she can design her life so she can do everything she wants to do. I call that a LIFE DESIGN MODEL.

Your Life Design Model

Life Design Models are a combination of time management and task organizing—and more. Life designs have always been at the heart of my work, because they're the essential underpinning for any happy and productive life. In my first book, *Wishcraft*, published in 1978, I said we must find clues "to your life design—to the discovery of what you'll be happiest doing and what you'll be best at." From the beginning, it's been clear that instead of trying to change yourself, you should arrange an environment so that it gives you what you need to function at your best.

In this book, I'll be suggesting Life Design Models for every different type of Scanner. Once you sense your natural patterns, you can choose a model to give shape to your life and remind you what steps to take next, like the diagrams of footsteps painted on the floor in a dance studio for each different kind of dance. They'll keep you moving until your life runs at its natural pace automatically, and I think you'll find them very helpful.

But they're not rules; they're only rough outlines, because your steps are unique. The number of things you love, the length of time you want to do them, and the career that's right for you are unique, so you won't find the perfect fit until you do your own adjustments.

In *Wishcraft*, I advised a Life Design Rehearsal to work out the rough spots. With Scanners, the process is no different—it's just that Scanners are interested in more things than other people. The richness of your interests affects every aspect of a Life Design Model: your schedule, where you keep your stuff, what manner of career will leave time for you to do everything you love or be an Umbrella that will include all your interests. As you'll see, I've given each Life Design Model its own name.

Carmen solved her problem by setting up a Life Design Model that fit both her need to be in Oregon for training to work with lions and tigers and her need to continue her successful career in North Carolina.

The Telecommuting Model:
How to be in two places at once

When Carmen told me she spent all her time at the computer, I asked, "If most of your work is on a computer, why do you have to be at the office at all? Can't you telecommute from Oregon?"

"I don't know," she said with some excitement in her voice. "Let me find out."

It took some wheeling and dealing because Carmen's boss was against tele-commuting at first, but she found literature that showed that telecommuters actually get more done and give their employers more results for their dollars. Carmen cinched the deal by landing a good account 2 hours from the tiger-training camp (something she'd worked on for months) and she agreed to fly back to the home office every 6 weeks to spend a week on-site.

But she kept her job and moved to the West Coast to start her training with the big cats. (I haven't heard from her, so I don't know what happened. I try not to be nervous about her silence.)

Helen, the woman who loved Africa but didn't want to live away from her aging parents, solved her problem with a different Life Design Model.

The Schoolteacher Life Design Model: Summers off

For the past 2 years since we first met, Helen has spent her summers in Africa and the rest of the year with her parents in Houston, using the Schoolteacher Model for organizing her year. This model has been around ever since humans started planting crops in climates that had winter. My father spent his child-hood in a Russian village, and his story was the same as any farm kid's in Wis-consin. Children went to school in the winter, when they weren't needed on the farm, but during the planting and growing seasons and until the harvest was over, they were too busy helping on their family farms. In the fall, they were able to return to school.

Since teachers had no students to teach during the summer, they used this time for their vacations, and this practice has continued to this day, even in metropolitan areas. It's an ideal arrangement for someone who wants to live in two different places or live two kinds of lives. But most of us forget about it, as this letter from a client shows.

> *Dear Barbara,*
>
> *I only spent 1 year in college before I had to go to work full-time, and for many years I grieved the loss of my dream of studying classical literature. As I got older, it seemed more and more impossible. How would I sign up at a university? I didn't have the time or the money. I tried to be a grown-up*

about it, but underneath I was disappointed. I still read books on my own, of course, but it wasn't the same.

And then, when I was 38, I started teaching elementary school (my third career!). What a revelation! Teachers get summers off! I had completely overlooked that. This summer I'm going to Oxford University in England for an adult education course in Greek Literature! We'll stay in students' quarters that were built in the Middle Ages! Why didn't I think of this before? How long has this been going on? And where have I been?

Incidentally, farmers are often free in the winter, and you can choose that version of the model if it suits you better. You could call that version the Farmer Life Design Model.

And if you're someone who wants to live both your lives at the same time, even on the same day, the Parallel Lives Life Design Model might be just what you need. Then you only have to change hats or move to a different room (or a different part of town) when you're ready to change your activities.

Of course, teachers and farmers have a livelihood part of the year that allows them to eat all year long, and you're going to need one, too.

Careers for Double Agents

If you want to lead two lives, a career that requires 9-to-5 days for 50 weeks a year simply isn't right for you. You need a less conventional source of income or an unusual job. Here are some options that might suit you. I've divided them into two groups. The first is for Double Agents like Helen, whose dreams include some kind of travel. The second is for those who want—or need—two or more different careers at the same time.

If your dreams include travel

1. Find jobs you can easily replace. A woman told me that before she was married she and a friend would take entry-level jobs in offices and work just long enough to earn money for a trip to Europe. "It was always easy to get jobs like that, so we didn't mind leaving, and neither of us was interested in building a career. We figured we'd get married and have lots of kids and we'd stay home forever, so we wanted to get our traveling in before that." She happened, however, to marry someone who led tours in Antarctica and collected fish in the South Pacific for places like Sea World, so she never did settle down, to her delight.

Tip: Set up your next job before you leave. If you're planning to lead your other life in a distant place, you can arrange to do freelance consulting work and line up a new job before you leave the country. It's very nice to know you don't have to find a job when you get back.

2. Be an independent worker. Daniel Pink, in his 2001 book, *Free Agent Nation,* describes some of the many ways independent workers are able to move through dozens of different environments every year. He mentions colorful names like permalancer (someone who begins as a contract or freelance worker and decides to keep that position even when offered a permanent job) and e-tirement (people who start Internet-based businesses after they retire) as well as "techo-cowboys, hired guns, nomads, gypsies, information backpackers, and portfolio workers."

Do those career descriptions sound unfamiliar or insecure? Pink reminds us these people are no different than plumbers, independent truckers, and carpet installers, who have traditionally had the most stable of careers. The money isn't bad, either.

Independent work includes the following:

Contract work: Another way to have some choice about when and where you lead your "other" life (or lives) is contract work. You can find opportunities on the job-listing sites on the Internet. Depending on your skills set, there are contract labor and temporary firms that place workers on a project-by-project basis.

Working on contract can be perfect for any kind of Scanner, and there's a lot more of that kind of work than there was 20 years ago. If you start out working through a placement agency, you can eventually work as an independent contractor and set your own (higher) rates. There's contract work out there for almost any vocation these days—techies, health-care workers, clerical, factory, etc.

I met a woman who worked in film production and another who set up corporate computer networks, and both of them managed to free up 6 months each year to follow all their other interests.

Temporary jobs: You can arrange to set aside a retirement fund and pay for your own health insurance when you have a temporary job. Scanners who love to keep their options open tell me they prefer temp jobs to permanent ones. Law firms, large banks, and big corporations always need proofreaders to check changes in contracts. There are temp agencies that deal with nothing but proof-readers. All you have to do is go in and take a few tests to show you can do detailed work, and they'll give you work right away (the night shift pays big money). Or you can find work on a more personal level, working for small or home businesses that need someone to do data entry or transcription.

e-lance jobs: An e-lancer is an independent worker who does everything via e-mail. My bookkeeper, who came to my house once a week for years, has become an e-lancer. I haven't seen her in person for a long time, but we communicate daily via e-mail. If she were overseas instead of a few miles away, I wouldn't know the difference.

3. Find highly paid short-term work to pay for the whole year. Work in these areas is usually found in one season rather than year around.

Fishing: A photographer I know spends the summer in Alaska working on a fishing boat. He makes high wages that allow him to be a photographer the rest of the year. (He takes some pretty amazing photos of work on a fishing boat, too.)

Tax preparer: You can be a tax preparer who works like a demon for 2 or 3 months during the tax season and be free all the rest of the year. Bill is an actor who prepares taxes for other actors during March and April, which leaves the rest of his year wide open for going on auditions or putting on his own plays. He wrote me this note:

> *Sometimes I go to the mountains with summer stock theater or go to other cities to see their repertory theaters or to study with a special teacher. And my clients are all actors, which is wonderful for me because I know how much most artistic people need help in this area. It creates a nice network, too, where we share important things (like who's auditioning, how to find a good manager, or how to talk to a casting director).*

Technical manual translator: That's what my son did for years. He'd work crazy hours for 6 months and save enough money to travel the world and do what he liked for a year (he's lived in Japan, Greece, Spain, and Germany). Then he'd repeat the schedule.

Gardener/ornamental horticulturist/landscaper: This is a job that allows you to travel in the winter (like the Farmer Model I mentioned above). You'd build up a client list and work mostly in the spring and summer, then pack up and head out to your second life the rest of the year.

4. Follow the sun. The Seasonal Life Design Model is a variation on the Double Agent for the Seasonal Scanner. These are people who manage three or more jobs, all of which they enjoy. A friend e-mailed me about someone he knew who was a Seasonal Scanner.

> *I had a ski instructor once who told me about a very cool way he found to do all the things he enjoyed, keep a lot of variety in his life, and even make a decent living. He repeated this program every year.*
>
> *He taught skiing in Vermont from December to March (he loved to teach); in March, he went to Australia to do underwater photography (he was a contributor to a diving magazine); in June, he'd go to Hawaii and surf (I don't think he did that professionally); and after that, he'd hit the slopes in Chile for their ski season and work as a test skier to demonstrate new equipment that the ski companies put out. That whole schedule paid for itself, and you could see by looking at him that the life suited him well.*

5. Find a portable job. Portable jobs come in all sizes and shapes and allow you to travel. There are programs for nurses that send them to different locations for a year and more. If you're in information technology and work with computers—or just if you speak English—you can set up a job before you go to a new place and carry those skills with you like Leena, who entered data for a hospital in the Midwest and always longed to go to Ghana.

"Ghana has hospitals," I said. "Why don't you contact them to see if they need your skills?" She started a Web site called WannagotoGhana for support and to get contact numbers and got a job in Ghana within a few months.

6. Find a job with built-in travel. Jobs with built-in travel have obvious advantages, but they don't always let you choose your location.

Simultaneous interpreter: I know a woman, originally from England, now living in Paris, who loves this work. She spends time in Central Asia at international business and governmental conferences—working with a team doing the kind of simultaneous interpretation that you see at the United Nations. She took a rigorous training course in Belgium that lasted over a year. "It's not the only way to get a license," she said, "but they refer you to good jobs, and they give you health benefits."

Assistant at international trade shows: There's a fabric show in Istanbul and another in New York as I write—and a hundred others all over the world, devoted to anything you can imagine. Manufacturers and buyers come from all over the world to buy and sell and see what's going on, and the companies that rent the space, set up the displays, and provide all the services need hundreds of assistants on every level. You can even walk in at the end of the show and offer to help individual companies break down their booths. I've been told by these people that they're so tired at the end of a conference they'd be grateful (and generous) to any helpers who showed up.

Worker with a global business chain: You can be a trainer for a corporation with offices all over the world, or you can work in the hospitality field for a hotel chain. A woman I met on a plane a few years ago told me she was a service manager at an American hotel based in Hong Kong, and on weekends she often went with friends to Katmandu in Nepal to relax!

What if you've got a passion that competes with an income-producing career? Did that Either/Or thinking sneak back in and give you these choices?

A: I must risk all for my art and do it full-time.
B: I can't give up security for art!

If so, remember the right answer is always, "none of the above."
Here are some better alternatives.

If you want (or need) more than one career

I saw an interesting discussion topic in the Scanner's section of my bulletin board recently: Subjects You'd Like to Study. Naturally I went to look, expecting to see variations on what I said as a freshman student in college—"Look at these amazing subjects; I have to study them all! Blowfish and aardvarks, philosophy and soil types, medieval shoe making!"

Instead I saw this: "Do you get thoughts about new careers every day? Yesterday the idea kept popping into my head that I'd like to go back to school to study culinary arts..."

Careers?! Who said anything about careers? And then I remembered that most Scanners—like most people in general—automatically believe every interest has to be a career.

As you know by now, this is a huge problem for a Scanner. For one thing, they have too many interests to make careers out of all of them. For another, very few careers will interest a Scanner for very long.

Fortunately, there are many alternatives.

1. Do one for money, the others for love: the Good Enough Job. The best friend of almost every type of Scanner is what I call the Good Enough Job. It isn't your dream job; it's the one that funds your dreams.

If a job isn't unpleasant, doesn't eat up more than 40 hours a week, pays well, and provides security—it can give you the freedom to do all the things you love *on your own time*. People complain about unfulfilling jobs until they understand what the Good Enough Job actually is, and then they feel very different about them.

Think of it: a job that doesn't bother you, whose only crime is that it's just not enough to fulfill your life. But it provides money and security and the freedom to fulfill your life in your free hours. That sounds like a great job to me.

But I want to love my job!

There are definitely jobs that people love, but you often run into problems when you try to turn everything you love into a job. This letter from my bulletin board explains it best.

> **Huey:** *I would love to just sit under a tree and read 19th-century novels all day. So I decided to become an editor, so I would "get paid to read all day." They made me read dreadful stuff; I hated it. Then I tried graduate school in English lit. They made me write papers; I hated it. So guess what I'm doing now? I work as a secretary, at a nice place, with congenial people, a pleasant walk from my house. And I spend every evening, every Saturday and Sunday, every holiday and vacation day, sitting under a tree reading 19th-century novels. I now tell everyone about my story. Because if you work 40 hours a week, you will still have at least 3.5 hours each evening, plus 12 hours or more each Saturday and Sunday, to sit under a tree and read novels (or whatever your idea of heaven is). You just have to accept the fact that you must find some sort of pleasant, mindless, easy job that will enable you to spend your time off doing exactly what you want.*
>
> *I've been told that I shouldn't be content with a "mindless" job, but I'm truly happy in mine, because I've accepted the fact that no one is going to pay me to do what I love (sit under a tree and read 19th-century novels), although as I said, I tried being an editor, a graduate student, and even working in a library (where, of course, I was fired for "reading on the job"!).*
>
> *So I've made my peace with that and do it on my own time.*

Artists and actors would agree with Huey completely. They're usually very good at coming up with smart ways to earn a living and pursue their art at the same time. Their income producers are all Good Enough Jobs. For example, Harmon trained to become an electrician so he could stay in the theater and have a good life, too. He's a freelancer, like most electricians, and takes jobs only when he wants to. "I used to be a waiter," he said. "That is *not* a Good Enough Job. It's too exhausting and often depressing because of the bosses. Since I became an electrician, I'm much happier. There's always work, and it always pays well."

2. Combine your favorite interests with your job. Sometimes a job will pay you to do many of the things you love.

State or National Park employee: If you love nature, you don't have to sacrifice any hope of a good job. You can work at everything from maintaining trails to taking tickets at the gate of a campground. It's a great job for someone who also likes to take photos or write or even have a part-time Internet business. Speaking of which...

3. Start your own business. If you start a very small service business, it won't require much investment, and there are ways to keep it from being time-consuming, too—such as making deliveries with your car, or turning a van into a pet washeteria, or taking cars in for overnight tune-ups and returning them to their owners before work the next morning, or being a language tutor (or any kind of tutor) over the telephone, and so on.

One mistake most people make is to do things according to the book. They'll try to write a business plan so they can get a loan, buy software for a marketing campaign, find an office—the works (and then pray that it pays off).

But you're a Scanner, and you know better. You've already had the experience of spending too much money on golf equipment only to have it gathering dust in your closet after 1 month of use. For that reason as much as any financial consideration, an enlightened Scanner is always careful to put her toe in the water instead of taking out a loan to buy the lake. The best way to test-drive a new business is to lower your investment and your expenses to almost nothing and then just give your idea a try. (Full disclosure here: My favorite business start-ups don't bring images of the stock exchange to mind; they bring up visions of pushcarts filled with apples and bananas.)

If you already have a business of your own, you can decide where you'll put your time. If you have a good staff or can hire someone to take your place (while you stay in contact by phone or computer), you have a lot of freedom.

This is what Peter, owner of a Toronto engineering firm, did when his "hobby" of acting in the theater started turning into a successful career: He hired a manager to share the workload in his business and started gradually shifting his work life from engineering to theater.

"I have a wonderful family, and I intend to take care of them, so even if I make good money in the theater, I'm not letting go of my business. Fame comes and goes, but engineering is forever," he laughed.

In the coming chapters, you'll find many other career options you can adapt to your particular needs as a Double Agent or a Seasonal Scanner or any variety on those types.

Now that you have some ideas for organizing your time and bringing in money, you need a special Scanner kit designed to help you accomplish all your personal goals and support your interests.

Some tools to help Double Agents

Here are some tools to keep you on track with your double (or quadruple) life. To start with, as a Double Agent you need to make sure your dream is always in sight, even if it's a half year away or more. Until your new lifestyle becomes a habit, you'll need activities connected with your other life and reminders so you know that you'll be doing what you love very soon.

Keeping your dreams front and center can be as easy as a putting a one-page calendar on the wall and having a couple of trunks (or boxes or closets or corners in your garage) someplace where you'll see them every day.

Your 2-year Wall Calendar Poster

Keeping your summer (or seasonal) visit to your other life front and center is as easy as drawing a calendar on a large sheet of paper and putting it on your wall. This one-page, poster-type calendar on the wall can be the difference between "I'll never get to do what I love," and "Only 84 days until I leave for Africa!" For most Scanners, I recommend a 6-year calendar. (You can learn more about that in Chapter 3, "Scanner Panic"). But for a Double Agent or Seasonal Scanner, I recommend posting a 2-year calendar, with each year broken into the four seasons. (A single year is all that's strictly necessary, but every time you see it, a 2-year calendar will confirm that you'll be able to live this wonderful life again the following year.)

One more thing: You should probably put up an identical calendar in many rooms in your home—and your office, too—until it becomes natural to think of your choices without it.

On the calendars, draw a wide band of bright color to block out your divisions of time. For instance: A band of yellow from the fall through the following spring might be your classroom teaching job during the year, and a band of blue would represent your scuba teaching job in the summer. It's important to be able to understand their meaning from across the room.

Your DESTINATION STEAMER TRUNKS

You should assign one place for all the gear you'll need in your other life just so your gear is easy to find. But if you also make this place interesting or beautiful, it will make you happy while you're waiting for your upcoming journey.

Helen keeps everything she loves about Africa—including her bona fide pith helmet with a sun-protecting scarf hanging down the back—in an antique brass-bound wooden trunk with decals of Africa and some replicas of antique steamship decals stuck all over it.

A duffle bag will do the trick almost as well.

If you go to more than one place (and this can include trips to a nearby park to take photos or to a rented studio to record a song), try having separate trunks for different areas, each one full of the things you love best about each place you go.

It helps to get everything you need ready so you can run out the door at a moment's notice. And although you may have plenty of time to assemble what you need for each life you're leading, the psychological effects of knowing you could take off for distant places at any time are truly wonderful. I have an area in my house for my spring and fall forays to my little village in Turkey. In it I have all the things I want to take with me (including a photo that I promised to give a sheep herder of his family sitting with two sheep in the open back of their brightly decorated little truck).

A Seasonal Scanner wrote the following note to me.

I've always had different areas in my garage for skis and climbing equipment—nothing very exciting. But now, over each pile of stuff in my garage I've put a bulletin board where I've pinned gorgeous National Geographic *photos of my other lives up there where I can see them so I never forget how wonderful they are. I've put up my 2-year calendars, big ones with each of my seasonal trips blocked out in a different color. I've actually painted them on cloth so I can fold them up and take them with me—and I put them up in every bedroom I sleep in so I see them when I first wake up!*

Your Scanner Daybook

If you must wait for months to travel to the place you love or if you're living the Parallel Lives Life Design Model and want to touch base with your art or poetry or designs after work each evening, use your Scanner Daybook as a way to make your visit. Sitting down with your Daybook opened wide, a favorite pen in your hand, and writing your memories or plans for what you want to do, drawing diagrams, or making sketches will help you visit your favorite place no matter how little time you may have.

When you've figured out how to pay for your double life and you've set up your Calendars and your Destination Steamer Trunks and you're writing in your Daybook, *your life will support your dreams.* When your life supports your dreams, something important changes in your thinking: All those Either/Or choices leave your head, and "all of the above" lives there now.

On the oppposite page is a list that will allow you to do a quick review of all the models, careers, and tools you'll need. When you're done looking at it (and perhaps putting a checkmark beside an item there for further investigation), I'd like you to turn to the next chapter. There you'll read about a Scanner with more than 2 or 4—or 10—interests pulling her in so many directions she's usually frozen in her tracks. I call this type Sybil.

HOW DOUBLE AGENTS DO
EVERYTHING THEY LOVE

Life Design Models for Double Agents

The Telecommuting Model
The Schoolteacher Model
The Farmer Model
The Seasonal Model
The Parallel Lives Model

Careers for Double Agents

Replaceable jobs
Independent work
Highly paid short-term work
Portable jobs
Jobs with built-in travel
The Good Enough Job
Your own small business

From Your Scanner Tool Kit

"Busting Open Either/Or Thinking" Game
Scanner Daybook
2-Year Wall Calendar Poster
Destination Steamer Trunks

Chapter 11

ARE YOU A SYBIL?

I'm pulled in so many different directions at once that I usually can't move at all.

I have half-finished books, businesses, board games, and Weblogs. I'll never have anything to show for any of my interests.

Whatever I do, I feel like I'm missing something else I want to do.

Are you a Sybil?

◈ Did you ever wish you were 20 people?
◈ Can you name all the projects you'd love to work on?
◈ Have you been interested in most of them for a long time?
◈ Do you have a major clutter problem; do you often mislay important parts of what you're doing?
◈ Would you love to finish a project before you move to another, but you've almost never done that?
◈ Do you love insights, revelations, discoveries that make you say, "I never knew that!"
◈ Are you afraid you'll never build a body of work, expertise, a reputation?

If you answered yes to most of those questions, you're a Sybil-type Scanner. Your list of interests is not endless, but unless you suddenly became 5, 10, or even 20 different people, you can't imagine any way to do everything on it.

You represent the largest group of Cyclical Scanners. You return to the same group of interests over and over, and each time you find them fresh and appealing. You're happy to try new things, too, but you really prefer to revisit what you already love, and a steady diet of novelty would leave you dissatisfied.

If you're a typical Sybil, you're usually surrounded by lots of "creative clutter." Sybil types can't always find their materials, because they have so many projects going on at the same time they can't keep track of them. All the same, most Sybil Scanners have very little tolerance for chaos and have bursts of organizing energy they find very satisfying. But order never lasts for long because when the creative urge comes, there is no patience for putting things away.

Like most Scanners, you're talented in many areas, and when you're using any of your talents, you're as happy as a child in a toy store. You've been told that you smile when you read, but you rarely read for long, because you'll get an idea and start creating a model or come up with a design for a small Internet business. Though you do well at your job, when it comes to personal projects, you're not goal-driven at all. You just enjoy mucking about in your favorite subjects.

That lack of goals is a problem for you, however. Because you're always starting over, you don't usually get very far with any of your projects, and down deep you long to have something to show for all the hours you spend with your interests. You wish you could present the world with a finished product or be an authority in one of your areas of interest. You've tried narrowing down your interests so you'd be able to go deeply into one of them at a time, hoping that would let you make some headway, but when you try to do that, you always feel stifled and like you're missing out on other, more interesting things.

Lynn's story

One evening not long ago, I settled in for a phone session with a woman named Lynn, who was having trouble because of her many interests. Lynn knew she was a Scanner and had already resolved any conflicts about choosing only one area of interest—she wanted to continue them all.

"I even have the perfect Good Enough Job," she said. "I call it the Great Enough Job! It gives me lots of time off and plenty of free choice about when I can do all my favorite things!"

"That's wonderful!" I said. "What's the problem?"

"I have two problems. First, I'm interested in too many things, and I want to do them all at once! No matter which of my projects I'm drawn to, if I pass another one on my way, I'm drawn to that one. They're all so appealing to me. But that means I usually don't do any of them.

"My other problem is that the years are passing, and I'm beginning to realize I'll never complete any of my great ideas. I won't have anything to show for all these interests. I can't tell you how many things I'll pick up for 5 minutes and put down again, thinking I'll really get into them one of these days. It's so odd. I'm finally free to do pretty much what I want, but I waste all my time doing things I don't care about. All that free choice and I'm stuck anyway!"

Freedom is not always a Sybil's friend

Lynn had hit on an important point that most of us miss: Freedom is not every Scanner's best friend. Sybil-type Scanners like Lynn are receptive, open-minded, and curious. They delight in unexpected connections and know they can look almost anywhere and make an exciting find. "Sounds like fun," I said.

"It is, for a while. And then it all falls down on my head. I become totally overwhelmed. That's not fun at all."

Clearly, Sybils need to replace some of that freedom with structure. But what kind of structure will work for someone with dozens of interests?

Can she find one underlying theme that all her interests have in common? Occasionally Sybils can do that, but for the most part, their interests are unrelated, often by choice. With this kind of problem, it looks like Scanners like Lynn will never finish anything and they'll never get the respect and admiration they secretly long for.

But appearances can be deceptive. Sybils can be the most productive of all the Scanners.

Lynn believed, as most people do, that if you can't focus on one subject you'll never accomplish anything, and her experience had borne that out. But I had a surprise for her.

"Scanners like you who keep returning to the same interests again and again are better designed to accomplish amazing things than anyone, even specialists," I told her.

"How?" she said, with disbelief. "I hardly pick up any of my interests anymore, and when I do, I put them down before I finish. How are you going to fix both of those problems?"

"They can both be fixed with the same solution," I said. "We just have to take away some of that freedom you've given yourself."

"Penal colony?" she asked, quizzically.

"No, just the right kind of project management. You need a schedule," I smiled.

"Maybe I need a mean teacher to make me buckle down," Lynn sighed.

"And a school bell to tell you when to change classes," I grinned.

"You know, that's not such a bad idea," she replied.

If someone like Lynn thinks she has to choose between her beloved projects, she's lost the battle before she's begun. But she obviously can't do them all at once. When you want to do everything right now, you really do need a schedule that lets you do one thing after another. But unless we find a way to match your schedule to the natural duration your interests require, it won't work.

"Don't tell me to stick with one thing for 6 months and then another. I tried that. It's suffocating."

"How about sticking with one thing for an *hour* and then another?" I asked.

"Like high school!" she exclaimed. "And college. You weren't joking about that school bell! I really do remember liking to hear the bell ring and heading over to a whole new class. I liked pulling out the new notebook and getting my books from the locker."

"You think an hour is about right for you?" I asked.

"Yes, at least it was back then. Any class that lasted longer, like science labs or drawing classes, made me uncomfortable. My mind would start wandering after about an hour."

This looked like a good fit, because Lynn already knew how long her interest duration was. If you're like Lynn, you can use the same Life Design Model she did.

The School Day Life Design Model

I read this letter to Lynn. It was from a client reporting in on her success with the School Day Model.

> I started a home business, a little public relations company. It wasn't entirely by choice, but now I'm in heaven! Every morning at breakfast, I study Asian

history. It's a hobby I've had for years but never had time for. Now I start my
days reading history and looking at maps. Then, after an hour or so, I move
to creative mode (is it the coffee?), and I work on speeches or brochures for my
advertising clients. Afternoons are for running my business. I meet online
with a virtual assistant, mostly troubleshooting and planning; twice a month,
I spend my afternoon on the phone with a coach to make sure I don't slack off
on marketing. (When I know we have an appointment coming up, I always
get my work done!)

In the evening, I have sessions with agency clients or watch an old movie.
I always fall asleep reading the latest nonfiction book. I could work at this
same schedule every day forever, but doing any of this for more than a few
hours wears me out.

"She sounds like my twin! I'm sold! But I wonder if I really need a school
bell," Lynn joked.

"I'm sure you can set something up with your kitchen timer, but you really
need a SCANNER PLANNER to write your schedule in."

"I'll get one tomorrow," she said.

"You might have to make your own," I said.

This could be true for you as well.

Your Scanner Planner

You know what a daily appointment planner is, but you can't go out and buy
what you need and you can't even draw a Scanner Planner yourself until you've
done a few tryouts with your Life Design Model. As you design your planner,
open your Scanner Daybook and select an area over on the right side of the
right-hand page to write down any thoughts that aren't connected to projects.
Be alert for fleeting memories of things you love but haven't done in a while,
such as singing, dancing, drawing, or reading one page of a favorite author—
even sitting outside for a few moments before you turn in for the night.

When your Scanner Planner is set up, you'll enter one of those activities at
the top of every page.

These entries will remind you to do all the things that have no purpose but
pleasure: to sing in your kitchen or to put on music and dance for a few minutes
or to draw a quick sketch of your coffee cup. These are such small things that

they're easily overlooked, but never underestimate them. They open up doors of sensation that can make the difference between an ordinary life and a glorious one. To a Scanner, they're like vitamins.

Now, give the School Day Life Design Model a try. Keep your pencil and eraser nearby and see if you can follow along with what Lynn did.

Make a list of your favorite projects. First, Lynn made a list of all those things she wished she could do right away.

- Start window greenhouses for my favorite herbs.
- Create a board game about famous travelers in history.
- Streamline my PR company and find more clients.
- Design and sew toys for my grandchildren.
- Write my memoirs.

Try out the model you've chosen. Anything can work on paper, but you have to really try out a schedule like this to see if it fits, so Lynn took 4 days to see if changing her projects every hour actually worked for her. When she got back to me, she was very enthusiastic. "I'm doing things I haven't done for years. I really love this," she said happily.

"It looks like the School Day Model suits you perfectly," I said.

"Well, not perfectly," she said.

Make Duration adjustments based on your tryout. "I must have changed since I was in school. One hour isn't enough for each of my interests. I'd prefer 2 hours."

"Well," I reminded her, "you've got five items on that list. That's a long day."

So she moved some activities around and made some adjustments.

Write up your adjusted schedule. Here's what Lynn wrote.

Monday to Friday

9:00 a.m.: Study history and take notes for a possible course in adult education program.

11:00 a.m.: Set up shelves for one window greenhouse, order seeds or buy soil and pots, or do some reading on the subject.

1:00 p.m.: Work with assistant on my public relations business.

3:00 pm: Work on my board game or go for a walk and record ideas for it.

Evenings: Design or cut patterns or sew latest toy while watching TV with family.

Saturday and Sunday

Morning: Write memoirs.

The rest of the day: Visit daughter and grandchild or do business maintenance—assemble press kits, do mailing list maintenance, or try out new software.

She drew up a week's worth of pages to reflect this schedule and made a number of copies. They represented her Scanner Planner.

"This Planner is having a very big effect on me," she said when she called in a week later. "It's keeping me honest, like an appointment with a doctor would. Once I see that I'm supposed to work on my board game, I really do it.

"What's new is that it doesn't just remind me to move to the next project, it gives me permission."

"Permission?" I asked.

"Yes. Part of the reason I wasn't doing what I loved was that it always made me feel a little guilty, like I had more important things to do. I never would have admitted that to myself until I used this Planner last week. Now, when it's time to do something I really enjoy that's just for me, I tell myself, 'Hey, it's on the schedule. I *have* to do it.' You know, I've really missed doing all these things. I used to look at the beautiful fabric and the pieces of my board game so sadly. I just couldn't figure out how to do it all. Now I'm having such a good time, I feel like I'm on vacation. I can't remember when I've treated myself so well. This is just great, and I never want to go back to where I was . . ."

But I could hear something in her voice.

"But . . .?" I queried.

"Well, we didn't exactly take care of my other problem," she said. "I don't want to be unappreciative and I can't tell you how much I love my new schedule, but . . ."

"What will you ever accomplish over the long haul?" I asked.

"Well, yes," she replied.

"You've only started having a real schedule and getting something done on each project every day, so you haven't seen the results yet," I said.

"Sure I have," Lynn said. "The results are dramatic! I'm having a great time, and I'm not stuck anymore. But I still don't see this going anywhere. I have this feeling that I'm doing a good job of amusing myself, but I'll never have anything to show for it."

"You mean a finished product of some kind?" I asked.

"Well, yes. It's what I've never been able to do. What will I ever have to show for myself? It sounds egotistical, but it matters to me. I'd like the world to know I'm here."

"What I meant by results wasn't that you felt good," I said. "I meant that when you add a little to something every day, after a while you can see it changing. If you stick to this schedule—or any good schedule—you're building something in small increments. That's how skyscrapers get built. Every day you move each part of the process forward a little, and every few days you build one floor. The following days you do the same, and you build another one on top of the first. If you keep it up, you've got a skyscraper."

"I do?" she said doubtfully.

"Well, you're a Scanner with more than one project. You might have five skyscrapers," I laughed. "If you continue to follow the schedule you created, in 1 year you could write the first draft of your memoirs, set up an herb garden in every window, prepare and teach a dozen history classes, and finish your board game—maybe even get it produced. You work on something a couple of hours every day and, over time, you could build the Great Wall of China—if you lived long enough."

"Of course," she said. "How did I miss that?"

Scanners and time—a reminder

Sybils are the best example of the Scanner's typical problem with time that I discussed in Chapter 3 ("Scanner Panic").

"It's easy for Scanners to forget about things like incremental changes, because they don't always understand time too well," I told Lynn. "They live in an endless Now. Especially Cyclical Scanners."

"I know," she said. "I thought that was a good thing. Everyone says you should live in the present."

"I don't think they knew about people who forget there's a future," I replied.

Which is another reason Sybils need schedules and calendars up on their walls where they can constantly see them. Visual ways of displaying time are just what a Sybil Scanner needs, not only to see where she's going, but also to remind her of how far she's come.

When Sybils don't notice what they've accomplished

I was working on a Life Design Model for Celeste, an artist whose work wasn't suited to the School Day Model, when the issue of accomplishment came up again.

"I go nowhere," she said. "I can only stick with the art for a few months, tops. I never have more than one or two pieces finished." Celeste creates, among other things, sculptures constructed from found objects. She builds fantastic pieces, some of them 6 feet tall, others much smaller, by working with great intensity for a few months. But then she gets completely tired of the process: "At some point, I can't look at another scrap and think of a sculpture. It looks like junk to me."

That's when Celeste usually picks up her guitar and spends her evenings writing songs and performing them in small clubs.

But after a few months, this, too, loses its charm. "Someone wanted to make a big production out of the songs, but by the time he came along, I was tired of making music. A year ago I'd been all excited about putting together a book about design but dropped that like I do everything else. Then, when I got bored with the singing scene, I got very interested in that book again." Other interests she returns to over and over include renovating her home, scuba diving, and baking.

"I don't stick with anything for more than a few months at most," she said regretfully, "and I don't have any choice about it. I never know when I'll get bored or excited about one of these things, and they're impossible to do without that excitement. But you can't plan anything that way. I should be having gallery shows and a CD of my music and a finished book by now, but I'd have to bite into something like a pit bull and never let go for that, and that's not going to happen."

Celeste is actually living her life according to her inner clock, which is a very practical idea when you have the freedom to do it. If you're like Celeste and find that a written schedule restricts your ability to respond to the unexpected arrival of a creative impulse, you need a different kind of Life Design Model, one that gives a name to what you're doing. To Celeste, impulse is creative fuel, and when she responds to it, she gets her best insights.

Every Scanner knows what it's like to be suddenly taken with a desire to stop what he's doing and pick up something else that calls to him. Often, he tries to resist these impulses or is ashamed when he gives in to them. If that's something you do, I advise you to just give in. Pick up any project that calls you and give it an hour, a day, or a week, however long it keeps you fascinated, and then put it away and get back to what you were doing.

This arrangement is called the Random Acts of Passion Life Design Model—and it might be just right for how your creativity operates.

But it won't take care of a Sybil's problem with progress. Celeste feels like she's going in circles, accomplishing nothing.

I remembered what she had told me when she first asked for a session some months earlier, and I reminded her of it. "Celeste, you wrote two one-act plays with music, you did the sets, and you performed in both of them. You've written and performed dozens of songs over the last 5 years. And 1 year ago, you sold two pieces of your artwork to interior designers for a lot of money!"

She nodded. "That's true! Why don't I ever remember that? Pretty good, isn't it? I have to remember the past better. But I still can't see ahead. I never have a sense of where I'm going."

Then I thought of something a potter had told me, one of those simple things that stick in your mind because they make so much sense: She always set herself the goal of finishing 1,000 pots each year, because it gave her a sense of direction and a goal to aim for. Maybe there was a way for Celeste to do something similar. And perhaps there was a way to adapt that idea into something like a progress report at the same time.

"Why don't you do that, Celeste? Can you set some yearly goals?"

"Even though I never know how long I'm going to do anything?" she asked.

"Sure," I answered. "I assume you get involved in each of your projects at least once a year, right? Just to make sure you're covered, you should set a goal that's more than 1 year away, and then, at the end of that time, schedule something big to celebrate its completion. If you scheduled a show, for example, you'd have to get something ready, wouldn't you?"

"That could be tricky," she said. "You really need a certain number of pieces for a show. I can't predict things like that."

"You could do something else, then, an event where people would show up so it would be a real deadline, not something you could ignore. How about a New Year's Eve Progress Report Party. Tell your friends to come with their goals, too."

That idea took Celeste's fancy. She set a 15-month goal of making and selling another sculpture, recording a CD with five new songs, writing two more performance pieces and coming up with some new ideas for sets, making some headway with her design book, and going scuba diving at least once.

I saw her 2 weeks later and asked how she was doing.

"Well, my goals may not be very ambitious, because I'm still not sure when I'll be working on anything," she said, "but setting this 15-month deadline has radically changed the way I work. I always tend to check my interest level so I can figure out what I'm into—the music or the sculpture or whatever—that's not new. But for the first time, I know where I am, how far along I am. I actually know what I want done before the end of the month! I've never had the ability to plan ahead except in school, which I always detested. I knew I couldn't do good creative work on command, so in my personal life I've always given myself complete freedom."

"You have too many talents for complete freedom," I smiled. "That only works for Picasso. He didn't write songs and novels."

She laughed. "Yes, he just got up every day and painted—or didn't. Ah, the simple life."

Celeste still ran into trouble with the unpredictability of the peaks and troughs of interest in each of her projects.

"That potter had a simpler life than I do," she said. "I wish I only had to do a thousand of any one thing. I'd know exactly what my priorities should be every day."

I recommended something I used for myself, the ROTATING PRIORITIES BOARD.

Rotating your priorities has a number of benefits. For someone like Celeste, it gives her life a shape and some structure by simply confirming the arrival of each interest. But if you've set a goal, seeing your priorities also serves as a gentle nudge by letting you know which of your projects could use some attention today.

I suggested that she use a simple chessboard, write each project on a sticky note, and arrange them like chess pieces.

"You can lead with a sticky note that says 'write a song' and let the other project sticky notes fall back behind this one," I suggested.

Celeste loved that idea and created a felt-covered chessboard big enough to be seen across the room, which she mounted on her wall right under her 15-MONTH GOAL CALENDAR. (The calendar was an ingenious grid that showed at a glance what percentage of each goal had been accomplished by how close it was to the final date and the New Year's Eve party.) For the Rotating

Priorities Board, she had sewn four Velcro-backed stuffed squares, each a different color, one for each of her passions, and she moved them around like chess pieces.

"I feel like I just got the compass for my life!" she said, pointing to the Goal Calendar and the Priority Board. "I know which way is north and which is south. I know how much I've still got to do, which I really like. I can't tell you what a difference that simple thing makes. Changing the order of what I'm working on actually feels good. I think, 'Okay, looks like music showed up; hello music,' and I move that piece to the front.

"I didn't know if priorities would work for me, because if I fell behind with the song writing, for instance, but my head was full of art, what would I do then? But the most amazing thing seems to be happening. When I look at the wall and see I've fallen behind in one of those areas, *it becomes interesting!* Even if it wasn't interesting before!"

The Rotating Priorities Board might do the same for you. Try it and see.

Getting organized

Unlike most other Sybils, Celeste wasn't disorganized and didn't have a clutter problem. She always knew where everything was. She did have to keep moving things out of the way when she wasn't working on them, which was a little inconvenient, but for the most part, her materials were under control.

This isn't the case with most Sybils. Disorganization and chaos stop most Sybils from being productive. If that sounds like you, here's another of my favorite Scanner tools that you might find useful.

The AVOCATION STATION

To spend as little time as possible getting ready and as much as possible actually working on one of your projects, you need to have all the parts available and ready to use immediately. For this, you can combine the Setup I suggested for Jeff, the busy parent in Chapter 5 ("Too Busy to Do What I Love"), with a very lovable piece of equipment I call the Avocation Station. Let me show you how it works.

"I can never find my to-do lists! Or the pieces to the beadwork I'm doing.

Or the articles I cut out for this report," a Sybil Scanner once told me. Because she was working in the School Day Model, she had about an hour for each project. "By the time I get everything ready to go, my hour is almost up. And then I have to put everything away again. I'm back to doing nothing!"

I imagine there are orderly, well-organized Scanners in the world, but there can't be very many of them. It's far more common to hear a Scanner mumbling, "Now, where did I put that lizard?" When you have lots of things going on at the same time and when many of them are in an unfinished state, it's to be expected that you'll have trouble assembling everything you need when you're ready to work on one of them. But if you're on a schedule, you can't waste precious time gathering everything together, and it would be so nice if you didn't have to clear off your workspace every time you stopped. Wouldn't it be great if you never had to gather up your tools and put them away again?

Enter the Avocation Station

I used to wish that I had a huge, empty room with rows of long tables against the walls and, on each table, everything I needed for one of my projects. Then I could leave everything out in the open on its own table and walk over to it and start working whenever the mood took me.

I don't have a room that large and I bet you don't, either, but the fantasy gave me the idea of Avocation Stations, and I started wondering what kind of arrangement could replace all those tables and take up less space. A rolling file cabinet might work for some of my projects, but it wasn't quite right for others.

Then, last month in a home furnishings catalog, I saw a little rolling stand with drawers and a couple of fun gadgets like a desk space that opened, a slot for large pages, a shelf for books. It was called a bill paying center, as I recall, but to me it was a dead ringer for an Avocation Station. I got visions of lining up 5 or 10 of them against one wall and wheeling out whichever one I wanted to work on at that moment.

If you're a Scanner with lots of projects going on at the same time, you should have some variation of those little pieces of furniture. You can make your own to suit yourself out of any small, rolling file cabinet or wire cart and keep a whole bunch of them ready to go.

Think of it! You'd never wonder where the glue was or the beads were, and you'd never have to put your scissors or magazines or recording devices or video camera "away" when you were done. Everything could be stored in its own movable work station.

Celeste decided to use an Avocation Station for each of her smaller sculptures-in-progress. She attached small wheels to four deep, two-drawer wooden file cabinets she found in a scrap yard and glued a large kitchen cutting board to the top of each one as a work surface. The bottle caps and hubcaps and other odd items she gathered for building materials went into the large bottom drawer, the glue and tools fit in a small upper drawer, and the piece she was working on sat on top. When she wanted to work on a piece, she wheeled the station to the electric outlet where she kept her welding materials. She did the same with her recording equipment and the files for her book-in-progress. And she rolled every project out of the way when it wasn't in use.

Lynn loved the idea, too. She put files for her history project in one Avocation Station and files for her memoirs in another.

"I love these! I'm going to start a business making them!" Lynn said and ran to her Scanner Daybook to write up the idea, with diagrams and measurements and explanations all over the pages.

I hope she really does it, because I'd like a few of those. But until then, you and I can make Avocation Stations from almost anything: a basket for craft materials, a tote bag for writing materials, or any other portable container that will hold everything you need for one of your projects.

Once your Avocation Stations are set up, the practical thing to do (and it's lots of fun, too) is to see if your Setups are complete by doing a test run. Bring out your KITCHEN TIMER and set it for 5 minutes. Then pull out one of your Avocation Stations and work on that project for 5 minutes only. If you find something's missing, write a note (or go get it, if you can).

In 5 minutes, when you hear the timer go "bing!" run to the next Avocation Station and repeat the process. If you keep moving fast, you won't take anything too seriously, and you'll spot any problems so you can fine-tune your setup for real use.

You'll also develop a wonderful game you can play anytime you've been so busy you've neglected your projects for too long and find that you miss doing them. Just set aside a half hour and do another high-speed Avocation Station test run, using that Kitchen Timer the same way you did before. You might write a few lines in your book, thread some more beads onto a piece of jewelry, pull out your camera and take a photo, and take a fresh look at a design you were working on. It will keep you in touch with all your projects, and if it feels like a guilty pleasure, tell yourself you're just checking the Setups to make sure they're working and ready.

You might want to write up the results of your first rounds with the Setup and Avocation Stations in your Scanner Daybook, just for the record. I think you'll enjoy remembering this day.

A package from Lynn

A few months after our discussion, I got a large envelope from Lynn in the mail. She had enclosed a folded red sheet of construction paper, which opened up into a little bulletin board with items stuck all over it. There were snapshots of two stuffed toys she'd made for her grandchild; a cartoon of a little book that said "Memoirs, 37 pages"; a dried sprig from a dill plant; and at the top, written in bold black letters, these words:

> *Doing Everything You Love Every Day, or How to Write a Book, Build an Herb Garden, Create a Board Game, Make Stuffed Toys, Study History, and Run a Home Business at the Same Time.*

There was a lovely letter about how well she was doing, and it ended: "P.S. Please return this sheet to me in the enclosed stamped self-addressed envelope so I can tape it into my Daybook."

Life Design Models for other kinds of Sybil Scanners

Sybils are the largest group of Cyclical Scanners, and they come in many sizes and shapes. If you're not like Lynn or Celeste, and their schedules won't work for you, consider one of the following alternatives.

The Physician Life Design Model: A physician might see patients on Monday and Tuesday, go into the hospital on Wednesday and Thursday, attend conferences a few times a month, and take 2 weeks in the winter to go with Doctors without Borders to Nepal to perform hundreds of cataract operations. But you don't have to be a doctor to follow this model. It's just right for any Sybil Scanner who likes to spend a few days on each project and do something different once or twice a year.

The Spy Life Design Model: If you've got projects that take you to very different environments and you've ever secretly wanted to be a spy who wears disguises, this model might suit you perfectly. I recently met a woman who designs and manufactures women's purses and bags. She's also an art dealer who specializes in African art. And she's attending graduate school for her master's in social work.

"I go to the factory to oversee the making of the purses and bags in my work clothes," she said. "If I have a sales meeting with a buyer or a show to go to, I have some fun and dress to kill! I wear different makeup and even a wig! And I have special outfits for art openings and different ones for school, too. And when I become a social worker, I'm going to come up with the perfect outfit for that environment, too."

More tools for Sybil Scanners

20 or 30 Three-Ring Binders: This is one of the most useful of all the tools for the Sybil Scanner. Almost all Scanners love using this system, but no one needs it more than Sybil Scanners. For one thing, it keeps all their projects organized. But there's an additional reason these binders are important to them.

Sybils can have extended surges of the creative phase, coming up with one good idea after another. (One client called them "idea spills"!) It's a waste of talent to slow any Scanner down and ask her to complete one idea before coming up with another. If she can pull out a Three-Ring Binder for every new idea, she'll be able to start them all as they come up. And the binders will provide a holding spot for later follow-up when the creative phase cools. This handy tool makes it possible to control almost any number of projects at once.

PROJECT BOXES: In case your ideas tend to be more 3-D—that is, if they include books or objects—you can use a portable file folder bin or set up Project Boxes to act just like those binders.

I realized how powerful this solution was in a recent telephone class I ran, when a woman named Clare told us her problem.

"I used to be a consultant for nonprofit organizations, and now I have a job I really love, teaching kids in grade school. But on the side I play with ideas for helping nonprofits make money, and I also have two little businesses of my own developing software. I've sent out e-mails and marketed most of my stuff for a long time, but suddenly, I'm getting lots of responses and I can't keep track of anything!"

You don't run into too many people with Clare's particular combination of activities, and I was sure she'd need a far more complex system for her projects, but I couldn't resist jumping in with the Three-Ring Binder Solution. "I know this is terrifically oversimplified," I apologized, "and I'm sure you'll get more sophisticated answers from other people on this call, but before I open the floor for suggestions I just want to suggest having a whole bunch of Three-Ring Binders with the name of each ongoing project on the spine and keeping them out in plain sight like I do."

While I was talking, I could hear other people responding on the line with interest, murmuring about the idea. I had assumed that my suggestion was such a primitive, low-tech notion that it would get a lukewarm reception at best. I was wrong. Everybody loved it.

Clare was extremely enthused. "That would really work! I love that idea!" she said. "It could make everything manageable."

Later, when the evaluations for the class came into my e-mail inbox, almost half the attendees wrote that one of the most valuable things about it was the suggestion that they put their projects in Three-Ring Binders!

I got this letter in my e-mail from one of the participants.

> *I've known for a long time that I'm a Scanner, but now I think the light went on. Having 20 or 30 projects to work on for a lifetime sounds just great! It makes me look at what I do during the day in a different light already. Today I made a cake for Grandpa's birthday (culinary work) while listening to a foreign CD (translation practice). When I play with the dog, it's animal behavior study; taking the recycling to the depot is now environmentalist work; reading this bulletin board trains me as a life skills counselor. All the activities that previously were "wasting time" now have a purpose.*

Careers for Sybil Scanners

Like Lynn, all Cyclical Scanners can grow into experts and authorities, because their expertise can accumulate through the years just like every other aspect of their projects. But while they're on their way, how can they pay the bills without taking too much time from all their beloved projects? Here are some careers that have worked well for Sybil Scanners.

Multiple income streams: This means using a number of different skills you enjoy to bring in all the income you need. If you can't earn enough money doing one thing you love, try getting five or six of them going at once and you might find you're doing very well. This is perfect for the Scanner whose favorite projects lend themselves to earning income.

The Good Enough Job: Sybils are often happiest with the Good Enough Job. It's a natural for you if your interests are the kind that can be done after work or on weekends. Remember, the Good Enough Job is a job that requires only 40 (or fewer) hours of your time per week, provides security, and has a nontoxic environment, meaning pleasant people to work with. A job like this is your own subsidy to the arts, so give it the affection it deserves.

A home business: Working at home running your own business might be ideal, where you'll wear all your favorite hats (and hire someone else to wear the ones you don't like as much). You can follow your natural rhythms, take energy naps and walks—and work on projects when you have the right level of attention.

Umbrella Careers: If you're looking for a career that will allow you to do many of the things you enjoy, you're talking about an Umbrella Career. If you like to write in addition to your other interests, consider being a freelance writer. Then you can write articles and even books on any subject that interests you.

Or, if you love information for its own sake (as many Scanners do), you can become a researcher, librarian, or information broker in one or more of the fields that interest you.

Consultant: If you find a job as a consultant in a field that interests you—such as animals or musical theater, for instance—you can build expertise and eventually command respect in that field. You can even become a guru if you create a teaching seminar or write a book about it. And you can still do all the other things you love on your own time.

Lynn's life today

I heard from Lynn again not long ago. Since she first learned how to organize her interests 2 years ago, her life is very different. She created a number of dolls based on historical figures from her history studies, set up a Web site where she discusses home greenhouses and specializes in heritage herbs, and runs regular publicity and promotion workshops at small business conferences (which she records and sells on her other Web site).

Let's see what happens when you try out some of these tools. I think you'll find yourself making a kind of progress you didn't realize was possible. You'll find the summary of them on the opposite page.

Now you're familiar with the Double Agent—a Scanner who takes months for each of her lives—and the Sybil—who can stay involved with one project for hours, weeks, or months. It's time to meet the fastest of the Cyclical Scanners: the Plate Spinner, who does all his projects simultaneously.

HOW SYBILS DO EVERYTHING THEY LOVE

Life Design Models for Sybils

The School Day Model
The Spy Model
The Physician Model
The Random Acts of Passion Model

Careers for Sybils

Multiple income streams
The Good Enough Job
Home business
Umbrella Career
Consultant

From Your Scanner Tool Kit

Scanner Planner
Scanner Daybook
15-Month Goal Calendar
Rotating Priorities Board
Setup
Avocation Station
Kitchen Timer
20 or 30 Three-Ring Binders
Project Boxes

Chapter 12

ARE YOU
A PLATE SPINNER?

Ed Sullivan used to have a man on his show who would put a plate on a pole, start it spinning, and hoist it up into the air. Then he'd put a plate on another pole and another until he had five or six plates spinning at the same time. I have always thought of myself as spinning plates like he did.

I have several dreams and try to keep them all organized. I have a paper diary, an electronic diary, to-do lists, electronic organizers—but none of them work. I'm more of a minute-to-minute person. Throw something at me and I can always catch it.

I'm the fixer at work; I like the challenge, but it doesn't leave any time for my own projects.

Are you a Plate Spinner?

- Do you often come up with solutions to problems faster than most people?
- Do you enjoy the challenge of keeping lots of projects going at once?
- Do you find it hard to say no when people ask you for help?
- Do you like learning only when it solves problems, not for its own sake?
- Does it feel good to be needed, to feel you're making a difference?
- Have you ever felt that your abilities have trapped you into a smaller life than you could be leading?

If you said yes, you're a Plate Spinner. You're energized by having many things going on at the same time. But you're not a typical multitasker, who solves her overload by giving only part of her attention to each task until she gets frazzled and inefficient. Doing many things at once is the first choice of a Plate Spinner, and when you move fast, you don't feel rushed. Plate Spinners are rarely overwhelmed because, for the most part, they think faster than other people. And like the Samurai in a Japanese film, a Plate Spinner is working on two levels—the task at hand and the task of sharpening her coordination.

You work on big projects in the same way. When the biographer Stuart Gilbert asked James Joyce which chapter of his classic novel *Ulysses* he was working on at the moment, like a true Plate Spinner, Joyce answered, "All of them."

For you, satisfaction comes from solving problems, often for other people. You're generous with help because it bothers you to see someone struggling with a problem you can easily fix. People depend on you. They often take advantage of you, too.

You might not think about it much, but you're capable of an entirely different and deeper kind of thought. You tend to neglect it, however, not because you have too much work but because nondirected thinking doesn't seem as important as problem solving.

"I need real-world problems to solve," Liam, an information technologist, told me. "Learning for its own sake is what vacations are for."

Problem solving has paid him well. When you're as good as Liam at devising new systems with one hand and putting out fires with the other, you'll always be too useful to others to do much else. And although you may work long hours, it feels good to know the place couldn't run without you.

But sometimes Liam, like many Plate Spinners, thinks about all his other sides—the ones he never gets to use.

"Today's workplace doesn't value anyone with a wide view. They see me as a troubleshooter, plain and simple," Liam said. He's presently a systems analyst at a major software company. "There's no way in the world I'll get the chance to use my other abilities at work."

"What would you like to do if you had more time?" I asked.

"All kinds of things," he said. "I really enjoyed helping a friend's teenager do her math this weekend! I had to figure out exactly what she wasn't getting; it was a real challenge, and then I understood she had math mixed up with *all* unsolvable problems. Being a teenager, she had a lot of those! I had to figure out how to show her that some problems could be solved, and with math the answer was guaranteed to be right. It was exciting! When she got it, I almost started laughing, I was so happy."

"You don't really get to use that brain of yours very much, do you?" I asked.

"Excuse me?" he said, astonished. "That's all I do! I'm worked to death! I hardly get home! I solve every kind of problem that's thrown at me during my workday, and my workday is sometimes 10 hours long! How can you say I don't get to use my brain?"

"I don't think you often get to use the part of your brain that makes you happy enough to laugh, like you did with your friend's kid," I said.

He was silent for a moment. "Well, maybe so," he admitted with a trace of weariness.

And here we find the Plate Spinners' real problem: They have a wide range of talents that go unused and that disuse is draining.

Hard work doesn't bother a Spinner. Liam works too many hours, but he can do twice the brain work of most people without breaking a sweat and enjoys pushing his limits. But too much of the same kind of problem solving creates a type of vitamin deficiency in someone like Liam.

"It's true that I'm not as relaxed or playful as I used to be," he admitted.

One woman said it very clearly. "If I keep using only one part of myself, I get worn out. Some part of me is bored even if I'm fully engaged."

And that's their dilemma. Because they're rarely asked to employ all their talents, Spinners are in the odd position of being both busy and bored, overworked and underused. I couldn't help wondering what ideas Liam would play with if he had time.

Do you have time for yourself?

If you're a great problem solver, you might be depriving yourself of all the other kinds of thinking your brain longs for. Do you agree with Liam that problem solving is the only worthwhile activity for you? Read this story, from another Spinner named Donna, and see what you think of the outcome.

"Everyone at the school and the church got so accustomed to having me solve problems they took it for granted. They loaded me up, and they figured there was nothing to it when I bailed them out of a tough situation. You'd be surprised how rarely I got a thank-you—instead, I'd get impatience that I didn't do a job faster," Donna wrote me. She was everyone's favorite volunteer because, like so many Spinners, she loves to make things work, pull rabbits out of hats, and create last-minute miracles.

If it weren't for the lack of appreciation and the heavy load of work people automatically dropped at her door, I think Donna would have given every spare minute to her volunteer efforts. But one day she pulled back and started taking time for herself.

"I never would have said no if they hadn't taken advantage and been so unappreciative. But I should have done it for myself! This feels like such a luxury, like I'm wasting time or something. But that's not right!" she said. "I forgot how much I love just sitting around and *thinking*!"

What was Donna thinking about? "Everything, anything. I love to learn anything, from books or magazines or the back of breakfast cereal boxes and that means thinking. When I cook or clean the house or go walking, I think almost the entire time. When I drew as a kid, I was *thinking* about what to draw. When I did magic tricks, I would have to *think* about how they worked. I loved thinking about math. I love to solve (mostly 3-D) types of puzzles, which involves *thinking* and rotating images in my mind.

"It's like being a kid playing outside when I'm not locked into the superficial level of practical problem solving. And it feels good, like my muscles feel when I go running."

How about you? Do you enjoy recreational thinking? Do you worry that maybe it's not allowed because it doesn't solve important problems? If you weren't spinning so many plates and solving so many problems, what would your brain enjoy doing?

Try this fantasy exercise

Pull out your Scanner Daybook and a pen and see if you can find 10 or 15 uninterrupted minutes. I'd like you to try this fantasy for yourself:

Imagine you're on a tiny desert isle alone, with nothing to do. A ship will be by in 2 or 3 days and you have enough to eat until then, but there's no one to talk to, nothing to work with, just a couple of days to pass while you look out to sea.

At first your mind might be empty, but give it a little time and when something comes to mind, pick up your pen and start writing.

What happened? Did you get bored or find your thinking slip into a different mode?

Liam couldn't think of anything at first, but then he started remembering some ideas he'd forgotten. And then the floodgates opened.

Liam wanted to organize international traveling children's theaters that visited small communities and auditioned local children for roles in each play.

"I heard of some people doing that in the United States, and the kids worked all year to get good grades so they'd be eligible to audition. It had an amazing effect on the kids. Some of them started to write plays when they didn't even like reading before that.

"There's a way to replicate traveling theaters in every region of the world. Even in the Gobi Desert, there's a tradition that could be thousands of years old, of traveling actors. It's such a big thing when they come to town. The theater could even be a school, if none existed."

He went on to draw some diagrams to show me a model he wanted to build that would help physics teachers explain the fifth and sixth dimensions. (I have to be honest and say I *think* that's what he said!) After that, he told me about a documentary he'd seen about Indians who lived in the Amazon basin of South America and played tiny flutes with a special, haunting tone, and he dreamed up some new musical instruments based on what he saw that would create a similar haunting sound.

The desert island fantasy had created an open space away from problem-solving and made room for his ideas to start flying.

He drew while he spoke. The pages he wrote on were soon covered with sketches and diagrams, and his face was lit up. He continued to eagerly explain his ideas, and he had a big smile on his face the whole time.

"Wow," I said when he slowed down. "You're a one-man marching band of good ideas!"

"Yes," he sighed, and he started looking serious again. "But they're just ideas. And that's what they'll have to remain."

His smile was gone. The look of excitement had disappeared, and he was caught in his conflict again.

"You look like recess just ended and it's back to the classroom."

"That's how I feel now while I reflect on my dissatisfaction," he smiled. "When I'm in those offices trouble shooting, I'm very high energy."

"Like a hockey player in a tough game?"

"Well, sort of."

"That's still not the feeling that made you laugh," I said.

He looked thoughtful, even a little curious. "Yes, it's different," he said.

I asked a question that was off the subject. "I've never understood alternating current, Liam. Can you explain it to me?"

He was a little surprised, but he made some attempts to enlighten me.

"Well, you could say it's an electric current that reverses direction on a regular basis. Why are you asking this all of a sudden?"

"I'm thinking up a Life Design Model that might bump you out of that one-track problem-solving mode, at least sometimes."

"Good idea, but I'd need a different job."

"You never know," I said.

The Alternating Current Life Design Model

This model has no calendar or schedule connected to it, and it can mean something as simple as remembering to step over to a window and look in the distance for a few minutes, just to see if another kind of brain wave would like a moment or two. Pulling out your index cards or Rolodex cards that make up your Portable Dream Deck is a good alternative, and if you work at home, you can schedule regular sit-downs with your Daybook.

"It's hard to care about things that don't have a real-life outcome," Liam said. "One kind of Scanner obviously just likes to learn. I confess I feel like those people are just fooling around when there's work to be done."

But, as theoretical scientists know, nondirected thinking can be an excellent way of finding things you didn't know you were looking for. The scientist father of a friend said it clearly.

> *Theoretical scientists come up with more original ideas than applied scientists, and we get nominated for more Nobel prizes. That's because we never assume anything, and we don't have a preconceived solution in our minds when we try to find answers to our biggest puzzles. Applied scientists, like those at disease research societies, are always looking for a cure, and they really have to be single-minded. But many cures are found by theoretical scientists who are not looking for them.*

Liam was smiling slightly. "It's a lot of fun to think about things in that nondirected way," he acknowledged. "But it's worlds away from what I'm comfortable with. I can relax and do that kind of thinking on long walks, but I usually move a lot faster than that the rest of the time."

But I wasn't talking about relaxing. I went to a computer to find an interview I'd done with another Plate Spinner and pulled it up on the screen for Liam to read.

Elizabeth's story

Elizabeth feels best when she's moving fast. In fact, it's actually painful for her to move at a slower pace. It's as big a strain for Elizabeth to use half her ability as it is for a car to climb a hill using half its cylinders. She wrote:

I have always had several things going at once. I get very bored and stressed if I try to do only one thing. For instance, when I was in high school I took dance, taught dance, and worked at a hamburger joint all while taking a full school load—you know, like physics and chemistry, etc. On top of that, I was responsible for the family dinner every evening as well as heavy housework.

When I went to college, I took 18 to 20 hours per semester, taught dance, studied dance, became a varsity gymnast, taught gymnastics, and became a gymnastics judge so I could judge meets. My first degree major was psychology with a biology minor. And darn it, since I still lived at home, I still had all those heavy household responsibilities!

I typically read three books at once—and, of course, magazines.

When things get hairy, and believe me, they get hairy, I don't burn out, I get extremely focused and take action. But it's not fun to be thrown in crisis mode. I can laugh at the pickle I've gotten myself into only after the crisis passes. I like my schedule to be full, challenging, and varied but not so tight that I'm late for things. I hate to be late! I have figured out that three things going at once are a nice balance for me, especially now that I'm raising children.

Liam was impressed. But what reminded me of Elizabeth as I described my Alternating Current Life Design Model was her final statement:

One key thing for me is I like for my entire "system" of mind and body to be completely used. I like to do things that are different from one another at the

same time. I like my body to be exercised fully. I like for my mind to be learn-
ing/doing/absorbing different things at the same time. Otherwise, I get fright-
fully bored, and I feel like part of me is "dying on the vine."

"Yes," Liam said. "I never thought of it that way. That's what I've been feeling!"

"How about using the Alternating Current Model for time-outs where you can develop all those great ideas of yours?" I suggested.

Liam seemed embarrassed. I looked at him questioningly.

The real problem

"I'm a fake," Liam said. "The real problem isn't that I have no time. The real problem is that I'd start one of those projects and have a great time, but after I designed it and understood it and gave it a try to see if it really worked, I'd lose interest and walk away."

"Oh, is that all?" I laughed. "That's not a problem. You just need to hand your projects off to someone else. Just teach others how to do them. In fact, teach some teachers how to do them so they can keep your idea going. Then you can go start something else."

His face lit up again, and he told me another of his ideas.

He wanted to work with the economies of impoverished mountain communities in the Himalayas (where he had spent a year after college). The idea involved new techniques for surface mining and a plan for setting up a mobile training unit that could go to any location and train the local people to teach everyone in the village how to do it.

"I love training teachers!" he said. "That really keeps you free, doesn't it?"

We were talking about the tool I mentioned in Chapter 4 ("Commitment Phobia"): the Learn, Try, Teach, Leave—LTTL—method of project management.

The LTTL System

People as fast as Plate Spinners often have Liam's dilemma of being stuck in one role when they were born to handle a dozen roles. The best use of a Plate

Spinner's talent is the LTTL System. Using this tool, someone like Liam is brought into a department to troubleshoot. He learns what he needs to know to fix the problems. Then he develops some new systems that he thinks will help the department and tries them out to make sure they work. Once he's sure they'll straighten out the problems, he teaches someone in the department how to use them. Then he heads off to another department, leaving employee manuals in his wake.

The Plate Spinner would be happy because he'd get to learn, to invent, and to test his inventions. He'd get to teach, too. And that would be all he'd be asked to do. This would be a delightful job for the Plate Spinner, and the boss would have a company that kept getting more and more productive.

Liam loved the idea, but he was pretty sure no one would hire him for a job like that. He was probably right. It looked like he'd have to start his own business one day—if he could get out from under his workload of 10-plus hours a day.

It looked impossible, but I had a plan.

Win hearts to start your own business

If you're a Plate Spinner, you can usually get a good job as a troubleshooter, but it's not easy to find one that lets you use all your talents or, as Elizabeth described it, your "entire system of mind and body." You might get lucky and find an exception, but few companies are set up to properly utilize a multi-talented Scanner. How do you make the transition to a business of your own?

You save your money, you win some hearts, and you build for your future.

Liam looked confused when I said that to him. "Win some hearts?" he asked.

That was what I'd said. Because I knew that if a Plate Spinner spends 99 percent of his time in problem-solving mode now, he'd spend 200 percent if he had his own business. And no Scanner is worse at delegating than the Plate Spinner.

The Success Teams I started in my first workshops back in the late 1970s are unbeatable when it comes to accountability and moral support. But the kind of team Liam needed had something else that was very special.

I'd read about this kind of support in a book about Jim Clark, the inventor of the first big Internet browser (Netscape) and, many believe, the man who created the "dot-com bubble" of the 1990s almost single-handedly. (You can read his story in *The Next, Next Thing* by Michael Lewis.)

Clark was a brilliant engineer who had attracted a following of dozens of other brilliant engineers because they loved the way he thought. Most of them worked for companies Clark had basically created and then cashed out from and abandoned. From the description, he sounded like a Spinner (on steroids!).

"Clark's inability to live without motion and change had gotten him to where he was," says the author. "He needed change even more than the money that came from the change." Clark had started out as an engineer, and back then, engineers weren't considered very important by the money people and were paid accordingly. But by 2000, when the book was written, Clark was worth hundreds of millions of dollars and about to be worth more.

He made his money by starting new companies, and he used the LTTL method I had described to Liam—but he left out a few letters.

It began when he walked out of a company that had tried to control him more than he liked, and he discovered, to his surprise, that the best engineers in that company followed him. They loved working with him. So he started the interesting system of operating his new companies in the Learn, Try, Teach, and Leave model, but he got rid of all the letters but the first and the last.

He "learned," or figured out, that there was a need for a new kind of software concept and told his engineers what he thought it should do. After that, he neither "tried" it out nor "taught" anything. He just "left." And the engineers did the rest.

Clark's story is amazing. It was far grander than anything Liam wanted, but the idea of winning over the hearts of those engineers and the power it gave Clark to make his ideas into reality wasn't lost on him.

"I never figured out how Clark got them to follow him," I said.

Liam smiled. "It's easy. All you have to do is respect them enough to give them their heads and just turn them loose to solve problems their own way. And you have to be smart enough to understand the value of their solutions. I'd follow anyone who did that for me, too."

"Ah," I said. "Well then, let me ask you something. Would anyone want to follow you?"

He laughed. "I'm a loner. I only know engineers when they come to me with problems."

"It's time to change that, don't you think?"

He shrugged.

I knew what I was up against. One thing I've noticed in Plate Spinners is that they're usually loners like Liam. They're so competent that they've never learned how to delegate and are impatient with people who don't do the job as well as they do.

Liam shrugged again when I said that to him. "So then, I guess you're the smartest engineer you know," I said.

"Well, you know, in my unit, at my company, probably yes."

"It's time to widen your social circle, isn't it?"

"No time," he said.

So I gave him a plan of action.

"First," I said, "start a class where you teach the best engineers in your present company how to solve their own problems. After a while, that will give you a little more time.

"Second, watch those same engineers to see who you'd love to work with when you leave this company."

"And what should I do with these people if they follow me out?" he said.

"Teach them to carry out those great ideas you told me," I answered.

"And how would I pay them?"

"You wouldn't. You'd have a company that would pay them."

"A Himalayan mining company? An international touring theater company? Those businesses wouldn't make enough money to pay the electric bills. Anyway, I wouldn't know which one to start first."

10 talents in search of a job description

"You should start all of them; you should be an incubator. That will use every part of you and every talent you've got. You should get funded as a nonprofit."

Liam finally laughed out loud and sat back. I knew I had stumbled on something a Plate Spinner like Liam would love to do: set up an incubator for a half-dozen creative companies and get them all started.

"You know you agree with me," I said and read a letter he had written me the week before.

> As I kid, I could explore. Today's working world isn't designed for Scanners who go off on tangents; it expects specialists to bury themselves in long-term projects, especially in technical fields like mine.

I feel like just a cog in the big machine, too far from the result to satisfy me, and there's not much chance of getting creative with technical projects. If you start getting creative, everyone gets unhappy. People like me aren't considered professional; we're seen as clever versions of janitors.

But where can you go where you won't be crammed into a limiting job? I've met other people like me; they're some of the most creative people, who could really make a big difference in the world if they were given a little freedom.

He listened thoughtfully while I read the letter.

"Have you really met other people like you, Liam?"

"Yes, a lot of them. I forgot all about them. A few even said I should give them a call if I had anything interesting in the works. That was a few years ago." He took out a pen and a small pad of paper and started writing. "I guess I'd better start setting up some Sunday afternoon baseball games and invite them to play."

That's how you get to create a project that uses every part of you: You find your people—not by networking, just by making it a habit to hang out and get to know the kinds of people who interest you the most. If you're someone who hires people for projects—for yourself or for the place you work—you're in a good position to be a talent scout. It can take a year or two, but when you're ready, you'll have your own version of Jim Clark's backup team.

So if you're someone who too often gets stuck putting out fires and wish you could do something more creative, you might want to consider alternating your high-powered plate spinning with some slower, more creative current—and throw away your Lone Ranger mask. Start keeping your eyes open for people who can help you.

You don't have to be a technician, and you don't always need brilliant engineers, either. Sometimes all you need is to hire an assistant.

In a recent Scanner workshop, a woman raised her hand and said, "My husband and I are both Scanners. We come up with 10 really good ideas a week! But we don't get our bills paid because we can't find them! We create huge messes and never get the small important things done, so we could never develop any of those ideas."

If their ideas are any good, it's a waste of their time and talent to go looking for their bills. And it's a big waste of money, too. When you're not good at something (like managing your business), you shouldn't hire yourself. And if you're good at ideas, you should arrange your life so that you can use the ideas.

I suggested she find a part-time assistant, maybe a "virtual" who worked entirely on the Internet. When a creative person does work that someone else could do, she's wasting her talents and depriving the rest of us who might benefit from those talents.

What if you don't have the money for an assistant? You do. If you took another job for an additional day a week and turned every cent over to the assistant, you'd still wind up ahead financially, because you can make things happen if an assistant takes the details off your hands. And you wouldn't be wearing out your sharp and shiny mind on work you're probably not that good at anyway.

Betting on a Plate Spinner

When Liam and I parted, I knew I had him thinking, but he wasn't sold. I had worked on him the best I could. I told him—as I tell you—to stand up and take responsibility for that unusual brain of his. Use it or lose it. Acknowledge what you need and fight to get it. Time is all you have. Don't waste your gifts when the world needs them. I gave it everything I had, and then I crossed my fingers and walked away.

I got another letter from him, a few weeks later.

> *I know I once told you that reading without purpose or a problem to solve was strictly for vacations. But I'm starting to wonder again about that. I think I've been depriving myself of learning and exploring. I'll pass them up to solve a problem every time. I'm beginning to see what that's costing me.*

I sent him an answer right away. "If you find a way to help the economies of small Himalayan villages and help physics teachers explain higher dimensions and help kids all over the world with your traveling theaters, it seems to me you'd be solving quite a few very important problems—and being creative at the same time. I think you'd better get your hands on about 20 or 30 Three-Ring Binders, just to catch the new ideas that will be showing up.

"Incidentally, you should look up what's available for your incubator at the

HOW PLATE SPINNERS DO EVERYTHING THEY LOVE

Life Design Models for Plate Spinners

The Alternating Current Model
The Learn, Try, Teach, Leave (LTTL) Model

Careers for Plate Spinners

Nonprofit incubator
Itinerant troubleshooter

From Your Scanner Tool Kit

Scanner Daybook
Portable Idea Deck
20 or 30 Three-Ring Binders

Foundation Library. I think it's online. It's never too soon to start preparing. Do you know how to write a grant proposal?"

He e-mailed me the next day. "Do I know how to write a grant proposal? No, but it looks like I'm going to learn, doesn't it? Oh, I meant to tell you, I've got a baseball game scheduled for this Sunday. I'll send photos."

I'm cheering for Liam.

I'm cheering for you, too.

Now let's take a look at the Scanners who don't circle around to pick up the same projects but move straight ahead. Some move slowly, like our Double Agent, spending months or years on one interest. And some of these Scanners move as fast as Plate Spinners.

They are called Sequential Scanners.

Chapter 13

ABOUT SEQUENTIAL SCANNERS

And now we get to the other type of Scanners, the ones who don't return to their interests over and over again—when they're finished, they don't look back.

> *Life is too short to do anything twice. Left to my own devices, I'd investigate some new field every few months and let the previous passion go without a thought.*

If you're someone who can't possibly make a list of everything you're interested in because you often don't know what that might be until you see it—and if you tried anyway, you're convinced your list would be endless—you're probably a Sequential Scanner.

Sequential types are searching for the next interesting thing, and they'll tell you in a moment that they don't want to return to previous interests.

"I'm ashamed to admit it," said one man, "but no matter how great a project is, there comes a time when it looks like an orange with all the juice sucked out and I'm looking for a new kind of fruit."

Sally gets interested in something new every few months. She devotes herself to her garden or learning a new computer program until she's satisfied with her level of accomplishment, and then she moves on. Of course, she won't let her geraniums die after that, but her passion will be for something new every time.

In the Sequential group, the Serial Specialist has the "slowest" duration. He stays with one project for years before moving on to the next. The "fastest" Sequential Scanner is the surprising High-Speed Indecisive, who looks like one creature but is actually another.

All Scanners love to learn—but some are trying to solve a puzzle that intrigues them, and when they get their answer, they're finished and can't be persuaded to go further. The Serial Specialist is like that. Others thrill to the challenge of mastering a skill and stay until they conquer their own limitations and achieve their very best, and that's typically a Serial Master. There are more kinds of Sequential Scanners than we realize.

They're a fascinating and brilliant bunch. If you find yourself among them, you'll be in good company.

Chapter 14

ARE YOU A SERIAL SPECIALIST?

I seem to last about 4 or 5 years at something, and then I'm ready for a change. It's very disconcerting to keep starting over.

I'm worried that I'll never build any stability. But after a certain time, I'm just not interested in my field anymore.

Are you a Serial Specialist?

❖ Does your work record look like it should belong to more than one person because you've changed directions so often?
❖ Do you immerse yourself deeply in a project or job for so long it looks to others like a permanent life choice?
❖ Do you find that once you get the hang of what you're doing, you're ready to leave and start somewhere else?
❖ Do you love exploring the culture inside a corporation, a hospital, a film production house, a Wall Street financial firm?
❖ Do you worry that your career changes will leave you without a body of work or a reputation as an expert in the long run?
❖ Did you ever think your problems might be solved if reincarnation were really true?

If you answered yes to those questions, you're a Serial Specialist.

On the surface, you don't appear to be a Scanner at all, because you commit completely to a field without any apparent problem and stay involved for years, exactly like a specialist. But then, often at the top of your game, you quit and start something new. Your family wonders if you're self-sabotaging or afraid of success, but being a true Scanner, you know that life is too short to do only one thing forever.

Serial Specialists often excel at whatever field they're in. It never occurs to your co-workers or bosses that you're only exploring. What are you looking for? Not the right career, that's for sure. One career will never be enough for you. You're after something more elusive and almost impossible for the people around you to understand.

Harry's story

When Harry won his award as the highest-selling real estate salesperson in his company, his family threw a party. From being an out-of-work graphic artist 4 years earlier (who was always underpaid even when he did work), Harry had become almost wealthy. Selling homes and business real estate came to him easily, and he had done his homework.

At the party, Harry's boss toasted the award winner, champagne in hand. "Harry studied the business of real estate, the history of the homes and businesses in our entire county, and even wrote his own newspaper column in the local paper. He had the first Web site in our state for viewing homes and making appointments. No one ever saw anything like him," he said. Harry smiled proudly.

"I don't know where you're going from here, Harry, but I hope you don't go after my job!" the boss laughed.

Harry laughed too. "Don't worry, Joe. I'm leaving real estate entirely."

The room fell silent.

His family was stunned. "What are you talking about, Harry?" they shouted.

"I want to be an English teacher in a high school. And I want to write a book about it."

Everyone was dumbfounded, even embarrassed. But to Harry it made perfect sense. "Why would I want to keep doing the same thing over and over?" he said.

"For the money!" his brother shouted out, and the room broke into relieved laughter. When things got quiet again, Harry, still smiling, said, "I have enough money. More than I need. Now I want to try something different."

That was 3 years before I first got to know Harry at a teachers' conference where I was speaking. Harry not only taught high school but had written a very decent account of it in a book-length manuscript. He's not sure he wants to publish it, because he says it was a learning experience that he wants to have again, but do even better the next time. But he won't be teaching school this time—he'll be traveling to an obscure island near the southern tip of South America and writing about the remnants of a small tribe of people who live there.

To Harry it was simple. You don't spend your life making money you don't need, and you don't waste time doing things you already know how to do.

Harry is a typical Scanner. He loves life, and he loves to learn. Since he was very young, he had the ability to bury himself in a subject for weeks, even years. He was obviously very smart, but more than that, he had a wide range of talents. He loved nature and math; he enjoyed taking things apart and putting them back together and designing new gimmicks for daily use; he could find his way around places he had never been when everyone else was lost; and he was kind and sensitive to people (his students loved him). It seemed there was nothing Harry couldn't do.

But the only thing that had stayed consistent throughout his life was searching for and finding an area that was almost completely foreign to him and stepping into it like an actor in a new role. What was his nectar, his Reward? He knew the answer right away. "It's simple. I want to live more than one life. I want to know what it's really like to be many different people," he explained. "I wanted the experience of being a rich, successful kid in real estate, and I got it. I loved that. Then I was ready for the next thing."

Edith's small business rescues

I met Edith on a telephone session last year. After we said our hellos, she asked a question that made me laugh.

"So where do I sign up for reincarnation? Because that's the only way I'll ever solve my problem," Edith said.

"You sound a lot like a Scanner," I replied.

But she didn't think so. "What do you call it when you stick with everything for about 5 years and then get tired of it?! That doesn't sound like a Scanner to me. I've done it three times already. I don't know what's the matter with me."

I was intrigued and asked her to tell the whole story.

"I was so excited about buying my first business, a fabric and sewing store. But once I moved in, the true condition of the business was revealed. It was an awful mess, unbelievable. We owed money and had money owed us, and both were overdue for almost a full year! I learned how to run a business under fire! I almost went bust every month. My husband said I should name the store the Perils of Pauline, because I always looked like I was tied to the tracks looking at an oncoming train! It's true I worked night and day to survive, and finally, after a few years, I did it!

"It was wonderful. I spent another year fine-tuning every aspect of the business and got things humming like a sewing machine. It was beautiful, beautiful to look at, beautiful to work in. I couldn't believe how smoothly things ran: I had loads of customers, I gave loads of sewing classes, the bookkeeping setup was perfect, and the bills were paid. I could finally sit in the store and look around with a big smile on my face.

"But after a few months of smiling, I realized I was bored. I started not wanting to go to work. I got maudlin, thinking my life was over. My family thought I was crazy. So did I."

"Maybe the part you loved was over," I suggested.

She sounded interested. "Well, taking care of those emergencies wasn't very restful, but it was always exciting, and it made me feel that I was doing something worthwhile. But listen, you can't just throw things out when they're finally working. I sold the place because we moved to another part of the country and then bought this very distressed little appliance store and started all over again! And when that store was in shape, instead of enjoying the fruits of my labors and relaxing a little, I wanted to sell again! I wonder if I really am one of those people who are afraid of success."

"Sounds like it's boredom you're afraid of," I suggested. "You work very hard to create success."

"Oh. Can you be afraid of boredom?"

"You sure can," I laughed. "It's like Kryptonite to Scanners. It makes them think their lives are over, like you did."

"Well, I'll be damned," she said, struck by this piece of information. "So what do you do? How do you deal with boredom?"

"You do everything in your power to avoid it," I said. "You did exactly the right thing."

"Well, blow me down," she said.

Why do Scanners turn their backs on success? Do they fear it? Are they afraid of commitment? Or is it something simpler than that?

Scanners just want to have fun

People who want to have fun are different from people who are ambitious. When you're ambitious, your goal is success, in whatever way your culture defines that word. You stick with something through thick and thin because your eye is on money or prestige or awards. For most of us, those are the recognized symbols of success. If you get them, everyone admires you. You're a winner.

But a Scanner's goal is something most people in our culture don't understand—and Scanners don't usually understand it, either. If you keep changing goals, or if you're like Harry and Edith and you walk out the door just when you've attained success, we all assume you have something wrong with you. It's incomprehensible that you'd value something more than success.

But that's exactly what Scanners do. If you ask them why they walked away from something they were passionately interested in and worked hard at, they'll tell you they lost interest in it. To everyone around them, that doesn't make any sense. Who cares? others ask. Do you have to be entertained all the time? Isn't it time to grow up? And Scanners don't know how to answer. They just know they can't do boring things. And they know that they really have no choice.

It's as though they're creatures in a science fiction story who fly on a beam of energy, and when they move off the beam, they sicken and fall to the ground. If they get back on that beam, their energy comes back, and they can fly again. For Scanners, that energy beam is almost always some kind of learning, which often involves problem solving and inventing, creating and thinking, or some other variation. What it feels like to a Scanner is fun.

Scanners love to learn more than they love to "know." That's why Harry wants to experience a new life and Edith wants to rescue a failing business. So Harry will never be a multimillionaire real estate mogul, and Edith will never own a hugely successful store. And they couldn't care less.

They pay a high price for that attitude in a culture that focuses on success.

Bella: *I have a cousin who's totally absorbed in becoming wealthy. I've never seen such focus in my life. When he's looking into some new way to do it— the stock market or import-export or whatever—he sometimes pulls me in to help with some new strategy he doesn't understand and I'm as interested as he is. But once I get it, I'm finished. And he stays interested.*

He might actually make a lot of money one of these days. My mom keeps saying, "Why don't you do that? You're smarter than he is." She's disappointed that I don't become a big success. But all I can think of is how miserable I'd be if I did what he does. I just don't care about the money. My family says I'm not ambitious. They think I'm neurotic—which means that I'm a loser.

And, when it comes to Scanners, why do I assume that these families have made a mistake? How do I know that Scanners are different from people who reject success for emotional reasons?

I know because when you reject what you really want, everything else feels like a poor substitute. But when Scanners reject something, they replace it with something they love more.

Thomas: *I love to search for new things to explore. I think I might find out something that maybe no one else knows, something they need. That means that I'm credible, relevant, needed, and have a reason for being here.*

Elsie: *The fascination I have with the unknown and the physical exploration of the unknown is so satisfying. That is why I do improvisational dance. Also the openness of improvisation is pure heaven.*

What do Serial Specialists want? What is it that Harry and Edith love more than money or prestige or success?

"I want to be Walter Mitty"

Harry, the real estate whiz who went on to become a high school teacher and a writer, said those words. He laughed, but he meant what he said. Walter Mitty is the character in a short story by James Thurber. He's a henpecked husband who continually daydreams of being a daring surgeon, heroic pilot, and dashing naval commander.

Harry knew the lines by heart: "Throw on the power lights! Rev her up to 8500! We're going through!" he said with great drama.

We smiled, and I asked, "Do you want a daredevil life?"

"No, just an interesting one," he answered.

"I *do* want a daredevil life," Edith said, almost surprised at her own words.

After some discussion, two interesting patterns emerged. Harry loved the experience of living different lives, understanding the inside of someone else's world through personal experience; Edith loved the excitement and intensity of taking on near-disasters and making them come out right. If Harry's a sociologist, Edith's a fireman.

They know what they love. But they have a problem, and it's a serious one that all Scanners worry about in one context or another. You can't keep changing careers and build any kind of financial security. And of course, you'll never be considered an expert at anything.

"I intend to lead a life that interests me and nothing else, if I possibly can," Harry said, "but one of these days, I'm going to need more than great memories. Is there any way to turn this all into something? Or will I have to settle down someday? I can't build a reputation or retirement funds if I keep this up. I could wind up nowhere, just like my family predicts."

Edith was worried, too. "You can never get financial security if you keep starting over."

So I told them about some Serial Specialists who found a way to climb the ladder to success without giving up being Scanners. Some had what I call Umbrella Careers.

Under one Umbrella Career, many different interests

One of them, Gloria, is a small-business consultant. She loves rescuing businesses like Edith does, and she has made a profession out of putting them back on their feet. She has an online magazine for one-person businesses and runs entrepreneur workshops for "small-time operators" all over the world, from Colorado to Siberia. But Gloria always had trouble sticking with one thing.

"I love clothes and wanted to be a fashion designer," she said. "I loved designing clothes and learning the manufacturing process, but then I lost interest, so I opened a small shop and really enjoyed it. But it was the same thing every day. I helped my brother start a small auto-repair shop for antique cars and found I was really interested in that, too. After a while, I realized that what I was interested in was business itself. Now I help small businesses in every field from doll hospitals to talent agencies. It never gets to be routine, and that's what I love most."

Another Scanner with an Umbrella Career is one of my favorite writers, Tracy Kidder.

I always talk about Kidder when I'm describing Sequential Scanners in my workshops and telephone classes. I first mentioned him in 1994 in my book *I Could Do Anything If I Only Knew What It Was,* in which I coined the word Scanners. Kidder is a perfect example of someone who, like Harry, is happiest when he can bury himself in one subject and one environment for a number of years. When he understands it to his satisfaction, he writes a book about it. Every book is about a completely different world. His first book, *The Soul of a New Machine*, is about the development of the first home computer. In his second book, *House*, about the design and construction of a private home, he spent almost every day for over 4 years with a family, their architect, and their builders, capturing a world no one had written about before. "I was like a fly on the wall," he said at a book reading. "The builders said they wished I'd wear a bell so they'd know when I was overhearing their discussions."

Kidder went on to write many books, and every one took him inside an entirely new and different environment. Yet he had one career only, and every book he writes builds that career. Every world he visits is new, but he never has to start his career from the bottom.

A writer or a journalist can have the same kind of career Tracy Kidder does, because, like consulting, writing is a perfect skill for an Umbrella Career. And Umbrella Careers are perfect for Serial Specialists.

Do you have any skills that could turn into Umbrella Careers?

Have your Scanner Daybook and a pen or pencil nearby in case the following list reminds you of a skill you have that could lead to an Umbrella Career. (Ask your friends and family if they can come up with something you can add to the list.) Here are some ideas to get you started.

Writer: You can spend years on one subject, write your book, and move to another.

Teacher: You can pick a field that broadly covers many of the areas you're

interested in—sociology, popular culture, economics, comparative literature—
and be paid to study everything in that field that appeals to you. You might also
be able to travel to other countries as a guest teacher.

Historian: Since everything has a history—businesses, dog breeding, families, and fashion—you can be hired to write histories of widely different worlds.

Public speaker: Most organizations need speakers on many different topics, so you can wear many hats as a public speaker and market yourself in all the
fields that interest you. Incidentally, you can record all your speeches and turn
them into books or booklets, reports, teleclasses, newsletters—whatever you
choose.

Troubleshooter: Although that's not a job title, you can take any job and
turn it into a troubleshooter position by volunteering to solve problems all
through the system. Pick someplace that interests you, like a zoo or the main
office of a chain of language schools, and you'll have fun and build a reputation, too.

Information broker: This is a fancy name for anyone who is asked to find
something out for somebody. If you work freelance and your clients are corporations or writers or small businesses or television shows, you can make money
and have a lot of variety, too. Scanner definition of variety: fun.

Journalist: This is a writer, of course, but one who moves between projects
faster than Tracy Kidder. If you're a Serial Specialist who doesn't want to stay
on one subject longer than a few months, you might prefer this Umbrella
Career.

Researcher: A variety of information broker, but you might also work in
one company instead of being self-employed and working with many.

Librarian: You'll be called on to provide answers to questions, and you'll
probably be paid less than many of the professions above, but library work has
the potential to become a "portable job" that allows you to take relatively long-
term positions anywhere in the world.

Personal assistant: If you work for a family that has art collections, phi-
lanthropies, and parties for influential people in many fields, you'll have one
group of experiences, and if you work for an actor or a professional athlete or
the family of a university professor, you'll have a wide variety of very different
experiences.

Foundation officer: If you have the job of reviewing grant requests in a
large philanthropy, you'll get to know about hundreds of wildly different programs every year, while keeping this one job title.

Business owner: Such as the owner of an adult education school who brings in teachers and offers evening classes in every subject under the sun. Or the owner of a company that reviews and advises public television stations which documentaries to put on the air.

Consultant: Which means that you leave behind all the parts of your present career that bore you and help other businesses with the parts you find most interesting.

Documentary film producer: You can start this as a hobby, but if you have a flair for it, your hobby can turn into a profession that is endlessly changing and new. You don't always have to compete in the small field that airs documentaries on television. If you're imaginative, you'll find yourself with as many opportunities to get paid for documentaries as the historian at the top of this list.

How do you turn your present profession into an Umbrella job?

I once met a woman who had a business degree and a high-paying job but was so bored with the repetitive work and the corporate world that she decided to quit and travel the world until her savings were gone. After that, she didn't know what she'd do.

She had already given notice when a friend told her of an opening with a documentary production house that needed a permanent employee to handle their budget department—and the employee had to be free to travel overseas. That was 6 years ago. Here's what she told me.

> *The process of producing documentaries is amazing. I never thought I'd stick in one career for so long, but each project is like getting a college degree in a totally different subject (and your parents don't get mad at you for changing majors!). I've been immersed in science, sports, politics, cultures, and nature, and I've met the most remarkable people you can think of. I've become an avid reader of history and an amateur photographer, too. I spent almost a year in Africa and Egypt, and it was just incredible.*

What if you're not a writer but wish you could create a book for each of your serial specialties? You can gather the information and the insights and hire someone else to write your book for you. There are lots of writers looking for specialists to work with. Some call themselves ghostwriters. You can find their ads in writers' magazines. On the other hand, if you love writing but can't or don't want to give up your present lifestyle to move into a different world, you can become one of those writers yourself!

Harry thought that was an intriguing idea: "I keep wanting people to know about the different worlds of work, from the inside. What I've learned is so fascinating, not anything like you'd expect." He hadn't considered being a speaker, but he was a teacher. "We're all hams," he smiled. "We love those captive audiences. I think every teacher can be a speaker." So we may be hearing from Harry one of these days.

The NEVER-ENDING RÉSUMÉ

Many Scanners complain that they have too many things on their résumés and it makes them look bad to an employer. But if you keep a private copy of your Never-Ending Résumé updated with every skill you acquire, you have a very useful tool.

You won't send it to a potential employer, at least not the whole thing, but you'll have your comprehensive list of skills and experiences in front of you at all times and can pick and choose what you like from it.

But the reason I suggest keeping one list with all your experiences is that this list will make you very aware of *anything* that can be translated into an Umbrella Career.

You may find that you're very good with people, even in locations where you don't speak their language. Or that people like your cooking more than you expected. Or that you're a good driver. Whatever you find, add it to the list. As you go through each Serial Specialty, pay attention. You might find niches and create careers in places no one ever thought of. Some people actually never have a job where they aren't thinking, "When I leave, could I come back as a consultant? Doing what?"

As a Serial Specialist, you'll accumulate knowledge in more fields every year, and you can use the skills and experiences from each of them to create a wide variety of consulting services—one in radio and another for public art installations, one for pediatricians and another for veterinarians.

I predict you'll have a glorious future.

HOW SERIAL SPECIALISTS DO EVERYTHING THEY LOVE

Life Design Model for Serial Specialists

The Walter Mitty Model

Careers for Serial Specialists

Umbrella Careers such as the following:

- ❖ Writer
- ❖ Teacher
- ❖ Historian
- ❖ Public speaker
- ❖ Troubleshooter
- ❖ Information broker
- ❖ Journalist
- ❖ Researcher
- ❖ Librarian
- ❖ Personal assistant
- ❖ Foundation officer
- ❖ Your own business
- ❖ Consultant
- ❖ Business skills

From Your Scanner Tool Kit

Scanner Daybook
The Never-Ending Résumé
Web E-Mail Account
Letters from the Field

A great tool for Serial Specialists

The one thing you should start doing today is to keep logs (and photos) of your experiences, even before you're sure what you can use them for. When you find the career that can use them all, you'll want them at hand.

But if you're like me, you can get lazy about writing, so let me suggest something that will make you keep records of your experiences in a painless way: Write letters to your friends from wherever you are. For this, I recommend a good Scanner tool:

A WEB E-MAIL ACCOUNT. This is one of the few tools for Scanners that is best done via computer, on the Internet. If you have a Web e-mail service (rather than one you can only open on your home computer), you can write letters to your friends or yourself from any Internet-enabled computer in the world.

Taking notes can be tedious, but writing about your adventures to a responsive friend might be the best conceivable way to record what you've done. Why? Because when you write a letter, you're not thinking of your English teacher; you're thinking of your reader. Almost everyone is a good writer in a letter. The language is immediate and unself-conscious, and you always have the patience to include the details. If you can find a friend who is responsive and appreciative—even better, one who is curious and asks lots of questions—you can almost painlessly gather together all the records you'll ever need. And one of these days, you'll find that Umbrella skill and you'll be very glad you've got those LETTERS FROM THE FIELD, lively, detailed records of your travels.

These are some of the ways to be the Serial Specialist you long to be and still look to all the world like a person with one profession and a steady salary. I bet you'll soon think of even more.

And now we meet another Serial Scanner, one with a distinctly different focus. This Scanner doesn't choose her subjects so she can visit different environments; she chooses them because she wants to master them.

Chapter 15

ARE YOU
A SERIAL MASTER?

I just won my third equestrian show jumping meet last month, and now I'm ready to look for something else. My teacher is disappointed, and my family thinks I'm crazy.

When I'm excelling at something, I'm on top of the world. But at some point I want to try something new. The problem is, I often don't know what that will be. That's when I feel lost.

I have done things (quite well, I might add) from performing taiko drumming to trading stocks, etc. I moved on when I found enough satisfaction of mastery, according to my own standard. It seems this should have value somewhere in the real world, but these personal triumphs don't add up to anything. I'll never find a career that works for me.

Are you a Serial Master?

❖ Do you love taking on a learning challenge? Do you look forward to the struggle against your own limits?

❖ Is it exhilarating to move from ignorance to competence and to realize you've done well because of your own efforts?

❖ Do you have less and less available time because you dislike leaving any hard-learned skill behind but continue taking on new ones?

◈ Have you ever wished you could clone yourself so you could keep learning new things?
◈ Do you get satisfaction from showing people how to do better? Do you wish you could change their view of their own limits?
◈ Do you enjoy being in the spotlight, giving demonstrations, getting respect and perhaps applause?

If you said yes to most of these questions, you are a Serial Master.

It's odd to put those two words together—Serial and Master—because, even more than "Serial Specialist," they seem to contradict each other. But the title fits you. Unlike a typical Scanner, you love to stick with things until you master them, but just like all Scanners, once you've gotten what you wanted, you get interested in something new.

For Serial Scanners, interests come and go, but the love of mastery always stays. You might take up sports or martial arts, but you also love the challenge of learning a musical instrument or a new language, even fitting into a foreign culture until you're almost a native—anything in which you can start from near-zero competence and work your way up to the very best you're capable of.

But you're a Scanner, there's no question about it. Because once you've achieved your best, you go looking for a new project. You love the conquest, but you love the process of becoming a master even more. The kind of learning you undertake is always difficult, but it's pure joy to you.

Tanya's story

Tanya runs her own martial arts school. She took it over when her teacher, a widely respected master, retired and moved to Japan. Being chosen to run the school was a great honor, but Tanya has mixed feelings about it: "If my teacher knew that I wanted to master other disciplines instead of devoting each day to perfecting karate, I know he'd be profoundly disappointed in me. I sometimes have dreams about it."

She never shared her feelings with her teacher, but she's known about them ever since she was a child. "I love finding a challenge that interests me and throwing myself into it," she told me. "I'm into mastering something, doing it until I'm as good as I can get. I got my black belt in Hop Ki Do last year, and I felt like a million bucks. I still love martial arts and don't ever want to give them up, but I've reached my limits. Believe me, I know that unmistakable feeling of 'I'm here, I did it.'"

What motivates a Serial Master?

Jerry, a graphic artist by trade, sent me this quote from Anaïs Nin, and it pretty much sums up the way most Serial Masters feel.

> It takes courage to push yourself to places that you have never been before . . . to test your limits . . . to break through barriers.

"That's what gets me out of bed in the morning," Jerry said. "I thought everyone felt that way or if they didn't, there was something wrong with them!" What excites Jerry is excellence.

Jerry: *I was more competitive when I was younger, and I always tested myself against others. Now that I'm older, I test myself against my own limits. Reaching them is gratifying, exhilarating.*

These days, I've started jumping into fields that have nothing to do with athletics. Last year, I was determined to play the clarinet! It was tough, the same feelings exactly of starting in a new sport or martial art, the feeling of ineptness, the stubbornness, the first sign that this might be learnable. I stayed with it until I was as good as I was going to get, enjoyed every minute of it, but after that I didn't do it very often.

Jezicka: *I set myself the challenge of learning the Czech language because I was impressed with a professor who was head of my local amnesty group and he advised it. I signed up and then discovered it was a course for graduate students in Slavic linguistics and that the course was actually being taught by someone else. Like most Americans, my knowledge of English grammar was rudimentary, and suddenly I was being told to memorize all seven case endings for masculine, feminine, and neuter nouns and for adjectives by the end of the week. I was in way over my head. But I just decided I was going to do it, and I ended up being quite fluent in Czech.*

When I finally went to Prague, I got involved with a small brewery and took on the challenge of learning how to make beer. I felt the same way, and I'm actually listed in an encyclopedia of beer as an expert on Czech beer!

My interviews show me something very interesting that I haven't seen before. People who try to master one field—tennis players or bridge players or poets, for example—say they have more in common with people who seek mastery in different fields than they have with casual hobbyists in their own. Those who love mastery understand each other perfectly, but they don't understand a casual or halfhearted effort. They agree on what's important: excellence, giving their very best.

For the most part, however, if you're someone who loves mastery for its own sake, you're at odds with your "practical" peers:

"What are you going to do with Czech?"

"You won an award in beer making! That's great! Get some financing and you can start your own brewery!"

But the Serial Master has already gotten the Reward she wanted and has moved on to other challenges.

The Repertoire Life Design Model

A Serial Master should never feel she's wasted the effort put into anything she learns, even if she doesn't continue to use it on a regular basis, because, like many Scanners, she's a collector. She collects knowledge of herself, of course, and knowledge of the detailed process of learning anything new. But Serial Masters also collect actual skills—languages, martial arts, even mountain climbing! And every one of these acquired skills increases her professional value, just as a musician increases his professional value by adding one piece of music after another to his repertoire.

Where will you perform this repertoire? Will you teach clarinet or lace making? You probably won't, although it will be fun to step forward on those occasions when someone asks a question no one but you can answer. But you don't want to teach any one thing over and over any more than you want to learn the same thing over and over. And, as you'll see in a moment, you can use every skill in your repertoire to create a fulfilling career—one that will support your love of mastery for its own sake.

Every Scanner should give mastery a try

We could all learn from Serial Masters, whether we care about challenging ourselves or not. As Serial Masters know, exercising your ability to do anything well—understanding math, listening to music, dancing to a swing band, or learning to juggle—might be as good for your overall health as pure physical exercise.

If you're not a Serial Master, it's not in your nature to enjoy mastering something just for its own sake. But every Scanner should try it just for exercise. It's good for you to learn how to spin a yo-yo or play a harmonica. It gives you a taste of the kind of stubborn tenacity you might need sometime in the future.

If you don't have much free time to undertake a stint with mastery (because you have so many other interests you care about more), just bring it into any quality time you want to spend with your kids or your nieces and nephews. Let them teach you how to become a very good yo-yo spinner; let them push you until you get it. Kids know quite a bit about mastering things and can teach you a lot.

What if they don't want to teach you how to use a yo-yo (or whatever else they know)? Pay them. Kids always need money, and you'll take it more seriously that way. Anyway, all teachers deserve to be paid.

If you *are* a Serial Master, however, you have a problem most other Scanners don't.

Once you've reached the limits of mastery that satisfy you and you're ready to move on, you are frequently stuck with nothing to do. While most Scanners see fascinating new projects beckoning to them from all sides, Serial Masters do not. They have a hard time finding another challenge. And they find that empty-handed feeling extremely uncomfortable.

Waiting to fall in love again

Mel: *I am now very much into weight training in the gym. I have been doing it consistently for 2 months now, and I can see results! I've considered becoming a fitness trainer, but I know I won't stick with it. I have this dread that when I'm finished, I won't be able to figure out what's next.*

Taylor: *It's such an empty feeling to be finished with something and not know what the next thing is. But I never know what's going to be exciting until I bump into it.*

Nancy: *When I master something, it seems to pave the way for more mastery (if I can hang glide, I can do anything!), but the next opportunity has not yet arrived, unfortunately, or has not been recognized.*

Part of the reason that Serial Masters despair during a hiatus is that they can't see any connection between the things they love, so they don't know where to look next. They often say that they have to "stumble onto" a new interest, "bump into" something, wait for the next opportunity to "arrive." I've often wondered why such focused and determined people wouldn't search more actively for something that's so important to them. It's as if they don't understand what the underlying magnetism is.

If you haven't already tried to analyze what draws you to one challenge or another, perhaps the following questions will help you. They have helped a number of my Serial Master clients to find their next interests.

❖ Describe the moment you first realized you were drawn to each of your earlier interests.
❖ Do you see anything these moments had in common?
❖ Was there anything you recognize as essential in all of them?
❖ Can you list areas you know you are definitely *not* interested in taking up?
❖ Do they have anything in common?

Give those questions a try and take some time to think about your answers. You might get some good insights that will point you directly to your next challenge.

But this kind of deliberate search isn't always helpful for Scanners, and they often report making mistakes when they try it. Some of them report they've established in advance what should be their next "ideal challenge" and sought it out, only to find it uninteresting.

"I looked at everything I had cared about before and was sure I'd love to learn ballroom dancing," Gayle said, "but it didn't do a thing for me. I felt like I was on a date my mom had arranged. No chemistry."

Gayle had put her finger on what every Serial Master's experience most resembles: finding the person you can fall in love with. Everyone knows the feeling, but nobody knows how to predict when it will happen. It's there or it's not. And so far, no one has figured out why.

That's why it's virtually impossible to plan ahead for the next perfect challenge. You, like most Serial Specialists, may have to put in your waiting time.

The only advice I can give you is the same I'd give someone who wants to fall in love: Get out into the action, visit lots of different places, and maximize your chances of encountering the person or challenge that you're looking for. I wish I could help you more.

But I do have a great idea for something that you can do while you wait.

Start working on your fabulous career

What fabulous career?

> **Michele:** *For such hard-working people, we Serial Masters seem to be the hardest to employ. Who's going to hire someone like us? As soon as we get really good at what we do, we're on our way out the door!*

Tanya, like many Serial Specialists, can't imagine what she'll do for a career if she leaves her school. "In martial arts, if you don't become a master in one specialized field and stick with it, you can't attract students. You don't have any way to earn a living. It's back to the typing pool."

In fact, there are a number of satisfying and lucrative careers that are just right for this kind of Scanner. One of my clients, a true Serial Master, became an agent for all the best teachers he had found in the fields he had mastered (yoga, tai chi, and meditation), and now he places his ex-teachers in the best spas in the country.

Another Serial Master works as a career and life coach for retired professional athletes, and though she has never been an athlete, she's very successful because she understands athletes very well.

Some Serial Masters simply change careers on their own.

> **Sarah:** *My father's best friend, John Gall, attended St. John's College, but only for long enough to get the curriculum of books—then he went off by himself for 3 years and studied them. He actually graduated from Yale. Then he got an MD and was certified in pediatrics. Then he went to Egypt with an expedition that x-rayed mummies—but what he actually did was to collect fingerprints from local people. (I'm not clear what this was for—something about genetics studies, I think . . .) Then he wrote a book called* General Systemantics—*which is now called* The Systems Bible *and still sells quite*

well. Then he and his first wife studied psychotherapy and started a private practice that concentrated on psychology and children. Then he wrote a novel on Queen Hatshepsut. And now, he says, he's just finished an autobiographical novel focused on his father, a powerful, conservative Washington lawyer. Fascinating fellow!

The most transferable skill Serial Masters have is their experience with excellence. Serial Masters are natural leaders who understand how to make people want to succeed. They're experts in pushing personal limits past anything a person thought he was capable of. They understand the actual machinery of striving for excellence inside and out, like a good mechanic understands an engine.

That means you could be a first-rate athletic coach or school teacher, but you might find that those professions would use too much of your time. While you need to earn a living and to have impact and be respected, your happiness and emotional health requires that you take on new challenges.

That's why I think the best-fitting, most lucrative, and least time-consuming career in the world for a Serial Master—the one that uses your amazing passion for personal excellence but still leaves you time to continue mastering new challenges—is being a motivational speaker.

Serial Specialists make first-rate gurus

Recently, I returned from making a presentation at a women's luncheon in Rochester, which was sponsored by the local hospital. It was fun, the women were delighted with having a speaker, it paid well, and I flew in and out on the same day. On the way to the airport, the booking agent who had brought me in told me some stories about the famous athletes she often got to speak at her events, and I wondered aloud what they would have to tell women?

"They've always conquered some personal challenges. It's very motivational, and everyone likes to be motivated," she said. I realized she was right. And no one in the world could motivate people like a Serial Master.

So I set up a program to help the Serial Masters I was working with take the first steps toward becoming motivational speakers. If you're interested in this subject, you might want to write down these steps and your responses in your Scanner Daybook.

Step 1: If you've ever taught any of the things you've studied, you've found that your students haven't always had your drive. What did you want them to understand that might change that?

Could you tell a story about how you messed up, and what was going on in your mind, and how you managed to hang in anyway? Or (and) how good every step started to feel?

Practice describing details like that by writing them down, and next time you're working on a new challenge, you might want to carry a recording device to talk into so you can catch the subtle things you feel when you're on the path to mastering something.

Step 2: Find a low-risk way to practice telling your story to a small group of people. If you know a high school coach, ask if she'd like you to talk to her students about how you learned what you did. If you're in the martial arts, like Tanya, the kids might actually listen. If your area of mastery is language or art or just learning how to achieve excellence (and what made that happen), anything you say on any subject is perfect for a high school.

In any case, you still have to keep their attention, and if you care about your message, you'll find a natural comedian or a great storyteller within you to do the job. Nothing trains you like a live audience. If you give your talk once, you won't learn much. If you give it 10 times, you'll learn everything you need to know about holding an audience.

Step 3: Start talking in front of larger groups, still for practice and for free. I'd avoid fun single groups or anything that's all about lighthearted party time. With a subject like excellence, you can try to find where you're really needed, like the parents of handicapped kids or the spouses from foreign countries who have to learn new ways of doing everything from language to driving. And of course, you can speak in front of conferences for schoolteachers themselves (so they can pass it on).

Step 4: Head over to Toastmasters International, an organization with branches in hundreds of locations, where you can practice making your talk short and punchy.

Step 5: Whenever you feel ready to start earning money as a speaker, contact the National Speakers Association and begin to learn the business side of this profession.

You'll make a great speaker if you're a Serial Master, even if you're not an extrovert. Why? You'll want to master this skill like any other, of course, but

HOW SERIAL MASTERS
DO EVERYTHING THEY LOVE

Life Design Model for Serial Masters

The Repertoire Model

Careers for Serial Masters

Talent agent
Career/life coach
Athletic coach
Teacher
Motivational speaker

From Your Scanner Tool Kit

Scanner Daybook

the major reasons you'll be good are, first, that you know what you're talking about, and second, you sincerely want people to hear it.

You know better than anyone, from personal experience, that doing things with excellence as your goal is more exciting and creative—even easier—than being half hearted and giving less than all you've got. And you know that if you could make people understand this, it would change their lives.

That gives you the drive and clarity of a great motivational speaker.

Eventually, you can build a lucrative career lecturing at corporations, at sales conferences, at teachers' conferences, even at fitness or fashion conferences about why undertaking a new challenge every few years is the best thing you can do to keep your mind sharp, your self-esteem high, and your fighting weight stable. (That's just a thought, but I bet it would work!)

Now it's time to meet the well-known Jack-of-All-Trades. He's a Scanner with a very different viewpoint from a Serial Master's, but you'll learn something essential from him.

Chapter 16

ARE YOU
A JACK-OF-ALL-TRADES?

I am good at a lot and great at nothing. I can't believe I'll ever find my passion.

I'm always hoping that the next thing I try will be the one: the one thing I shine at, my calling, my brilliant career.

Are you a Jack-of-All-Trades?

❖ Do you have more certificates and degrees than most people—all in different disciplines?
❖ Are you good at just about everything you try?
❖ Have you ever thought your problem would be solved if you were good at only one thing?
❖ Do bosses and teachers try to keep you on board?
❖ Do you notice that other people are passionate about things you merely like?
❖ Would you rather learn how to plant a garden, work with friends to paint a house, or just have a great day with your family than any job you can think of?

If you said yes to most of those questions, you're a Jack-of-All-Trades, and chances are it's caused you some discomfort until now.

That's because no one, including you, has ever tried to figure out why you always move from trade to trade and never become a master. You only know that you enjoy learning for its own sake, and because many things come very easily to you, you sometimes underestimate their value (after all, "important" things have to be hard, don't they?).

It also feels like every door is open, and the number of choices can be bewildering.

You don't fear hard work; in fact, you take real pride in doing a good job and enjoy being seen as capable and reliable. You're social and friendly, and you like being helpful to others. Because you're typically conscientious and easygoing, employers, teachers, and colleagues often try to recruit you to sign up on a permanent basis.

But you're still looking for your great passion and have often complained that being good at almost everything isn't the same as being great at one thing. You wish you were passionate about something so you could finally pick a career.

However, you might be looking in the wrong place because, in fact, Jacks can be *very* passionate. It's just that they're rarely passionate about a career.

Looking for love in all the wrong places

Phil keeps trying. Each time he signs up for a course of study or steps into a new job, he's determined to make a permanent commitment because he wants to stop searching and settle down with one career and one lifestyle. At first, everything looks wonderful. He can see himself being happy and working with people he'll like. But after a short time, he sees that something about the situation won't fill the bill, and he starts planning his getaway.

Phil tried business school and did well in all his classes, but he realized that he didn't share his classmates' interest in getting rich or making VP, so after a few semesters he left. He considered becoming a scuba-diving instructor because he loves the sea, is a natural swimmer, and loves sea animals. He thought he had it right that time, so he went to the Bahamas and started his training. The instructor noticed right away that he had the temperament and physical ability to dive professionally, and told him so. For 1 month Phil learned rapidly, but a familiar feeling was creeping into his heart.

"I didn't like it as much as I expected," he told me. "Not as a way of life. And this was very disappointing. I knew my search wasn't over."

Because Phil has a natural ability with languages, he lived overseas for a number of years. "I taught English in Japan right out of college," he said, "and liked a lot of things about it. I'd take the students out of the classroom and we'd go on field trips, or I'd teach them to sing Bob Dylan songs. The head of the school asked me to open and run an additional school, but that same feeling crept up on me: Is this it? Is this what I really want?"

Photographer, tour guide, importer-exporter—one after another, Phil tried different fields, but they all came up the same.

"All my friends have settled down into careers and I'm the only one still floating. I just don't know what's the matter with me."

He's not alone.

Martha: *I am now 51 years old and never, ever have found that one burning passion in life that others seem to find. It was frustrating to me to see friends and colleagues catch fire and dedicate themselves totally to their goal. Meanwhile, I kicked around for almost 20 years in the family business, got a degree in psychology, tried social work for a while. Quit that, got a degree in computer science. Have worked in that for 15 years. Now getting ready to quit and get my teaching degree, so I can teach math in high school/junior college. I have always been very successful at what I do, but I get really bored and disenchanted after a while.*

I have actually liked my choices and like a lot of the hobbies I do (golf, reading, bodybuilding, geology, travel), but none of them is an overriding passion, and I get bored if I delve too long or don't look into new things.

A drawback that I have seen with this lifestyle is that you have to "start at the bottom" numerous times in your life.

Deborah: *I really like learning "how," understanding the language of a new field—but once I do, the desire to bury myself in that field is gone. I'm coming to the conclusion that I may never "bury" myself in any field at all.*

It looks like a dead end, doesn't it? How can you overcome the inevitable disenchantment? Jacks have so much talent, but that's not all they have—they are the ones who show up and deliver. They do the job. With all these qualities, they should be hugely successful in business or the arts or some profession. But they rarely are. Why?

Because "fields" and "professions" aren't what matter to Jacks at all. They aren't really looking for the right career, although they sincerely believe they are. In fact, a Jack is satisfied with any pleasant job if the pay, the hours, and the co-workers are decent. He can even tolerate detail work, which others might not. That's because a Jack-of-All-Trades cares primarily about his surroundings, including the people he works with. It's not winning that matters, either. In fact, Jacks don't care much about success at all. They just want to be happy. Lionel is a good example.

> *When I think about why I tried one thing and then another, it was never primarily ambition. When I went to get the computer science certificate, I thought, "This will not only give me a lucrative job, but I'll be around smart people like my high school friends. I'll see how far my brain can go and just have a great time." Turned out not to be the case (for me), so I kept on looking.*

How Phil found his career

One day Phil took a low-paying proofreading job at a small advertising agency. He did such a good job at catching and fixing editing mistakes that he was soon promoted to editor. One day he was walking through the office and was called over to help brainstorm slogans for an ad, something he often did on his own for fun. He did such a good job that he was called in to every session and was soon promoted to copywriter.

When he saw some proofreading come back that he'd already done, Phil created a system to cut out the duplication of effort that existed in the proof-reading process. He also wrote a procedure manual for one of the computer systems as he was learning it.

Since he spoke a number of languages, he was often put on the phone with foreign clients and dealt with them so successfully he was asked to take over the job of entertaining them when they came to town. Because Phil loved night-clubs and music and joking with friends, he was always a big hit with the foreign clients and knew all the best restaurants and most interesting sightseeing. (He found a museum of shoes for one client's daughters!)

He was given three salary raises in his first year.

"How would you like to be the general manager of this place?" the boss asked him.

"Not at all," he answered, to the boss's surprise.

"Well, what do you want?"

"I like things the way they are," Phil said. "This is a friendly place and everything is interesting. You let me do lots of different things. I have no complaints."

In our interview, he told me, "I liked stepping in and saving the day. I've done so many things, I usually know how to solve odd problems. I guess that's my most marketable skill."

Phil is right about that. If there were a job title called Most Valuable Player on the Team, he'd have all the qualifications. Almost without exception, this type of Scanner is gifted at something you don't find on career lists: Catching the ball in a team situation. Bailing out the other players. Saving the day.

Hilary, another Jack-of-All-Trades, was very happy to find this out. She wrote:

> Until you told me I was a "rescuer," I had no idea what pattern or theme ran through anything I did. And even then, I'd have assumed that meant I should be a psychotherapist or a doctor, but I wouldn't like studying for those fields; too isolating. I like stepping in and solving problems, seeing smiles, and hanging out with the people.

Mark, another Jack-type Scanner, agreed: "If I'd been the type, I probably would have been a wastrel, a fraternity boy airhead in beer-guzzling contests. I know I'm not stupid, but I'd rather not be a serious type. 'Fix the problem and then let's play.' That's my motto."

If you're a Jack-of-All-Trades, keep in mind that there's nothing missing from your résumé—you've just been looking in the wrong place or, rather, applying the wrong criteria to your abilities. It's not a title or a huge salary you want: More than almost any other Scanner type, what matters to you is happiness. If you make that your main objective, success will come quicker than you think.

What about that passion you were looking for?

Are Jacks doomed to never have passion? Not at all. You might be very close to finding it. You just have to stop looking for it in any special occupation. As much as you may enjoy training for a career, your passion is probably waiting somewhere else.

Phil found his somewhere he hadn't even been looking: He and his wife had a baby, and he realized that he was born to be a father. He used the Internet to find editing and proofreading work and gave up all work that took him away from the house, so he could stay home with his little boy. "I want to be here so I can play with him and watch him grow up," he said.

He loves to cook and often has friends over to dinner. When the baby was born, Phil picked up the guitar after a long hiatus and started playing tunes for him, which gave them both a lot of pleasure. Jake, one of the friends who often came to dinner with his two children, heard Phil play and persuaded him to join his band. Now Phil is performing and writing songs.

Jake is another amiable Jack-of-All-Trades who knows how to do just about everything Phil doesn't, and they spend many happy hours recording their songs, creating graphics for the covers and their Web site (Jake does the graphics, Phil writes the copy), and visiting clubs and restaurants to drum up gigs.

"The kids always come with us," Phil smiled. "I'm sure they get us business, just because they're so cute.

"This was completely unexpected," he said. "I searched for years and couldn't find what I wanted. And then I discovered two passions in the same year: Now I'm a happy, singing daddy. My wife loves it!"

So what's the career solution for Jacks-of-All-Trades? Because they're a modern-day version of the Renaissance's Universal Man—the courtly fellow who dueled and danced equally well—they won't fit into any defined profession. They'll always enjoy learning new skills, being involved in team projects. So where should they look for work? The answer is: anywhere they like.

Your career can be anything at all

It doesn't matter what job you enter or at what level. Like Phil, you'll probably be promoted when they see what you can do. If you don't have the needed skills, you'll learn them fast, because you know how to learn. It's one of those metaskills you've picked up in your travels. And as long as the people treat you and each other reasonably well, you'll be contented. If things get unpleasant, you'll probably leave, but in most cases, you won't have much trouble finding another job. Everybody needs someone like you, and you'll always enjoy being the capable one, the go-to guy, the helper.

But that doesn't mean you can't continue to explore new fields if that's fun for you. Just don't sign up and start writing checks. If you happen to see a career or a business or some certificate program that looks interesting, find a way to try it out without committing too much of your time or money. If nothing else comes of it, you'll have a chance to learn new things and make new friends.

Tryouts can be very simple and easy to do. This story by a Scanner will illustrate one of the many kinds of Career Tryout.

> *For one pre-Christmas season, I worked at a department store photo studio ("McPhoto" to me). I did it to see if I could be comfortable taking pix of people (as compared to my usual landscape photography). I thought I'd like taking pix of babies and kids, but it's such an unnatural environment for them that the photos were run-of-the-mill. But with one family, I worked surprisingly well. It was a woman who had just had a birthday, and I could see she was uncomfortable with getting older. She came with her two teenagers, who were barely speaking to each other. I had them laughing and teasing each other in no time. And I got better photos than I'd ever gotten of people before. Guess it goes to show we really need to get out there to try stuff and stop researching things to death!*

Often the best way for a Jack to try out careers is to take a contract job. While most Scanners take contract work in one field—their main motivation being to have free time to do what they really love—Jacks can sign up for a project because they enjoy doing different kinds of work and picking up new knowledge.

"It's the best thing in the world if you can get hired to work on a project basis. You meet new people, learn how to do interesting things, and when you leave, no one ever gives you a hard time," one client told me.

What about your passion?

Keep shopping; you'll find it. But it will probably never be connected to a career, a school, or a certificate, not even status or money. It will almost always be connected with good friends, a good home and family life, and some intense interest, like gardening, small business, sailing, or a band like Phil's.

Think about it. What would a good life look like to you? Forget the status symbols and titles that mattered to your friends and see what you really need to make you happy. Think back to the good times in your life and see if you can isolate the elements that mattered most to you. They count more than anything else, especially to a Scanner like you who wants nothing more than to rack up one happy day after another. If you keep these elements in mind, you'll know what you're looking for and can work toward getting them into your life now.

Your Life Design Models

The best Life Design Model for a Jack-of-All-Trades is the MVP (Most Valuable Player) Model.

This is a great career model for you because it means you can change interests and jobs when you choose, without any of the usual stress about finding the "right" career. When you live by the MVP Life Design Model, you never again will feel that any past choice has been a mistake or that there's anything wrong with leaving to find something new, because every new thing you do adds to your skills and your value. The knowledge you gain will be needed by the people around you sooner or later, and you'll be glad to share it.

But above and beyond work, Jacks are happiest with an additional Life Design Model.

The Good Life Model

Jacks have many talents, but they have to admit that their greatest talent is knowing how to live a good life. That's why the Good Life Model is best for most Jacks-of-All-Trades. It means that whatever comes Jack's way, the first question won't have to be, "Will this lead to success?" From now on, he only has to ask, "Will this make me happy?" More consciously than any other type of Scanner, having good days with good people is what Jack really wants, and if he sets up the Good Life as his operating model, he won't forget that.

Tools for Jacks-of-All-Trades

When it comes to organizing your space, you tend to be the Scanner with the smallest clutter problem. You often don't need to work with a calendar, either! You don't manufacture ideas at a high speed, and you tend to put the ones that interest you into action: If you think building a shed would be a great idea, you'll do it. This makes the Scanner Daybook less urgent for you than for Scanners who fear they'll lose their best ideas.

But, like all other Scanners, you start a lot of things—in your case, you'll have artifacts from one career or another—so you will need a way to wrap up your projects and create a visual place to show what you've done on your travels through life. Depending on what kinds of things we're talking about, you'll want the Scanner's Finish and some version of the Life's Work Bookshelf.

How about a collage of all your certificates in a large, framed picture to show off what you've learned? Add photographs of the things you've done and the places you've been, to remind yourself that you're not just a helpful person who's good at a lot of things—you're a highly accomplished person in your own right.

And leave plenty of space for the untried "trades" you're going to learn in the future, because your exploring isn't over. Talent always wants something new to learn.

Chapter 17

ARE YOU A WANDERER?

Every week I get inspired to do something. Some project, some way to be the new me!!! I'm completely committed to it for a week or two, then I lose interest and find yet another, really cool thing to be obsessed about. I seem to wander from one area to another, randomly. What will I ever do with my life?

If only I could use all the things I learned in my exploring instead of wasting them. Is that ever a possibility?

Are you a Wanderer?

- Have you always gotten interested in unrelated activities for no apparent reason?
- Are you intrigued by things that people around you find boring?
- Do you like trying on new jobs and lifestyles?
- Do you love adventure and new experiences: people, places, sensations?
- Do you lack a sense of direction in your life and see only the next move?
- Do you wish you had a map and a destination?

The Wanderer is a great lover of random experience and allows herself to move toward whatever looks attractive and give it a try. Unlike the Jack-of-All-Trades, she doesn't have a plan and doesn't want one. Wanderers are never at an event for a specific purpose. They only know it's fascinating.

The Wanderer keeps an open mind and isn't confused by labels. If you're a Wanderer, you've never had the same concerns of many people who struggle to understand how they can use their interests to create professions for themselves. You've never asked yourself questions like: What do you call someone who likes animals, or someone who explains things well, or someone who's a good organizer? Is this a career? Is that a hobby? What do you call a person who just likes to talk to people? Is that a therapist? Are such skills even remotely relevant to any job search?

As a Wanderer, you never have these thoughts; you appreciate experience for its own sake. As a result, you can see opportunities where others see nothing.

But Wanderers do need to find an underlying theme for their seemingly random interests, or eventually they become concerned.

Gary's story

I was interested in so many things it was ridiculous. I looked into anthropology and truck driving and art history and found them all equally fascinating. I really enjoyed working in my dad's lunch truck in factory parking lots (he was delighted but thought I was crazy) and always wanted to know what it was like inside the building. Career testing suggested I be a sociologist, but there was something so limiting about that idea. They also suggested getting a PhD in industrial psychology. The title depressed me.

One summer I worked at a resort as a golf caddy during an academic conference of some kind and managed to get some fascinating interviews with mathematicians—for no reason at all. I just wanted to know what made them like math. (They said no one had ever asked them that question before!) I didn't understand much of the math, but I understood how much they loved it. I was always asking people about what kind of work they did just because I was so curious.

But I could never explain what I was doing. I was always probing to see why people liked things that I didn't. I didn't actually want to be a biologist or a composer or a corporate employee or a welder. I just wanted to know what it felt like to be one. Once I got a glimpse of that, I was finished. But for all my interest in other people's work, I never found anything interesting enough to make my profession.

At 37, I was beginning to get uncomfortable when I was asked what I did for a living.

If you're like Gary, your meanderings can be incomprehensible to an out-sider (or even to you!), but there's much method in your madness, and if you know how to look for it, a theme will always reveal itself.

How will you ever find your true path?

You know what it feels like to be fascinated by this mystery or that one, but have you ever tried to identify what all your interests have in common? If you think they're not related in any way, you need to look more deeply. Wanderers who are looking for a career—or trying to justify their lack of one to uneasy families—need to begin a conscious search for the underlying theme that pulls them to all their interests. By keeping their eyes open for what they enjoy about anything that interests them (and keeping a record in their Scanner Daybook), they might find that at the heart of all their interests is a common theme. The most important question a Wanderer can ask during any activity that attracts him is this: *What element, if it were missing, would have made my exploration unin-teresting?*

Try it yourself. Flip back through the pages of your Scanner Daybook and ask yourself that question of everything you found exciting enough to write about. What was the essential part? What would have caused you to feel no excitement? It's not easy to find the answer, but I promise you, it's in there. Once you find it, you can continue to enjoy yourself as a Wanderer, but you'll also realize (often with startling clarity) exactly what you want to do with your life.

Here's what some Scanners found.

> **Maureen:** *My favorite things have a theme of paradox and unknowability or the individual in a new and strange environment of some kind, dealing with challenges. Also, I definitely need the sense of adventure and open-endedness in my interests. The thing that prevents me from sticking with something, I think, is that once something becomes routine or a known quan-tity, I have seen its limitations. For instance, I loved anthropology as a way to explain the world. Then I decided I found its limit and moved on.*

Do you see a theme? I think Maureen is interested in learning how to explain the world. She could become a popularizer, teaching what she found with anthropology, then moving on to another course of study. Her explorations could take her through literature and astronomy, religion and geology—a path that would make no sense to outsiders but make perfect sense to Maureen.

Janet: *Oh! Yes! That's what really got me interested in Eastern European literature—it was the absurdists! Odd juxtapositions and paradox—it just gets me quivering with excitement like a kid before Christmas!*

Could Janet write a book or a play, or could she teach absurdist literature in a college? Or could she perform an evening on the stage, in front of an audience, sitting and talking about the deliciousness of the odd juxtapositions and paradoxes she's found in her travels?

Meg: *I love uncharted places. Once I've charted them, I'm not interested anymore.*

Does that mean Meg is some kind of mapmaker—or the explorer who takes careful notes and sends her findings back to the mapmaker? What kinds of unknown areas draw her, and to what use could she put her careful notes and findings?

Eleanor, a 35-year-old client, was angry with herself for never sticking with any of her personal interests.

"I wish I had stuck with Spanish," she told me. "But I dropped out after a year because I was bored. That happened with so many things. A few years ago, I had this fascination for algebra. No other part of math, not geometry or numbers, just algebra. Then I developed the same fascination for Braille and then sign language for the deaf. But I didn't stick with any of that. Instead I got interested in the sign language of Native Americans. I thought I'd study anthropology, but suddenly I simply *had* to learn how to read music. Music! I'm not a musician! I don't know what's the matter with me. If I'd stuck with Spanish, I could have been somewhere by now."

"Where would you be?" I asked.

"Well, I'd be a teacher. Bilingual studies. Or I'd teach Spanish."

"Is that what you'd like to do?"

She sighed. "No, it isn't. It sounds boring," she admitted.

"Good thing you dropped out early," I smiled.

She wasn't amused. "But what am I supposed to do, work in an insurance company forever? My life is going nowhere."

"Maybe all those things you're interested in have something in common. Take a look at them. What interested you most about each of them?"

"I'm not sure. It's hard to put my finger on it. They seemed so exciting until I understood them, how they worked—whatever that means—and then I wanted to move on."

"Could you possibly be interested in code?" I asked on a hunch, and she sat forward, her eyes wide with interest. We had stumbled on something important. After a little more back and forth, it became clear that she was interested in linguistics. She remembered that ever since childhood she'd been fascinated with one or another aspect of linguistics but had never realized it.

"I read *The Man Who Listened to Horses* in high school, especially the part where he learns how horses communicate with each other. I read that over and over, and I was so excited I couldn't sleep!" At my urging, she signed up for a linguistics class at Barnard College in New York the next day.

Gary, who you met at the beginning of this chapter, had looked into more careers than anyone he'd ever met, but though they were all interesting, none of them led to a career. Eventually, he forced himself to become a social worker because he liked helping people, but the work was never as satisfying as he had hoped.

Then one day he sat in on a meeting the employment counselor was having with a group of her clients and, to his surprise, found he was able to help almost all of them identify *their* best careers.

Why? Because Gary knew about more kinds of work than anyone in the department. He'd done nothing but research careers most of his adult life! "I never realized that I was interested in *careers*. Not *a* career! Right in front of me, but I never saw it." Gary became a life coach and has never been happier.

Finding a common theme to your changing interests

If you're a Wanderer, there's a very good chance that you also have an underlying theme in all the things you do. If you can find what they have in common, you might be able to locate a career or avocation that all your interests had been pointing to, like Gary and Eleanor did.

Themes are not always obvious. If you've searched before by making a list of all the things you've been interested in and you still had trouble figuring out what on earth your interests have in common, try making an "Everything I Don't Want" list.

1. First, make the longest list you can of careers or avocations that do not interest you. Start with everything you rejected on your own and then add all the misguided suggestions that family members, friends, and acquaintances have made. Look through a newspaper or weekly newsmagazines to find more careers. If you feel ambitious, look on job sites on the Internet. Just be sure to keep occupations that look interesting *off* the list.

2. Now go down the list and, next to each entry, write a comment on why you don't want that occupation by noting what's missing. Rather than listing all the negative elements (like "too regimented" or "don't like the subject"), try to form statements around what you like that isn't there. For example, you might list "lacks freedom" or "has no interesting content" and any other good elements that aren't there.

3. When you're finished, read all your comments and see what patterns emerge.

Eleanor, who loved linguistics, would have found most of her rejected items lacking in unique world views or fresh ways of explaining what they do. Gary, who was interested in every career under the sun, might have crossed off only jobs he had already tried and written "nothing new to learn here." Their searches are particularly subtle, and you should find your themes much easier to find.

> **Cara:** *I always thought there was nothing I wasn't curious about, but once I started making my not-interested list, my viewpoint changed completely! That list of subjects I didn't care about got longer and longer. I wasn't interested in society or cars or engineering—it was amazing and oddly liberating.*
>
> *And when I was pretty much finished, all that was left were areas of creativity.*

Try it for yourself and see what all your wanderings show you about what you need to keep your energy high. You'll find all those Rewards we talked about in earlier chapters, the magnetic forces that pull you and keep your mind awake and healthy.

Jane: *I love being on the brink of discovery, not having any idea what's coming. Once I know the answer, the exciting part is over for me.*

Fernando: *What was missing in the list was something complex enough to require lots of learning, maybe the chance to come up with a new connection or something no one else has ever thought of before!*

Very useful discoveries. But how can they help a Wanderer decide what to do with his life?

What will a Wanderer do for a career?

Let's look at each of these answers one by one and see if they suggest any careers.

Cara, who saw that everything that interests her has to involve creativity, needed to find out exactly what "creative activity" meant to her. In her case, it meant solving business problems, and she noticed that her wanderings were always from one business to another. Others might see they were drawn to work that allowed them to create new physical environments or come up with new systems.

Jane realized she was born to be an "advance scout" of some kind. She learned that marketing research companies often send scouts to locations all over the world to see if local communities would be receptive to a certain kind of business. Also she learned that journalists accompany explorers of all kinds, such as anthropologists venturing into little-known cultures or medical researchers looking for new cures, so journalists can be advance scouts, as well.

"I love the realization that I haven't been walking in circles, that I've really been on a path that led somewhere, that there was a theme in everything that interested me," she said.

Fernando, whose wandering had usually been through different fields of teaching, realized he loved to make discoveries. He finally understood why no area of teaching had ever held him for long: As soon as he made his discoveries in math, theater, or history, he'd move to another specialty. This gave him the key he had been looking for.

Instead of continuing to wander through different fields, he changed the way he taught every subject. "It's all about discoveries," he said. "I break every class into teams, and each one is given a complex issue in that subject to work out, and they have to come up with something they didn't know—an 'Aha!' moment.

"Once they've done that, they can stop studying and then present their discovery in such a way that the rest of us will feel very enlightened. I have fun coming up with the questions for each team. They're learning important skills, and it never stops being interesting to me!"

If you already have a career that provides you with security and you hesitate to leave it, or if you long for such a career but have rejected it as a dead end, consider taking another look. Without knowing it, you might have been looking at a different kind of Umbrella Career, one I call the Ticket to Ride career, and it could be just what a Wanderer needs.

I mean careers like accountant, lawyer, computer information technologist, or nurse. Most people don't realize it, but even conventional careers can take you where you want to go.

For instance, a lawyer can represent astronauts, home-business owners, authors, actors, deep-sea divers, and inventors. Lawyers interested in business often become business brokers, because they have clients investors want to meet.

And the picture of the poor accountant, poring over his budget and payroll books until late into the night, isn't always accurate.

In one of my workshops, a man stood and told the following story.

I trained as an accountant because, although I had dozens of things I was interested in, I didn't know what to do for a career. But every aspect of the work was so dreary that I knew very early I had made a serious mistake. I was on the verge of chucking the whole thing and starting over in a new field when I got offered an assignment to a government construction project in India to get their books in order for an audit so they could bring in investors. I figured I'd be bored with the accounting as usual (I'd done construction jobs like this in the States, and they're usually pretty routine), but I figured at least I'd be in a new country and could do some interesting things on my own time, so I gave it a chance.

What I didn't expect was how an ordinary construction audit job, if you do it in a completely different culture, can be so incredibly interesting! For example, I had to assess a cost for a very expensive pet Australian emu, a bird that sat in a cage on the grounds, and the salary of the foreman's teenage son who did nothing but care for it.

At first I thought this was some kind of "under the table" favoritism, but then I realized that this bird contributed enormously to the efficient functioning of the company! According to folklore, emus have some mysterious mechanism that senses the coming of rain from hundreds of miles away, long before anyone else knows it's coming.

The workers were all trainees from different parts of India, and they weren't comfortable with each other or the foreman, either. But they all knew the importance of monsoons, and this emu turned them into a community. They'd talk to the foreman's son about the bird—practicing the local language at the same time so they could start talking to each other. And before long, they were friendly with the foreman and cooperative with each other. It was a stroke of genius on the foreman's part.

That was just plain fun to research. I had to talk to a number of people at the British embassy, a zoo expert, an anthropologist, and an Australian priest! Of course, it was still a bit of a challenge finding a column to put that expense into! I finished that job before I was anywhere near bored, and for me, that was very unusual. Then I got sent to Siberia! And then Uzbekistan!

Now I've even reactivated some things I used to love, like photography. I find myself suddenly interested in shooting family scenes in different countries. I also make a lot more friends than I used to; somehow, it's become easier. So, when you add travel to my profession, real travel to unusual places, it becomes a completely different experience.

What happens when a Wanderer doesn't find any theme but curiosity?

After all, the truest Wanderers just follow their interests randomly, and the only thing that drives them is a love of adventure or a fascination for the unknown. What becomes of these people? Their families think they're going nowhere and will end up with nothing. Is that true?

The "I Might Need That Someday" Life Design Model

Wanderers are open to experiences, but when something they try turns out to be important later, they feel their wanderings have been justified. They like to say, "You never know what will come of this new adventure. Someday I might need what I find." Tatania started with a scene in a movie and made a friend who, years later, introduced her to her husband.

> **Tatania:** *Just to show you how silly the beginnings of really big things can be—a whole long train of events in my life actually started with a single scene in a movie called* The Stunt Man, *in which Peter O'Toole plays a mad film director. That took me into a fascination with Peter O'Toole, to films and movie making, to writing a screenplay (with side trips off into a few things like the Gullwing Mercedes, which my main character used to own), to poetry (an old interest), to reading plays and acting myself, which led me to Tom Stoppard's work. From there I managed to meet Stoppard and learn about his friend Václav Havel, who was then in jail. Because my interest in film and political prisoners had led me to make a proposal for a film festival of "banned" films, I stopped off in London on the same trip and did some research at the British Film Institute. And there I made a friend who, many years later in another country, introduced me to my husband—just before he went onstage in a theater production of one of Havel's plays.*

Some successful and well-known people started out as Wanderers, like Steve Jobs, CEO of Apple Computers. In a graduation speech, he explained how his travels gave him experiences that turned out to be very useful later in his life.

> *I had no idea what I wanted to do with my life and no idea how college was going to help me figure it out . . . so I decided to drop out and trust that it would all work out okay. . . . The minute I dropped out, I could stop taking the required classes that didn't interest me and begin dropping in on the ones that looked interesting . . . . And much of what I stumbled into by following my curiosity and intuition turned out to be priceless later on. Let me give you one example:*
>
> *Reed College at that time offered perhaps the best calligraphy instruc-*

tion in the country. Throughout the campus every poster, every label on every drawer was beautifully hand calligraphed. Because I had dropped out and didn't have to take the normal classes, I decided to take a calligraphy class to learn how to do this. I learned about serif and sans serif typefaces, about varying the amount of space between different letter combinations, about what makes great typography great. It was beautiful, historical, artistically subtle in a way that science can't capture, and I found it fascinating.

None of this had even a hope of any practical application in my life. But 10 years later, when we were designing the first Macintosh computer, it all came back to me. And we designed it all into the Mac. It was the first computer with beautiful typography. If I had never dropped in on that single course in college, the Mac would never have had multiple typefaces or proportionally spaced fonts. And since Windows just copied the Mac, it's likely that no personal computer would have them. . . . Of course it was impossible to connect the dots looking forward when I was in college. But it was very, very clear looking backward 10 years later.

Until you find your home, like these other Wanderer-type Scanners above have done, you should continue to wander and trust your instincts. If something interests you, follow it. Always assume there's a good reason for any attraction you feel and that sooner or later, the answer will show itself.

Wandering is the way your mind works best. You're good at getting to a crossroads and following your instincts to find the right direction. You're a little like the Greek hero Odysseus.

The Odysseus Life Design Model

Odysseus wasn't exploring, and he wasn't wandering. He was just trying to get home, but in a way, so are you. He knew where his home was, and you're still looking for yours, but you both have similar ways of traveling: You stop off in different places for a while and then continue on your way. This model will allow you to keep wandering as you wish but will remind you to always stay alert to any signs that will help you find your home—the vacation that will satisfy your soul.

The Itinerant Minister Life Design Model

Years ago, in rural areas all over the world, communities often couldn't support preachers or judges or doctors. Instead, they welcomed traveling professionals to visit them when they passed through their area. These travelers sold their services on the road: They typically rode a horse from one town to another, staying a week or longer in someone's home where they were given room and board. That home served as the center for church services, courtrooms, or surgeries.

If you were an itinerant professional, what skills could you get paid for—and what could you learn that would add to your skills bank for the next town?

You can translate this into a lifestyle by doing nothing more than following your nose. Wanderers are drawn by curiosity. They love to move toward the unknown. If you combine that urge to explore with a project that belongs to any new place you go, you'll enjoy your wanderings more than a mere tourist.

For example, let's take a look at a Wanderer par excellence. You've probably heard of him.

Studs Terkel

Studs Terkel is in his nineties as I write these words. He's written gripping books on many subjects: making a living (*Working*), racism (*Race*), the Great Depression (*Hard Times*), World War II (*The Good War*), the movies (*The Spectator: Talk about Movies and Plays with the People Who Make Them*). And recently, *Will the Circle Be Unbroken?*, a meditation on death and dying.

But Studs didn't start out as a writer. He began as a radio performer in the 1930s. Circumstances drove him, in 1949, to begin a brief television career as an actor. After an impressive debut as a bartender on *Saturday Squares,* he was given a chance to develop his own show. *Studs' Place* was a weekly comedy that focused on the lives of working-class Americans in a Chicago restaurant.

The show didn't last, and in 1950, he moved back to radio in Chicago. These days he has a radio show called *West Coast Live*. Each week, he interviews famous and not-so-famous people, as he has done for so many decades. Some of his interviewees have included philosopher Bertrand Russell, painter Jacob Lawrence, dancer and choreographer Martha Graham, all the biggest film stars, and even a member of the Ku Klux Klan who later tore up his Klan card and became a civil rights supporter.

Terkel's wanderings taught him radio and television, acting and writing, but his theme, his first love, and his greatest gift is listening to people. A brief glimpse into his book *Working* will show you a level of interviewing mixed with commentary (a form he developed) that you've never seen before.

Terkel hasn't retired. He still travels and uses his remarkable ability to interview people whose voices fascinate him, and us.

Wanderers are usually going somewhere, but they just don't know it

A UCLA college friend of mine is a perfect example. Richard was in college, but he knew only one thing: He loved movies. Since he was very young, he spent all his spare time at the movies. He saw the same pictures over and over and could repeat every word in many of them. He didn't know how to turn that into a career, but he intended to try.

So he took every film-connected class the university offered, one after another: acting, casting, film editing, even special effects, animation, monster modeling, and writing and editing film scores. He wrote a few screenplays that weren't bad and even earned money one summer as a drama coach.

Richard was reasonably good at everything he studied but not really interested in sticking with any of the subjects after the first class or two.

By the time he graduated, he was discouraged and switched to business school. He enjoyed business school to a point but knew he wasn't like the other students, who were much more enthused than he was by the prospects of earning money and creating successful businesses.

Then one day he was sitting in the cafeteria and overheard a student talking about investments in the arts. A lightbulb went on in his head.

He suddenly saw that he had unwittingly accrued all the training, skills, and many of the credentials needed to become a film producer! He knew movies backward and forward. He had a keen sense for talent and good scripts. And he had become friends with a large group of people who would make great investors. He's been a film producer for a long time now and still loves it.

Themes can be maddeningly evasive, and you can't always find them right away, but you can see how important they are. If you find the hidden commonality, you can find the vocation you truly love. You simply have to commit yourself to the search. Start paying attention when you're drawn to one area or when you lose interest in another, and keep a keen watch for important clues.

Until you find where you belong, you might need sources of income that will allow you to continue wandering.

Careers for Wanderers

Income streams: A series of part-time jobs can be often enjoyable for Wanderers if the sources of cash are inventive or unusual. Jane picked up so many skills in her wandering that she now works as a seamstress in an antique-clothing boutique 1 day a week and designs and maintains lawns and gardens 3 days a week in the summer (not at all in the winter). And on weekends, she drives through the suburbs in her little white van with a sign on the side that says, "Children's Barber—get your kid's hair cut—right here, right now."

Expertise for sale: Contrary to popular belief, Wanderers seem to always be able to get work, simply by selling their skills and knowledge, often in informal ways. Your wandering may have given you more marketable skills than you realize. Try both versions of this exercise, Sing for Your Supper, to get some ideas for yourself.

Survival skills: Imagine you've been stranded far from civilization with a small group of people and you may be there for years. To survive, each person must have a number of skills that will help the community's survival. List all the skills you could contribute.

Teach what you know: You're on an educational cruise and none of the other teachers have shown up. You find that you've forgotten to bring money or credit cards and may have to ride out the cruise in steerage, unless you can figure out something to teach. If you had to teach something, what would it be? Write a list of everything you could conceivably teach in that setting.

Incidentally, take time to notice if you enjoy teaching more than you realized, as long as it's in an informal structure, because it can be the perfect career for a Wanderer. If you find yourself enthused about telling people things they don't know, you're a teacher. And if schoolrooms aren't your favorite place, you can earn a living with all the knowledge you've gathered in the very old-fashioned Itinerant Minister Life Design Model.

Now, what did you discover in this exercise? Which skills will help you find your vocation? Are you a tool maker, an inventor, a problem solver, a natural scientist? Can you help people tell their stories, find their talents, or start small businesses?

Do this exercise a few more times and see if it begins to point the way to the right career for you.

Now, which tools will help you get the most value from your travels?

Keep track of your wanderings

Be sure to record all your explorations in your Scanner Daybook or write daily Letters from the Field to your friends about what you're doing, teaching, or learning wherever you are—and print out a copy for yourself. This not only will help you find the hidden theme in everything you love but also could lead to the *Worlds I Have Seen* book you might write one day. A Wanderer's tales are always fascinating, and all you have to do is tell what happened! Your stories could be more useful to others than you imagine. I believe we all owe a report of our times, our travels, and our viewpoints to generations that follow us.

And for those times when you start to feel doubts about this wandering path you've chosen, just take as your motto something Robert Frost said:

> A scholar is someone who sticks to things.
> A poet is someone who uses whatever sticks to him.

You see, you're not someone without direction; you're an investigator, and the whole investigative process consists of learning a little bit about everything that looks interesting to you. If you respect your natural curiosity, you'll come to trust your enthusiasm. It knows something about you. Your trail of enthusiasms is the most precise instrument you have for locating where you'd find the deepest satisfaction in your life.

Your wandering can be unnerving to the people watching you, because they assume you're going nowhere. But as many explorers have found, wandering can be the best way of finding something really excellent that you didn't know you were looking for.

Final thought: The horse knows the way home

In the days before automobiles, people in horse-drawn wagons used to sleep if they were tired. They didn't worry about getting lost, because the horse knew the way home. Your heart knows the way to your gifts. You can trust it to take you to them.

Now, let's turn to our next Scanner, the Sampler. If you're a Wanderer, you'll understand a Sampler's curiosity—but her Life Design Model will show a completely different focus than yours.

Chapter 18

ARE YOU A SAMPLER?

I have nice friends, a nice family, and a nice life, and I don't mind my job. But there is that nagging feeling that something is missing. When I go looking for what that could be, many things look good, but nothing looks exciting. I wish I knew what I was looking for.

My job is okay, but it's really not enough. I wish I had a way of bringing more interesting things into my life. But I don't want to go back to school. I don't think that would solve the problem anyway.

Are you a Sampler?

- Have you ever thought you wanted to experience just about everything?
- If you had your way, would you never do anything twice?
- Does the idea of being an expert sound narrow and boring to you?
- Do you prefer to learn by doing, rather than reading or hearing about something?
- Once you know how something is done, are you ready to move on?
- Do friends and family think you lack ambition?
- Do you wish you'd live 200 years so you could learn everything that interests you?

If you not only said yes to some of these questions but actually became happy when you saw them (it's wonderful to finally be understood, isn't it?), chances are you're a Sampler. Samplers, maybe more than any other Scanners I talk with, are delighted to hear that it's okay to want to try everything.

I've always thought I was weird or something! I just "want to know." I'll look something up, research it, do it for a while, get bored with it, and want to do something else. When I was younger, my dad said I should become a professional student.

I love it when I find something in which I can positively lose myself! Of course, I've never figured out what to do with all this stuff. It fascinates me and then it's gone.

Once I've done something, I don't ever want to do it again. People ask if I'm going to do one of these things for a living, but it wouldn't make sense. So what's the matter with me? I'll never have a résumé I can show anyone!

Every one of these comments comes from a Sampler. A Sampler is someone who looks for a special kind of richness in her life and finds that there are very few ways to fill it.

The Sampler knows something is missing

For one thing, there's not enough variety for you in the ordinary job—or in the average life, for that matter. You want more excitement in your life but not the jumping-out-of-planes variety. In fact, you have a hard time explaining what's not there.

You're clear that you want more creativity in your life, not in any special area, but in as many as possible—but you don't know how to make that happen. You may have gone to college, or not, but you know that college classes aren't the answer. What you're looking for and where to get it, though, are far from clear.

When I first spoke to Sharleen on the phone, she was frustrated that she'd never get to try all the things she wanted. I asked her for some examples.

"Well, for one thing, I'd love to learn to weave a Navajo rug; I'd like to understand the symbols and how the wool is made, what they use for the dye, that kind of thing."

"Okay," I said. "And then?"

"Well, I'd like to keep the rug I wove. And put it on my wall. And look at it. I would really understand that rug, you know?"

"Yes, you would," I agreed. "Much more than if you'd bought it in a store. And what would you want to do after that?"

"Then I'd like to do something completely different."

Before contacting me, Sharleen had almost given up. Although she didn't hate her job, it left her empty at the end of the day. She'd tried going to school in the evenings but couldn't find anything that really interested her, and she didn't want to get a degree. After our brief discussion on the phone, I asked her to write me an e-mail telling me all the things she might want to do. This was her answer:

I've given your question a lot of thought, and although I know the answer, I've hesitated to send it to you. That's because my list is full of things that have nothing to do with each other. And they're odd things. People think I'm crazy and I'm afraid you will, too. But here goes.

I want to build a house—a small beach house or a country house, just a few rooms. I don't want to be a carpenter; I just want to do it once. And it would be fun to live there for a few weeks, just to see if I'd done a decent job.

I've always wanted to write and illustrate a children's book, but all I hear is how hard it is to get published. I don't want to get published; I just want to write the book. This is so hard to explain to anyone.

I wish I knew how to read music so I could actually put together a little 10-minute classical piece for a chamber orchestra. I'm not even a musician, but someone once explained the sonata form to me, and that's like the recipe for classical music. I'd love to see what it's like to make one. I wouldn't care if I wrote something stupid or impossible for a real orchestra to perform, although I'd like to hear what I had done somehow, maybe on a computer. It's just that I want to understand it. I know I'd hear classical music differently if I did that.

I realized this years ago when I took a painting class in college. We learned how to do the same paints and glazes as Renaissance painters, and it was intense and so fabulous. And when I was through, I could visit museums and for the first time really see what the painter had done. I had taken art appreciation, but this was a hundred times better. I could see every brush stroke after I took that painting class. It has continued to be among the best things in my life, just looking at paintings.

Where is the school that will teach me the things I really want to know?

Where is the school for Sharleen?

Sharleen's letter reminded me of something I had forgotten. Years earlier, I had also wanted to find a school like the one she wished for. For a time, I audited classes at a nearby college, but when my life got busy and I began traveling as part of my work, I had to stop.

But I came up with an unusual way to feed my love of learning.

A client of mine, an opera singer, told me her singing teacher would send her to a dictionary to look up all the words in any aria she was learning, and he even required her to search the word for its roots. I thought it was a brilliant teaching method and wished I could learn more about it. I called a few friends to see if they would come over to hear this teacher speak at my house. They loved the idea, so I invited him to give a talk and the whole thing was set up.

He was a fascinating lecturer. He felt that songs were poetry and that poetry is about the meaning of words. He thought most people had gone off track by focusing on the psychology of the character instead. I couldn't remember hearing a more interesting lecture in college, and everyone in the room hung on every word the teacher said.

We all brought food to eat and some money to pay him, so he was enthused by the opportunity. When he finished, he said he was pleased and surprised at everyone's receptiveness.

"Are you all opera lovers?" he asked.

All the eyes that had watched him so attentively suddenly looked embarrassed. Not one of them loved opera.

"Poetry?" he ventured, hopefully. No one looked any less embarrassed.

"I guess they love stretching their minds," I ventured, and they all looked up thoughtfully.

"You hardly ever get to think about such interesting things after you leave school," one of them said.

"Let's do this again," another nodded.

"I'd like to do the next one," Richard, a painter, said. "I want to explain why I think you can see music and hear paintings." Everyone picked up their heads with interest and signed up at once.

After that, we had a meeting once a month for over 2 years. A rising poet talked to us about why working at a Fortune 500 company like he did was actually a great thing for a poet to do. Another member took us to a dance studio, where her parents gave a demonstration of what they called Old Smoothie Dancing and gave us a fox-trot lesson. Another gave a talk on the nature of creativity. It was simply wonderful. We decided to call these evenings SOIREES.

The Soiree: An important tool for Samplers

The Soiree can also be called Lifelong Learning in Your Living Room.

Of course, if we had lived a hundred years earlier, we would have seen a grander kind of informal learning. Those were the days of town hall lectures, when the great scientists, philosophers, and politicians of the day came to town halls and opera houses and gave lectures, or chautauquas, which were open to the public and often packed to the rafters. Before cinema, these ever-popular chautauqua lectures were held across the country. In fact, Mark Twain made his living on the lecture circuit after he went broke in the publishing business.

The chautauqua lectures usually included an expert in his or her field (for example, a flautist might lecture on Chinese flute music and give some pleasing demonstrations). A scientist might lecture on electricity and demonstrate some simple generators. Speakers lectured on "authentic Sioux Indian music" and played some examples. Chautauquas fed the learning hunger of the nonacademic general population. And then they disappeared.

Looking back, it sounds so appealing. But even in our Soirees we had a great time. We invited instructors who were passionate about their subjects, eager to tell us about them, and happy to answer any questions. The evenings were better than any formal class. Our informal little evenings became the perfect postgraduate school for Samplers.

"Your Soirees sound simply fantastic," Sharleen said. "That's exactly what I mean! I want to do so many things that I can't possibly head for a university and sign up for a master's degree, but I want to study something a little more deeply than you did in a Soiree. One night isn't enough for me."

"Why don't you set up a Quarterly Creative Project," I suggested, "and find a place where you can learn whatever you want, for 3 months or so?" Sharleen murmured her approval as the possibilities started sinking in.

The Quarterly Creative Project Life Design Model

The idea of Quarterly Creative Projects isn't mine. It's something I read at least 15 years ago on a pre-Internet bulletin board, and it's so inspired I never forgot it.

With Sharleen and countless others, that simple idea has changed a wistful longing into some of the most exciting experiences that Samplers have ever had.

"That's such a perfect time frame for me!" she said. "I'll just take on a Quarterly Creative Project! I can stick with one thing and do it in all my spare time. I love calling it that. It has a name. I can't tell you how much that helps!"

And so we went searching.

The first thing we found was a Navajo weaving project not far from where Sharleen lived in Arizona. She found she could arrange for classes on the weekends and that it would take her a few months to finish a 6-by-8-foot rug, which was just what she wanted. She signed up at a local museum for some evening sessions to help her learn about the symbols as well. I got weekly reports via e-mail, and after 3 months had passed, she contacted me to say the rug was finished and, though it was an amateur effort, she had never loved looking at any rug more than that one.

"That's really great. It sounds like you found exactly what you wanted."

"I certainly did," she said.

"So . . ." I hesitated.

She knew what I was thinking. "So, what do I do now?" she said.

"Can you build a house on a beach?" I asked tentatively.

"No," she said. "But I can *learn* how to build a house! Thanks for reminding me." And she went off to volunteer with Habitat for Humanity. Before the week was out, she had also signed up for a one-night adult education class in the installation of solar panels for small summer houses and hired the teacher to give a weekend hands-on class on building an energy-efficient cottage. She had already launched a campaign to bring in other students to share the tuition fee she had offered him. Sharleen was on fire.

That was 2 years ago. In the following 2 years, Sharleen has done the following:

◈ Written, illustrated, hand-lettered, and bound one children's book
◈ Helped build three houses with Habitat for Humanity

- Installed solar panels in a friend's home
- Taken a 3-month course in conversational Swahili
- Taken two 3-month courses in African dancing (she might never stop that project)
- Spent 3 months with a community theater learning how to build sets and the next 3 months working with lights and special effects
- Taken a 3-month course in sewing and another in costume design
- Spent 3 months learning how to ride horseback

She wrote:

> *Now I know how it feels to speak Swahili. I haven't mastered it and don't intend to try, but it's opened my mind to such a different way of putting language together! And now I can visit many places that felt off-limits to me before, from local African restaurants to Africa itself; I can go to African theater or help a teacher friend create a program for her class on African heritage.*
>
> *That's not all, Barbara. I can go to conferences about writing children's books. I can walk into any community theater and help out—they see me as an insider, and I found that I absolutely love working in the theater. It's a kind of team project that I just don't have in my life. It's so creative and so much fun, and the hair-raising deadlines before each performance always keep things exciting.*

The Quarterly Creative Project Model has set many Sampler Scanners like Sharleen free. It allows you to work on your own projects in your own time, and it's successful because the structure is both sensible and clear. But the Quarterly Creative Project also requires that you have a certain kind of career.

Careers for Samplers

The Good Enough Job: As you recall, the Good Enough Job can be a relatively mindless but not unpleasant job that leaves you enough time to pursue your interests on your own time. It's perfect for the Sampler, who's pouring all her creative energy into her after-work creative projects. The Good Enough Job takes all the pressure off having to turn a profit from the things you love to do. You're free to do them for your own reasons. You don't have to justify your interests either, simply call them hobbies, as in, "Don't worry, it's only a hobby." As long as you've got a job, most people will leave you alone.

But some Good Enough Jobs are more than pleasant; they're quite wonderful on their own. And they will still support all your other passions. (The Good Enough Job can be so good that I've even considered changing its name to the Great Enough Career or setting up a Life Design Model called the Having Your Cake and Eating It Too Model—but for the sake of simplicity, I resisted.)

Here's an example: My friend Kelley decided in his forties to become a chiropractor and now has a successful practice in a small town in upstate New York. He loves his work, but he's also interested in many other fields. He loves the "gentler" martial arts, like tai chi, which he teaches on weekday evenings. For a few years, he studied astronomy, then astrology and tarot at a desk in his attic—and painted the ceiling to look like the night sky. (His wife, as a joke, made him a magician's cape and a cone-shaped hat with stars all over it.) For 2 years, he managed a rock band. At the same time, he returned to his childhood love of Beethoven piano sonatas and keeps a grand piano in his office, which he plays whenever he has a free hour. For a while, he gave concerts all around his county and in New York City as well.

This year, he has become passionate about a new kind of exercise program he's developed and that he hopes will soon be released nationally. He does all this while continuing to enjoy his practice as a chiropractor.

There are many others who enjoy their careers but don't limit themselves to them. I read with great interest an article in *New York* magazine (August 22, 2005) about the world-renowned pediatric neurosurgeon James Goodrich, who led the celebrated team that successfully separated a pair of head-joined twins in August 2004. Goodrich is passionate about his work and has dedicated years to studying everything about his field. If anyone appears to have made a single, focused choice in life, it's Dr. Goodrich.

When I turned to the second page of the article, I found something I didn't expect. It seems that Dr. Goodrich runs a mail-order antiquarian-book business out of his New York apartment in addition to practicing medicine.

And that's not all, according to the article: "Every 3 or 4 years, I pick a goal to learn something new," Goodrich says of his obsessive curiosity. "I started out with wine, then it was books, then it was bonsai trees, then it became the didgeridoo [an Australian Aboriginal musical instrument consisting of a long, thick wooden pipe that the player blows into, creating a deep reverberating humming sound].

It's the way I approached the twins. I sit down and learn everything possible..."

Temporary jobs: There are jobs for people who like to sample jobs—also known as temps. Some temps (like temporary CEOs and "corporate samurai," who can turn around an ailing company) earn as much as $5,000 a day.

Adult education schools: One job that might be made to order for a Sampler is to work for one of the adult education schools that exist in many cities. I started my speaking career at one of them: the Learning Annex, in New York City. The school invites people to give a one-night class at a space in a hotel or school on any subject in which they have some expertise, and the catalog offers everything from samba to classes in Photoshop. I suspect the seats are filled with Samplers. But on several occasions, some of the assistants who take the tickets and handle the logistics have said to me that they love their jobs because they get to listen to every lecturer.

If you don't have anything like this in your town, you might want to start an adult school of your own. Of course, you'd have to find the teachers and listen to them all. But for a Sampler, that's like going to a party.

The Smorgasbord Life Design Model

This Life Design Model is named after the traditional Swedish banquet table packed with morsels of dozens of different kinds of food where you take what you like, as much as you like, in any order or combination you choose. If you want just a taste or a glimpse of something and you have the imagination to create a whole world from a tiny fragment, this model will work for you. It's best for Samplers who prefer not to have a structured time-management style. These Samplers love to travel as much as they can to learn about other cultures, or they take a cooking class on one night and a sword-fighting class on another. To a specialist, a Sampler's level of interest is incomprehensible. To a Sampler, however, a specialist misses too many wonderful things in life, and the Sampler understands that *the only way to do it all is to do it small.*

The Everything 101 Life Design Model

If your areas of curiosity are mostly taught in universities or found in books, this might be a good model for you. Sometimes your explorations take a full semester. One Sampler said, "I take one beginning survey class every semester in any department that looks intriguing. The classes are usually fantastic. I get an overview of that whole field, something a specialist might not care about, but it's the only part I want to know."

Sometimes you simply take an armful of books home from the library and read the introductions, the final chapters, and the index at the back. I get insights into very complex books I'd never be able to read all the way through. Somebody once asked if I was a lifelong learner, and I said I'm more of a lifelong amateur.

A true lifelong learner you should know about is Cornelius Hirschberg, whose book, *The Priceless Gift,* never leaves my bedside table. Hirschberg was a self-taught man who studied math, philosophy, music, literature, astronomy, physics, history, and languages for 45 years as he traveled to and from his job on the New York subways. Almost no one seems to know about him (I found out about him quite by accident in a used-book store many years ago). He wrote only this one book, published in 1960.

In it he carefully and modestly explained exactly why we should all study everything, just like he did, and he set out a program of study to help us do it. If you've ever wanted to know everything and looked at a "great books" list only to become overwhelmed by the impossibility of ever reading them, let good Cornelius Hirschberg set your course of study. *The Priceless Gift* is a book unlike any I've ever come across. If Mr. Hirschberg had known about Scanners, he wouldn't have understood why I single them out. I think he'd say to us, "Good start. I wish everyone would do what you're doing."

Your Life's Work Bookshelf

Samplers typically love to learn about new things by doing them, and they often end each project with something they've made—a glazed pot, a woven rug, or the first draft of a novel they wrote as part of a 30-day online challenge (with the National Novel Writing Month; see www.NaNoWriMo.org). Most Samplers like to keep the things they've made, so they can find themselves with a lot of stuff.

Where can a Sampler keep all these objects?

On display!

You're not supposed to put the results of your samplings away in a box in the basement and forget about them. They're a record of where you've been and what you learned, and like books, they should be on a shelf where you can see them often. The Scanner's Life's Work Bookshelf usually serves this purpose nicely.

You read about your Life's Work Bookshelf in Chapter 8 ("I Never Finish Anything"), but let me remind you that it doesn't have to be a bookshelf. It's anything that can be considered a display space, where you can keep your completed projects for viewing.

Its purpose is for you to display and admire these records of your travels. Most Scanners need to be reminded that they've been spending their time learning how to do new things. Even more, the items can be seen as keepsakes or souvenirs of happy time well spent.

The PRIVATE MUSEUM

Some Scanners go way beyond my bookshelf idea and come up with very creative ways to acknowledge their output.

> **Rudy:** *I now have a little museum in my ex–storage room, devoted to a show of my most interesting artifacts from the last few years: There's a stained-glass piece I made in an art class, a video of the reading of the one-person play I wrote and performed at the local school (it's set up in a small TV-set VHS player and ready to be played with the touch of a button), an audio recording of me giving speeches at Toastmasters trying to be a guru (set up on an old cassette player and ready to hear), and two examples of my attempts at learning how to cartoon, nicely framed and hung on the walls.*

The Annual SHOW-AND-TELL PARTY

Some Samplers throw a Show-and-Tell Party for their friends and families.

> **Lita:** *Last January, I threw a New Year's Day party with a theme (I called it Lita's Creative Life) at my parents' house and invited all my friends. I stood up in front of them like a student in a classroom doing show-and-tell. I picked up one funny thing after another that I had made during the year and told them the quick story behind each. (I used a clock timer and kept my stories to 3 minutes each, because I had so many things to show!) I had fashion draw-*

ings and a fringed shirt I had made in a sewing class. I had a lot of stuff. I even recited a short poem in Spanish (which I had studied for 1 month!).

My friends and parents were totally inspired and want to start bringing their own stuff next time, so I'm going to have a party like this every year! Good idea, right?

I thought that was a very good idea.

Next, we come to our last Scanner type: the High-Speed Indecisive. She's like a Sampler but changes interests even more frequently.

Chapter 19

ARE YOU A HIGH-SPEED INDECISIVE?

I start and stop things so often it would make your head spin...and it makes me feel like a failure.

Everything is interesting. I can be completely absorbed in one thing, and suddenly I'm wondering what else there is to do! I hand things off so fast I never get past the surface of anything.

I completely understand the wanting-something-new syndrome!!! I am so good at it. I could be in the middle of something that is all inspiring, all consuming, and just in the middle of it I can stop and think, what next?

Are you a High-Speed Indecisive?

- Do you love to bite off more than you can chew?
- Do you dislike having to finish one thing before you start another?
- Do you quickly grasp new ideas before others even notice them?
- Do you feel guilty because you drop new interests so quickly?
- Do you see potential where others see nothing?
- Do you secretly suspect you're not looking for one right thing at all?
- When you're forced to conform, do you feel like you've been put in a small cage where you can't stretch to your full length?
- Do you wish you could find a career that lets you change one interest for another at least once a day?

If you said yes to most of these questions, you are a High-Speed Indecisive, maybe the most misunderstood of all Scanners. You get pulled away from your latest project sooner than other Scanners, not because you've lost interest, but because you see something more fascinating. You don't even have to be triggered by seeing something. You're just as likely to drop what you're doing because the possibility occurred to you that something else might be going on.

Your behavior wasn't a problem when you were young, because children often move from one activity to another in a short time; as long as you were able to get involved with each one, your parents had little cause for concern. Like children (and other Scanners), the High-Speed Indecisive is usually having a very entertaining time and typically enjoys everything she does.

But when the High-Speed Indecisive gets older, her constant switching from one subject to another stops being accepted. Like most Scanners, High-Speeders are sensitive to disapproval; they soon stop enjoying what is interesting and start worrying about what is "right." As an adult, the High-Speeder has stopped having fun and is trying to win respect. After all, what about a career? Where on earth will someone who swaps one interest for another a dozen times in one week be valued? Can there be a career out there that pays for a High-Speeder's talents?

What are the High-Speed Indecisive's real talents?

Even the High-Speeder assumes his behavior is some kind of learning disability. Because he can't settle on any one interest, he makes no progress in any direction, and he's in danger of becoming the most paralyzed and least productive of all Scanners. It's hard to figure out what talent this Scanner might have—unless you take a closer look.

Jason, a 47-year-old postal worker, explained his situation to me in our first session.

"No matter what I'm doing—going through a pile of magazines, looking at seed packages for a vegetable garden, or walking through a flea market—my wife says I always appear to be in a hurry, looking urgently for something I really need," he said. "But that's not what I'm doing, really. I'm just enjoying how things are made, wondering what they were used for, imagining what could be done with them, that kind of thing."

Jason is intelligent and works well below his abilities because he can't settle on anything else for long. "Everything looks good for a little while," he told me. "All my life people have told me to make up my mind, that I was indecisive and immature or I had a case of attention deficit disorder. I've been tested for every kind of learning disability and attention disorder in the book, but the results are never definite. I used to enjoy sorting the mail because I'd win speed contests with my fellow workers, tossing letters into the right slot faster than anyone else. Now I've taken a job delivering mail, just walking all day. It's not too bad. I think the exercise is essential. But I know I could do a lot more with my life."

Jason's style of thinking clearly hampers his ability to accomplish anything. For him (and for you?) this is obviously a big problem.

But it may also be his greatest talent.

No Scanner has an eye for potential like the High-Speed Indecisive

Many Scanners have extremely fast responses. Plate Spinners, for instance—the fastest of the Cyclical Scanners (those who return to the same interests over and over again)—can move like lightning, keeping a dozen projects in play at the same time. High-Speeders are different. They're not usually adept at the Plate Spinner's gift. A High-Speeder's talent isn't for keeping things moving; it's for spotting gold.

Instead of trying to explain this radical notion, I read Jason a letter I'd just received in the mail. He listened with great interest.

> The best job I ever had was putting together a huge book about all the colleges in the United States. It was a huge undertaking, and we weren't working with computers at that time. But I could whiz through every informational package the colleges had sent and see exactly what was wonderful about every school. My bosses were so impressed they gave me assistants to get the details about fees and tuition, that sort of thing. I was left to describe the strengths of each school, and they were so easy to see! This one was in a beautiful location, had a great-looking campus, or had a great history. That one had total geniuses in their history department and small classes to boot! I wanted to go to every one of those schools! And the book was a great success. Most of the schools sent thank-you notes and asked to be able to use what I had written.

When I looked up at Jason, his face had changed.

"That's an amazing letter," he said carefully. "I've never heard anyone say anything like that before."

"It changes everything," I agreed. "What if you were to put a High-Speed Indecisive in a situation where a quick search for potential is exactly what's called for? Would you be good at something like what was described in that letter?"

"You bet I would!" he answered. "And the best part is that I wouldn't have to decide which of the schools is the best! That's the most remarkable part about a job like that! It never occurred to me that you could look at a hundred interesting things and not have to decide between them. It feels very radical!"

Assessing without having to choose does feel like a radical concept, but it shouldn't. Clearly, when you have a natural ability to see the potential in just about anything, you're not going to be good at decision making. But Jason was beginning to realize that maybe he wasn't supposed to be making decisions at all!

We tried to think of professions a High-Speed Indecisive would enjoy and excel at; a place where his Scanner style would be valued. We singled out these four prerequisites.

❖ It wouldn't require Jason to choose "this or that" but rather to get involved in everything.
❖ It would endlessly provide variety.
❖ It would value someone who can create enthusiasm in others.
❖ It would reward quick assessments, fast work, quick thinking.

Jason was exuberant. He pulled a pen and a small pad of paper out of his pocket, and we started tossing ideas back and forth as fast as we thought of them, without much discussion.

"Let's see, you can switch to different subjects if you're a tour guide and take people to your favorite museums or film festivals or fashion shows," he said.

"Or a researcher in a television news room," I responded. "That's faster."

"Yes, I like that. I could put out fires! Why didn't I think of that? I like the variety and the challenge of figuring out something new, fixing something, as long as it doesn't take too long. Some kind of troubleshooter's assembly line," he grinned. "I think it would be fun to assemble a catalog, like the woman who researched the colleges," he said, writing it down while he continued talking. "Of anything. Toys. Clothes. Camping equipment. That could be fun."

"That's a splendid idea. You could also write a little blurb about what's good about each item. You could actually do that after the items were selected by someone else and put in the catalog."

"I'd also be able to describe how each item could be put to great use," he nodded, writing on the paper. "I swear, I look at something and I see a business or a design or a gimmick or a time-saver. If I had the patience, I'd be an inventor."

"You could also become a presenter in product development departments in corporations, teaching their staffs how to spot potential. You could present new books at publishers' sales meetings to get the salespeople enthused about your books!"

He wrote it down, saying, "I could be a speaker at toy conferences, showing them how to evaluate toys. That would be fun!"

We came up with even more ideas, and it was like hitting a Ping-Pong ball back and forth: I offered a doubtful suggestion about being a fast-talking auctioneer (that would be high speed but not really about potential), a stockbroker on the exchange floor, or a reader who takes the first look at the "slush pile" in the office of an overworked magazine or literary journal. ("I wouldn't have the patience to read the whole thing," Jason said. "Neither does anyone else," I answered.)

A High-Speed Indecisive could also write abstracts of proposals that come in to film production companies—or grants that come in to nonprofit foundations.

"I never had the slightest idea there were so many things I'd be good at," Jason said. "I'm starting to feel talented instead of handicapped."

He looked back at his very full piece of paper and said, almost to himself, "And the things I like best on this list are just what I do now: Look at something, see all the good things about it, and then look at something else and do the same thing." Then he looked up again, a bit worried.

"The only thing I can't seem to do is to write up an evaluation. I get too impatient. I don't even have the patience to speak it into a recorder."

We had run into a problem.

This was the one place that Jason's speed could create trouble for him. Write-ups of his remarkable insights and evaluations were basically what he'd be able to sell. He also needed to learn how to accumulate the information his mind produced so easily instead of letting it fly out of his memory. Writing things down slowly would give Jason the little bit of retraining he needed.

He knew this. We both sat silently. And then I got an idea.

"Do you draw, Jason?" I asked.

"A little," he said.

"Do you draw fast?"

"No, I don't," he said. "Drawing is one thing I do very slowly, and for some reason, I don't mind. A therapist once said drawing for me was like singing for someone who stutters; it makes their stutter go away."

"This is very good. Then you can do a da Vinci Write-Up and you'll be home safe," I grinned.

High-Speeders benefit from writing up every idea just like da Vinci did, as a way to work out their ideas and to remember what they'd been thinking about. It may be even more important for a High-Speed Indecisive than for any other Scanner, because when a High-Speeder's ideas are lost, he starts to forget who he is and gets in danger of letting other people define him.

And who knows? The High-Speeder just might start picking up where he left off if each idea weren't lost as soon as a new one takes over. Jason had never tried this, and I thought it might suit him more than he expected. (Drawing can be the perfect device for making you slow down when you're moving too fast.)

"You really do have to capture your new ideas and hold them until you're ready for them, Jason. Using the da Vinci Write-Up is like putting a glass dish over a beautiful beetle so it doesn't run away."

"I could try that," he said.

I gave him another assignment to take with him and told him to call me after he finished so we'd see where he was. If you're a High-Speed Indecisive, you should try it, too.

Your CATALOG OF IDEAS WITH POTENTIAL

This can go right in today's (and tomorrow's) pages in your Scanner Daybook, but I'd like you to use a special layout: Fit at least 10 ideas on any double page, laid out like a catalog of clothes or camping supplies. Put the heading at the top: "Catalog of Interesting Ideas." And then, with a fine-point pen, make a small sketch or draw an icon that represents the idea. It doesn't matter what the sketch is, as long as you understand it.

Now, under the sketch, in 10 lines or less, write up a description that sells the idea, as if you were a manufacturer and this product was actually in the catalog you sent out to your customers.

With a little practice, you'll be great at it. For inspiration, check out back issues of the *Whole Earth Catalogue*. Published irregularly between 1968 and 1998, this big, beautiful, black-and-white catalog of goodies was a collection the likes of which no one had ever seen before. Stewart Brand, who put together this great oversize book with a team of enthusiastic founders, said its purpose was to provide education and access to tools so the reader could find his own inspiration, shape his own environment, and share his adventure with whoever was interested. Steve Jobs of Apple Computer called it the conceptual forerunner of a Web search engine. It was about everything.

I got this description from Wikipedia (a wonderful Web site for Scanners): "With the Catalog opened flat, the reader might find the large page on the left to be full of text and intriguing illustrations from a volume of Joseph Needham's *Science and Civilization in China*, showing and explaining an astronomical clock tower or a chain-pump windmill. While on the right-hand page are an excellent review of a beginner's guide to modern technology (*The Way Things Work*) and a review of *The Engineers' Illustrated Thesaurus*, on another pair of pages, the left-hand reviews books on accounting and on moonlighting jobs, while the one on the right bears an article in which some people tell the story of the community credit union they founded. Another pair depict and discuss different forms of kayaks, inflatable dinghies, and houseboats."

The *Whole Earth Catalogue* could have been the Scanner's bible. Assembling it had to be the work of a High-Speed Indecisive.

When Jason came for his next session, he was grinning from ear to ear and had his Daybook under his arm—a huge black drawing book with blank pages 17 by 24 inches in size that he'd gotten at an art supply store. "I have definitely found my career," he laughed and opened the book for me to see.

What he had done was delightful. Jason had an unexpected gift for cartooning, and his drawings were witty and appealingly unself-conscious. He was very good with a fine-lined sketching pen. One sketch was of a stick figure standing on a biplane and waving a flag that said, "See the hidden valleys of California!" Under it, he had written what amounted to a short story about how he'd once seen some valleys from a small plane and was stunned by their beauty, and how you should rent a plane, take your camera, and go see those mountains. He actually wrote long, tiny lines of words. The whole two-page spread looked like a work of art.

It also looked a bit like the beautiful *Whole Earth Catalogue*.

HOW HIGH-SPEED INDECISIVES DO EVERYTHING THEY LOVE

Life Design Model for High-Speed Indecisives

The City Desk Reporter Model

Careers for High-Speed Indecisives

Freelance writer

Researcher in a newsroom

Troubleshooter

Catalog compiler/copywriter

Inventor

Abstract writer

Stockbroker

Slush-pile reader

From Your Scanner Tool Kit

Scanner Daybook

Da Vinci Write-Up

Catalog of Ideas with Potential

The City Desk Reporter Life Design Model

Instead of trying to force-fit yourself into an ordinary job, you might want to step into this model. On a daily newspaper, a reporter on the city desk has to deal with dozens of stories, deciding which to cover and which to ignore, and before the daily deadline, which ones should go into tomorrow's newspaper. Being able to make fast assessments of the potential of each story is a definite asset.

If you're a High-Speed Indecisive, you won't have to do much changing to adopt this model; its framework validates the way you naturally operate and is a good corrective for the ways you've been taught to think about yourself.

But what if you don't want a career?

What if you just want to be comfortable falling madly in love with something on Monday and forgetting it by Wednesday—usually because you've fallen madly in love with something else? One Scanner figured it out very nicely:

> *One thing that I've learned to do is just relax into the fun of something and ignore the "what on earth is the point of Viking graffiti?!" sort of voices that might come to challenge me. (Did you know that on one of the islands of Orkney, in the north of Scotland, there are some runes that when translated turned out to be Viking graffiti? Eight feet up a wall it says: "A tall Viking wrote this." You gotta love that.)*
>
> *It's like relaxing into a warm bubble bath. A shower would be more sensible and economical but not half as much fun.*

I hope you see High-Speed Indecisives (and yourself, in particular) differently than you did before. You're not someone who can't make up his mind; you're a high-quality idea producer. No one should have a brainstorming without you.

YOUR BEST WORK

Now you've almost completed the Refuse to Choose Program, and you understand that you can do *everything* you want to do. No more restrictions, no more embarrassment about transferring your passionate curiosity from what you loved yesterday to what you love today—and what you will love tomorrow. You understand now that you have the freedom to explore every interest and the right to drop it whenever you wish. You're a Scanner, which means you will always be curious and passionate about many different things. You are poised to do something extraordinary.

In fact, you need to do something extraordinary or you will never be satisfied—and it may seem more impossible now than when you first opened this book. What am I talking about?

You need to throw yourself heart and soul into something you love and give it your very best effort. You need to push past your boredom barriers and take at least one of your passions to the absolute limit you're capable of.

Yes, that's what I said. If you look at the opening pages of this book, you'll see two quotes. One is from a Scanner who's afraid she'll never fully use what's inside her. The other is from an artist who reminds us that we all long for the chance to do our very best.

You will never be satisfied with yourself or your life if you don't choose something to which you can give your very best. Being a Scanner doesn't mean only that you're drawn to many things. It also means that you have powerful talents that want to be used.

How can you do it? How can you choose only one thing to work on? How can you push through the boredom barrier? Does this mean you have to stop being a Scanner and turn into a specialist?

I'm going to answer every one of those questions and show you exactly what to do right now.

How will you ever choose something worth your best efforts?

You can't go wrong if you simply select anything you really love to do.

At all costs, do not try to find something "important" or "worth doing." That will lead you into more inner conflicts than you'll find in a Russian novel. Pick something that you're enthused about, something you love enough to want to get it right. Pick something you'd like to share with the world. Think of this project as a present you want to leave behind when you go.

Don't worry about it too much. Your first attempts at accomplishing something might be valuable only because they teach you about yourself and how you work. You might not finish them at all.

But you have to learn how to throw your heart into something you love and not ask for it back until you have something to present to the world.

As enthusiastic as you may be about every passion, an active mind doesn't get refreshment from producing nothing. Scanners actually grow tired when they're underused. So you'll have to give hard work another look, because inside you there are highly original works waiting to be brought into the world. Nothing will do that but starting and finishing at least one of them—or all of them, one at a time.

But will you still get to play like a Scanner?

Of course! You must never stop being a Scanner who snoops into all kinds of new things and doesn't even *think* of finishing them. Returning to full Scanner mode between your Best Work projects is an essential part of the process. It all fits together. Here's the whole routine for living a full Scanner life that includes Best Work projects.

First, select your project and decide on your goal

Pick something that appeals to you and wholeheartedly throw yourself into it. Hold nothing back. Complete a book, produce a play, build a computer, pass an exam, or set up your home as an art gallery and schedule an open house for your own paintings.

Decide exactly what your finished product will look like: If you complete a book, your finished product will be a 200-page manuscript. If you produce a play, your goal might be met with a performance of your play in a theater with a full audience. What if your selection of a project is a bit lightweight? What if you only want to create the perfect cheesecake or the perfect wardrobe? That's perfectly all right. Something wonderful happens when you're doing a Best Work project, no matter how "unimportant" it may seem: The more time and effort you give it, the more meaningful it becomes.

Second, schedule a date for a Real Deadline

For example, with a book manuscript (unless you have a wonderful publisher to hound you), you might set a date to give a reading at someone's home or at a local bookstore.

A performance of your play can also happen in a private home, if that works for you. Otherwise, part of your project will be finding a theater and handling promotion. The computer you build might be a birthday present for someone, and it would have to be delivered on that date. The date of the open house for your art show would be on the invitations you sent out, and you'll have to be ready when the people show up.

Here are some other Real Deadlines:

Teach a class. If I want to create an audio program about a given subject, I schedule a telephone class and notify my mailing list of the date well in advance. I book someone to record my class, too. I might work on the material in a leisurely way for months, but when the date draws near I start scrambling to get everything polished and clear. I'm not a detail person ordinarily, but I double-and triple-check to make sure the class will be recorded, the phone numbers are all correct, and a final announcement with the right information goes out to my mailing list.

Schedule a Show-and-Tell Party. If your goal was to build a ship in a bottle or write a really good poem, you could create a Real Deadline by setting a date and inviting your friends to a Show-and-Tell Party where they could come to admire your work. I'm all for potluck at this kind of party because those last minutes before the deadline are precious for putting the finishing touches on what you're presenting. If being the star of the show is too immodest for you, invite everyone to bring something of their own to show off as well and give them each 10 minutes to stand in front of the group and present their "party piece."

Schedule a Makeover Party. A variation of the Show-and-Tell Party can be used to do a makeover on a room in your house, your garden, or yourself! Send a letter or an e-mail of a "before" photo showing the present condition of whatever you want to change and include a date for a live viewing of the "after" makeover. If you know people are coming on that date to see what you've done, you'll do it.

Set up a contest. You can expand the idea of a Makeover Party by inviting all your friends to send out their "before" photos and arranging for a panel of judges to decide who came closest to achieving his goal.

Third, get to work

It would be grand if you could push the rest of your life aside and work on this project night and day, but it's a luxury few of us have. All the same, you'll have to move some things aside so you can devote yourself wholeheartedly to this project every moment you're involved in doing it. A halfhearted effort is a waste of your time and can even be demoralizing.

I advise you to make a simple DOWN-TO-THE-WIRE TEAR-OFF CALENDAR—one that fits on the wall near your work space is best—by stapling together enough sheets so you have one for every day between the start and the completion of your project. If you've set up your Real Deadline for 70 days from today, for example, you'd have 70 sheets of paper stapled together. The first sheet would say "70," meaning you have 70 days left to complete your project. When you tear that one off, you'll see the sheet that says "69," and the next day "68," and so on, right up to the sheet that says "Today!!!"

Are you experiencing a little stress when you contemplate that calendar?

I know. That's what it's for. Deadlines drive you into action precisely because they create stress. But between now and the moment of truth, you are going to be in love, dedicated to something you care about, and allowed to focus on your own work and to put yourself first. Remember: You're not going in front of a firing squad on the final day; you're going to be immensely proud of yourself for your accomplishment.

Fourth, attend your
Real Deadline/Grand Finale event

Tear off the last sheet on your Down-to-the-Wire Tear-Off Calendar—the one that says "Today"—pick up your splendid boat in a bottle, and head for your rendezvous with destiny. Someone will be waiting for you somewhere or showing up at your house today. Carry your finished work with you and walk on stage for your Grand Finale. Whatever you set up for your Real Deadline happens now, on the date you arranged. Be sure you've assembled an appreciative audience. No critics allowed.

Fifth, bask in your own glory

After the applause has died down and the confetti has been swept up, it's time for a period of solid Basking. Put the finished product where you can see it and fall in love with your wonderful brain and your perfectly disciplined character every time your eyes fall on it. One good place (if it will fit) is your Life's Work Bookshelf.

Pick a shelf above or below the ones where you keep the packages and parcels that represent your Scanner's Finishes and label the shelf "My Best Work." On that shelf you can now place your manuscript or the playbill and video (if you have one) from your play or the photos of the party where everyone tasted your history-making cheesecake or the piece of paper with your number if you ran in a marathon.

Add a small card with the name of the project ("The Eating of the World's Best Cheesecake," for example) and the beginning and ending dates prominently displayed on it.

And be sure to salute your work (or wave hello) every time you pass it.

And then what?

Now return to full Scanning mode

You've been on an invigorating, even grueling, journey and now you're home again in Scanner Land. Pull out your Scanner Daybook and leave it open for writing up anything new you get a crush on. Bring out your magazines, leaf through them, and save anything that intrigues you; even create a Three-Ring Binder for it. Go anywhere, study anything, start anything—and remember: *You don't have to finish anything when you're in Scanning Mode.* You've worked hard and must go back to filling your creativity reservoirs with new energy and lots of sunshine.

And then, in 6 weeks or 6 months or even 6 years (you'll know what's right for you), pick another project that you love, roll up your sleeves, set a new Real Deadline, and do it all over again.

That's all there is to the entire process.

If, in the future, during one of your Best Work scenarios, you should have a moment when you can't remember why you, a Scanner, agreed to do this high-intensity, exhaustive (and exhausting), single-minded activity, just pick up this book again and turn to the quote at the very front and read it to yourself slowly.

For now, I'll put it right here:

Through all the world there goes one long cry from the heart of the artist: Give me the chance to do my very best!

If those words ring true, reading them in the middle of a tough stretch will remind you that you decided to give yourself that chance.

I tip my hat to you.

HOW DO SCANNERS
EARN A LIVING?

Someone on my bulletin board just alerted me to a career she thought might be perfect for a Scanner. She saw it in the *Aberdeen* (Scotland) *Press and Journal.*

Seamus McSporran (his real name), age 62, lives on the tiny Scottish island of Gigha just off the Mull of Kintyre. Population 100. Mr. McSporran currently holds down 14 different jobs at the same time, namely:

Police officer
Fire officer
Postmaster
Pier master
Shopkeeper
Ambulance driver
School bus driver
Taxi driver
Petrol (gas) pump attendant
Registrar of births, marriages, and deaths
Insurance agent
Rent collector
Undertaker

And he also runs his own bed-and-breakfast establishment.
    Today, Mr. McSporran has announced he is retiring.

If Mr. McSporran's work life sounds interesting to you, I have some bad news and some good news. The bad news is that the article is from April 2000, and I'm pretty sure Mr. McSporran's positions have been filled by now. The good news is that not everyone really enjoys doing that many different activities. If his replacement wasn't a Scanner, the positions might have opened up again.

Of course, there are lots of other jobs for Scanners that might be a bit easier to find. In the following pages you'll find great jobs for superfast thinkers (Plate Spinners and High-Speed Indecisives), who like to keep lots of balls in the air at the same time—jobs like reporters on busy newspapers or in TV newsrooms, on-site disaster management people, and troubleshooters in the technical fields. You'll read about great jobs for people who love to learn all the time (Samplers), as librarians, researchers, and consultants; for people who need weekly variety (Samplers) or yearly variety (Serial Specialists); and for people who won't leave until they get it right (Serial Masters) and then will *always* leave. There are jobs for people who need weeks or months of freedom from any work, and jobs for Scanners who love to travel.

There are two kinds of jobs that are right for Scanners

The Good Enough Job mentioned in Chapter 11 ("Are You a Double Agent?") is one kind of job for a Scanner. I hope you've taken a more tolerant view of such a job now that you understand the benefits of subsidizing your own fun.

Now, let's look at the other kind: paid work that's endlessly interesting and will keep a Scanner happily absorbed forever. If you're a Scanner, you enjoy the learning phase of every new activity so much that you race through it and get to the boring part all too soon. After that, most jobs become intolerable, even depressing. But there are many jobs with so much variety built into them that they never get boring.

I've put together a small sample of the many such occupations that are available, so you'll understand that the world is full of good ways to earn a living without sacrificing who you are—because, if you're like most Scanners, you assume that what you want is not available.

For me "the right career" doesn't exist. It would have to satisfy my creative part, be challenging, and be sometimes solitary, sometimes social.

I know that job exists, because I have it. When I design workshops or do-it-yourself kits or do problem solving with clients or work on my books or even take long walks, I satisfy my creative part; I'm always challenged and sometimes solitary, sometimes social. I always knew that designing and running workshops was something I enjoyed enormously. I love making people laugh and, even more, showing them how important and unique they are. What I didn't know was that being a speaker is the most highly paid and least labor-intensive job I can think of. If I merely liked it instead of loving it, I'd do it anyway, because it leaves me so much free time to write books (one of my great loves), travel to my second home in a little village in central Turkey where I teach e-commerce to the village weavers (another of my great loves), and use my spare time to read history and geography books (yet another of my great loves).

> *I feel like a lot of people under one skin: an artist and a businesswoman, a spiritual guide and a teacher...finding a job that would satisfy me is impossible. I'm doomed to hold jobs I detest.*

If this Scanner looks a little further, she'll find many people who are artists and businesswomen, spiritual guides and teachers. Mindy Stricke, a talented photographer, started teaching to pay her rent when she lost her office job a few years ago. Since she didn't have a darkroom, she gave her students lessons in how to *see*. She has a remarkable eye, and her classes were nothing short of inspiring. To earn a little extra money, she started taking portraits of friends to put on Internet dating sites. She did such an amazing job that all the friends got dozens of calls the day after they put up her photos. When the word got out, she was interviewed by CNN and appeared in the *New York Times*. Now she's a businesswoman with a number of assistants, being courted by the Internet dating sites to take pictures of their clients.

Let's see, artist, businesswoman, spiritual guide, and teacher. I think Mindy's job covers all that. (You can find her site at www.singleshots.com, if you're curious.)

Jobs for those who love travel

> *I love travel. And all of the fiber arts. And fitness. And kids. And philanthropy. I have never found a way to do most of those things, much less make money at them!*

I don't know anyone doing all of the things this Scanner is interested in, but my project in central Turkey covers travel and the fiber arts and philanthropy. I'm not sure she really wants to be paid for fitness, but if she does, she can work for (or create) a fitness program for children. There are people who do that. You can find them all over the Internet.

I haven't been able to figure out how to turn anything I enjoy into anything other than a hobby. What I enjoy most is reading about ancient (world) history, listening to innovative music (from around the world), surfing the Internet, watching movies, learning about tropical fish . . . How could I turn any of these things into a career?

I know of people earning money doing everything this Scanner mentioned. They tutor ancient history on the telephone or by chatting on the Internet with students in schools all over the country or, for that matter, anywhere in the world (like children of actors on location or servicemen and -women stationed in places like Germany or Asia). This Scanner can be paid via the Internet as well. He can start adult education classes in his town or lecture all over the country to active retirees. He can create a Learning Vacation at an existing resort and invite other speakers (which would make him a booking agent). Or he can teach on a cruise ship, if he likes that environment. If he builds a mailing list from any speaking engagements, he can give regular telephone conference-call classes and fill them up by sending e-mails to fans who have already heard him speak.

He can also do Internet research for small businesses that don't have the time to do it themselves. One woman did this very successfully by using the low-tech personal touch to get clients: She put up small posters in the center of her town offering Internet research for a week, and then walked into each small shop to show them how they could improve their businesses with her help. "These are mostly one-person businesses that can't afford the Internet researchers that the big corporations use," she told me. When we spoke, she had four clients and was expecting more.

There really are people who make money watching movies, though to be honest, I don't think they have as much fun as people who watch movies for pleasure. However, there are a number of movie fans who have Weblogs and e-zines on the Internet that have attracted large followings. One of them is selling advertising to film studios, because his following is large enough to interest them.

I had a friend who was a "fish collector" for a big-city aquarium. An engineer with no special credentials except some scuba-diving experience, he went out on a special ship equipped for oceanography studies and spent so much time in the South Pacific that he fell in love with it. Now he and his wife live on their sailboat in Hawaii and Australia much of the year. They support themselves by inventing interesting gadgets and toys for places like the Sharper Image.

> *I love the theater, but I'd hate to be stuck in some dinner theater in Podunk. I need to see the world! And what about teaching and fashion design? I want to do those, too!*

If you love the theater, teaching, and fashion and you love to travel, look at these suggestions from my bulletin board.

> *Go on the road with a theater group. The Broadway musical touring production my friend is on employs several people who are dressers. The dressers do exactly what it sounds like: They dress the cast. What a job! (She has also designed and sewn costumes for this show.)*
>
> *There are two kids who perform on this production, and because they're traveling, they need to have a tutor to teach them.*
>
> *There's a couple that travels with the show whose job it is to sell show-related merchandise in the lobby. You'd think these would be people employed by the theaters where the shows are booked, but in fact they are employed by the touring company.*
>
> *For all of these Broadway-related jobs, contact a Broadway touring company or the unions, like the dressers union.*

Jobs for those who love to learn

> *I've got nothing against work and I'd love to find a job I could really get into, but what about all the things I wanted to learn? Do I have to forget them?*

If you've ever said, "I wish I could get paid to go to school," you might be able to get that wish. I heard of someone who has a job taking dictation of classroom lectures for foreign or handicapped students.

It's also possible to work in a college or university's offices if you have the skills. The pay isn't always great, but you can often get benefits—and one of the perks is usually the freedom to take as many classes as you like.

If you have the right credentials (or you're willing to get them), you can get a job teaching—and still audit as many classes as you like, in any department you choose. There are courtesy exchanges between most teaching institutions so that you can attend classes in schools other than your own.

> *What do you call someone who spends all her time on the Internet, looking up things for no good reason except that it's fascinating? I call her unemploy-able me.*

How about "highly paid information broker"? That's just a fancy way of saying you look things up for people and get paid for it! One of the keys to this is the ability to boil down or package information in executive summary–type reports. Some technical writing experience might come in handy, but it's not necessary.

Jobs for those who love to share ideas

> *I know I'll never be an expert (and wouldn't want to be) or some fancy PhD, but isn't there some way I could share all the wonderful things I learn with rest of the world?*

If you love to tell everyone what you've learned, you're a popularizer—a very fine enterprise for both you and your audiences. You can (and should) offer school assembly performances or go on the lecture circuit for special groups like the elderly, kids at risk, single moms, or others whose lives you might change by opening up their minds to what you love.

If that appeals to you, it means that you're a communicator, teacher, explainer, enthusiast, and an absolute Santa Claus to other Scanners. Popular-izers write pop science books and produce shows for *Nova* and the Discovery Channel. Anyone who has ever had the sheer thrill of learning from a book, a documentary, or a teacher who is truly excited by his subject can tell you how wonderful popularizers are. Of course, there are also specialists who are pas-sionate about their subjects, but teaching the same thing year after year often wears them down. A Scanner, on the other hand, maintains enthusiasm because she's always falling in love with something new, and her classes change every semester.

Jobs for those who don't want jobs

I don't really want a profession, but that world is fascinating to me. How can I be a professional without having a profession?

Lots of Scanners are fascinated by professions and businesses. You can write about professions by being a journalist, or you can learn about them by working for an Internet job site, matching employees with employers. You might enjoy heading up an association for professionals. Did you know there's an organization called Mompreneurs, serving moms with businesses? And one of those moms earns her money by running the Mompreneurs association. I've met a number of people who earn their living by running associations. One of them is a high-school classmate who runs the alumni association. Another travels through Russia and Eastern Europe teaching small business skills and starts new chapters of the American Association of University Women wherever she goes.

There's a company called Lawternatives, too, which shows not only that lawyers are looking for alternatives but also that someone who is interested in professions has created a career out of helping them find those alternatives. And, of course, there's Gary in Chapter 18 ("Are You a Wanderer?"), who realized his job-changing was the result of being fascinated by many different professions and so he became a career counselor.

Jobs for serial professionals (aka freelancers)

You probably know about freelance writers (they write most of the articles you read in magazines), but there are also freelance executives, pilots, cooks on sailboats, artists, film producers, and performers. One of my clients became a successful freelance writer, with articles to her credit about subjects as varied as infant development and parenting, inventions, collecting art, and popular science for preteens. Another is a designer-for-hire who is known for creating wildly imaginative sets for interactive performances (with original songs and dances) at school assemblies on subjects that range from recycling and nutrition to conflict management. A third became a romance novelist with 31 books to her credit at this writing. Her books feature musicians, mathematicians, Olympic athletes, mountain climbers, journalists, artists, and sociologists. She loves doing the research (which often includes spending time in the company of real-life musicians, mathematicians, Olympic athletes, etc.), and anytime she's interested in a new field, she creates a new character that specializes in it.

Jobs for experts

Scanners are often torn between needing variety and wanting to be experts in one field. Few of them realize it's possible to be an authority in a number of fields. Writers like Isaac Azimov, for instance, turn out books on many subjects. Azimov is best known for his science fiction novels, but he also wrote books about Greek and Roman history, two guides to the Bible, and many other subjects. (The great variety of information covered in Asimov's writings once prompted Kurt Vonnegut to ask, "How does it feel to know everything?")

But you don't have to be a writer to be an expert in many fields. You can be a compiler. One of my all-time favorite jobs for Scanners who want to be experts is to investigate any area that interests them—roses, autos, babies, insomnia—and compile what I call a moles and gophers book about it—and then move to a different topic and do the same. I got this idea years ago from a book about how to succeed in direct mail. It described a book called *100 Ways to Get Rid of Moles and Gophers*. The author knew nothing about moles and gophers when he started.

He walked up to people he saw watering their lawns, asked how they got rid of moles and gophers, and wrote down their answers. When he had 100 different techniques, he listed them, printed up his book, and sold it through the want ads. (Today you can do the same at less expense with an e-book that can be downloaded from your Web site.)

Where will your buyers come from? If you used a subject like moles and gophers, you'd advertise in landscaping magazines or write short articles in online magazines that specialized in lawns.

Combo jobs

My interests don't seem to have anything to do with each other. How could I possibly turn them into a job?

My cousin Mary loves to travel. She also loves homes and can't resist visiting every house with a "for sale" sign, even when she isn't in the market to buy. Another one of her hobbies is taking photographs of the wilderness. She's been advised to be a travel agent ("Hate it," she said) or a real estate broker ("Never. Can't stand to sell!") or to take photos of people instead of nature so she could make some money from it ("I don't want to take portraits, and anyway I'm no good at it," she told me).

But Mary found a career she adores as a location scout for a major film company. Her job requires her to search and photograph interiors of dozens of local houses in Los Angeles to be used as backgrounds for feature films, and it also requires her to find and photograph jungle locations in the hills of Thailand for action films. Her ability to take good photos of scenery and her willingness to go tromping around in both bug-infested jungles and manicured Beverly Hills homes make her very good at what she does and very popular with film producers.

Tryout jobs

I'd love to try something like acting without making a permanent commitment. Is there any way to do that?

Acting/soap opera writing: In our newspaper this week, it was reported that people giving dinner parties are hiring actors/amateurs to attend, dressed and behaving as normal guests. Their job is to have an argument or lover's tiff partway through the night or to behave obnoxiously to some of the other guests. This is supposed to spice up the dinner party and make it more memorable.

Performing, clowning: There are people who get paid to dress up in funny clothes and go to parties, conventions, or corporate sales meetings! Contact incentive houses, such as Maritz in St. Louis, Carlson in Minneapolis, McGettigan's in Philadelphia. These organizations work with vendors who provide talent for corporate meetings, trade shows, and so on. Or contact caterers and conference centers.

Jobs for people who love to read

I could read all day and all night. I thought about being a librarian, but you need a fancy degree, don't you?

My area offers classes at a local community college in library technology, which goes toward a certificate in this field but isn't a master's program. The certificate helps you get jobs as an assistant librarian but might also help you to create a job classification that wouldn't require a master of library science degree. The classes here are offered on weekends and include lots of library-computer courses.

I was a librarian for 5 years in a rural library, and I loved it. One of my friends is a librarian with the park service, and another is an archivist with a big museum. They are very happy with their work.

The beautiful thing about being a librarian these days is the range of skills necessary. The American Library Association (www.ala.org) shares lots of information about how technological advances have changed the library sciences.

While computer skills may be a new area of training, bibliographic instruction is alive and well but with a different name and a different focus. Information literacy is the byword, whether that means instruction in finding citations in print indexes or using an online database, searching the Web, or sending an e-mail to get information.

Variety jobs

A Scanner posted this comment on my bulletin board:

What I care mostly about is variety. Give me that and I can do almost any job.

She got these answers:

I worked in corporate training, where I designed and wrote training on a variety of subject matters. It was a great job for me, because although the process was always the same—analysis, design, development, testing, implementation, evaluation—the subject matter changed, and even more as I changed jobs and companies.

I'm an advertising copywriter who comes up with publicity campaigns for all types of businesses. There's always something interesting to learn.

Survival jobs for Scanners

See if any of these survival-type jobs might be interesting for a short while—at which point you can try another. Again, I'm talking about variations on the Good Enough Job.

An ideal Good Enough Job uses very little time, pays well, and uses some talents you enjoy. If you have nice people around you or an entertaining environment, that's a bonus. This job is not high-priced transportation; it's a mule. It will get you where you want to go.

Tour guide: You can lead a tour group through almost anywhere. Do you know something special about an area where you live? Become the expert, advertise in the local paper, get the local chamber of commerce to list you on their Web site, leave brochures with local hotels. You can show visitors bird nesting areas, old movie theaters, or rose gardens—whatever you think might have an audience.

Wild Women Adventures started when two wild women—Carol Rivendell and Martha Lindt—decided that women should have some fun traveling and shouldn't have to do it alone. According to their story in *Success for Less: 100 Low-Cost Businesses You Can Start Today*, by Rob and Terry Adams, their start-up was $5,000, and their Carmen Miranda–esque style and sly marketing sense set them apart from the rest.

Personal assistant: This is not at all the same as being an administrative or executive assistant (though there may be some administrative duties included in your daily schedule). Personal assistants look after the private affairs of people who simply don't have the time to do it for themselves. Duties include booking travel arrangements, returning birthday gifts, picking up the dry cleaning, walking the dog, paying bills, or food shopping. I have a friend who used to be a personal assistant to stars, and he would take the cat to the vet, make hotel and entertainment arrangements for their guests who came to town, even put together their photo albums. He's honest and dependable and has a great reputation, so he works all the time. How did he start out? Through a friend of a friend, he met a star he admired and said, "If you ever need a personal assistant, it would be an honor to work for you." The next day he was hired. He's been working at that job for 15 years, making a very good living.

Tutoring service: Is there one subject you're really good in? Math? English? Creative writing? You could make really good money as a tutor. Advertise at schools or call your local school board and let them know. Some departments—English, math, science—will provide lists of tutors available. Lisa is an actress who just happens to be really good at math—calculus, to be specific. She makes an exceptionally good living tutoring junior high school kids in New York City. If you live near a school, visit their office and find out how you can get on their list.

Expediter: If you like to read or listen to music (or audio books) on your headphones, get a job as an expediter. They stand in line for their bosses, fill out forms, head down to the dock to oversee unloading technicalities, and so on. They need patience, but if you're a reader, getting paid for standing in line a few hours is just fine. You're reading standing up, that's all. (Or you can bring a folding camp stool.)

I know someone who is paid very well to be an expediter. She works for insurance companies and building contractors and basically stands in line to get permits for them. She's got the personality for it and doesn't become impatient waiting in line for hours to get something signed. Expediters get paid a lot of money because they push along—they *expedite*—the horrific and sometimes infuriating practice of processing paperwork, which could otherwise hold up someone's valuable business.

House sitter (or "anything" sitter): People want to be able to go away and know that their house, apartment, dog, and plants will be in good working order when they get back. A house sitter would take in the mail, open the windows, generally occupy the space to ward off intruders, and whatever else is needed to maintain the home until the owners get back. Word of mouth will get most of these jobs. Or run an advertisement in the local paper or get an application through an agency, like www. housecarers.com.

Résumé tutorial for Scanners

Now you've gotten a sense of the wide variety of careers and opportunities that exist for interesting people like you. In order to get them, you're going to need that little document so many Scanners dread, the résumé. Don't worry, this is a process you're going to enjoy.

Your THREE SCANNER RÉSUMÉS

Scanners have résumés they don't want to show a prospective employer. With so many different jobs written down, how will anyone take them seriously?

There are dozens of books in the stores right now that will show you how to write a skills-and-achievements résumé (rather than a list of jobs) that illustrates what you're really capable of. But I don't believe you should have a résumé; I think you should have *three* of them! Let me describe each one and why you need it.

The first is the Résumé for the Man. This résumé is for the world that doesn't understand Scanners but does pay salaries. This is your typical résumé, respectable and lucid, and you use it when you really need a job. It's full of dignified bragging about all the important things you've done and the kinds of things you're exceptionally good at. Just be sure not to list anything you dislike doing just because you know how to do it. Unless you're on the verge of being thrown out of your home and haven't laid by any canned goods, that skill could get you hired and make you very unhappy.

Second is the Résumé for Your Dream Job. First, imagine the classified ad you wish would show up in the newspaper, the one with the happiest parts of your Scanner's life listed as requirements. Next, write the résumé that would get you that delightful job. Make a list of every relevant skill or experience in your history.

Then call up everyone you know and read them your Dream Job Résumé and ask them if they've ever heard of a job that could use those skills. You'll be surprised at how many people know of careers you never heard of. You might find an entirely new direction in your professional life with this technique.

If you get an interesting lead, do your research and then write up the résumé that could get you that job—and see if you can get an appointment for an interview. If that's totally impossible, fax it in anyway and add a section called What I Could Do for You.

Here's what I mean: If you could make everyone work together well and develop their skills, or if you could bring in more business to the company, or if you could set up systems to simplify the work or back up any of their tech support, say so. Sometimes people need to be told what your skills can do for them.

Caveat: Unless you're in dire financial straits, try as hard as you can to get a smart boss. Smart bosses like smart people. Second-rate bosses resent them.

Finally, you need the Résumé from Heaven, which isn't about a career at all—it's about how you should live your life, using the very best of what's inside you. It says, in effect, "I have these talents, these experiences, these special sensibilities. I'm looking for a life in which I can enjoy myself, make a contribution, and use the best parts of me."

That means you have to list all the things you've done that show the best parts of you, chronologically, like you'd do in an ordinary résumé.

In all likelihood, that résumé won't get you a job, but that's not what it's for. It *could* get you a life, however, by reminding you who you are.

One part of that life might include working at a job like this:

> *As a Scanner, my new bookstore job is turning out to be just the right prescription! Always new books, new ideas, new people, new things to learn. Hiring a Scanner to work in a bookstore is like hiring a bumblebee to work in a flower nursery. In addition to working on the floor, I've been employed to design a Web site for this small, independent, locally owned bookstore. Not only do I get to consume lots of information, but I can contribute in a creative way too. I work in an environment where my brainstorming and ideas are appreciated and valued. What luck!*

Let me close with a few more letters from Scanners who have found the work that suits them.

Letters from the Field sent by happily employed Scanners

Dear Barbara,

I love being a Scanner. I think it's the best thing a person can be.

Right now my focus is on starting a nonprofit, and my focus has been strongly ongoing in that area for about 2 years now. I also work a full-time job on the side.

The work of growing an organization from scratch, from the cells of my brain, is fascinating. Wonderful work for a Scanner! I have so many different things to do for the organization that anytime I'm bored or frustrated with the current focus, I just switch to something else.

My whole outlook on life has changed—I used to be stuck on finding "the" job/career of my dream plus making lots of money. This is still not a bad idea, but now I see that there are so many things in life waiting for me to discover and have fun with. I want to enjoy them without mixing them with money. In terms of money, which we all need, I will always find it one way or the other. I actually enjoy temping, liking the idea of working one day for one day's pay—it feels very free for me. Also with temping, I have more freedom in terms of arranging my time. I do have an IRA account, so I am thinking about my later days, but I do believe active fun and money just don't stop after a certain age.

Signed, Nancy

This letter is from a Scanner (of the Sampler variety) who will soon be gainfully employed.

Dear Barbara,

I thought I loved research and thought I should be a librarian or some sort of researcher. They are still options, but I realized what I really love is learning about anything and everything.

I've recently decided to go to court reporting school, and I'm hoping to come out as either a "closed captionist," a reporter taking depositions or working in a courtroom, or a steno interpreter, where you sit in college (and high school, I just found out) classes and take the notes of the lecture. I'd never before found something with so many delicious possibilities! I love the idea of being "in the real world" and being a fly on the wall.

Plan C? Of course, I have one. If none of that works out, I'm going to walk into a private detective's office and do the legwork. I don't want to hide in bushes and spy on married men, but I wouldn't mind using my "street smarts" to interview people or find hard-to-find information!

Signed, Susie B.

I hope you're starting to see how many career possibilities exist for multitalented Scanners like you. (There are many more on my bulletin board at www. barbarasher.com.) It's important to realize that you don't have to take jobs that aren't right for you.

TOOLS FOR SCANNERS

Dear Scanners (and friends and families of Scanners),

I'm finding new information about you (and me) every day. To keep up with the latest news, to ask questions and find a community of wonderful, interesting Scanners, and to add your story to all the others, be sure to come to my bulletin board at www.barbarasher.com. Click on the link to the bulletin board and scroll down to find:

Refuse to Choose: The Forum for Scanners

What should you do when you want to do everything? If you're fascinated by everything, and you've been called a dabbler, dilettante, undisciplined, indecisive, etc., this forum is for you.

Moderator: Barbara Sher

While you're on the site, check out "What Some Very Smart People Say about Scanners," a collection of thoughts from esteemed researchers about Scanners. Here's a quick look:

If you feel foolish because you're magnetized by mystery instead of being down-to-earth: You're in good company. Here's a quote from someone who felt the same way.

> *The most beautiful thing is to gaze at a mystery and say why is this here? How does it work? . . . The important thing is not to stop questioning. Curiosity has its own reason for existing. One cannot help but be in awe when he contemplates the mysteries of eternity, of life, of the marvelous structure of reality. It is enough if one tries merely to comprehend a little of this mystery every day. Never lose a holy curiosity.*

Who said this? Albert Einstein.

For more, go to **www.barbarasher.com**. I'll see you there!

Signed,
Barbara Sher, Scanner